INTRODUCING
SOCIAL
NETWORKS

ISM   Introducing Statistical Methods

Series editor: Daniel B. Wright, *University of Bristol*

This series provides accessible but in-depth introductions to statistical methods that are not covered in any detail in standard introductory courses. The books are aimed both at the beginning researcher who needs to know how to use a particular technique and the established researcher who wishes to keep up to date with recent developments in statistical data analysis.

Editorial board

Glynis Breakwell, *University of Surrey*

Jan de Leeuw, *University of California, Los Angeles*

Colm O'Muircheartaigh, *London School of Economics*

Willem Saris, *Universiteit van Amsterdam*

Howard Schuman, *University of Michigan*

Karl van Meter, *Centre National de la Recherche Scientifique, Paris*

Other titles in this series

Introducing Multilevel Modeling
Ita Kreft and Jan de Leeuw

INTRODUCING SOCIAL NETWORKS

ALAIN DEGENNE
MICHEL FORSÉ

Translated by
ARTHUR BORGES

SAGE Publications
London • Thousand Oaks • New Delhi

SAGE Publications Ltd
6 Bonhill Street
London EC2A 4PU

SAGE Publications Inc.
2455 Teller Road
Thousand Oaks, California 91320

SAGE Publications India Pvt Ltd
32, M-Block Market
Greater Kailash – I
New Delhi 110 048

British Library Cataloguing in Publication data

A catalogue record for this book is available
from the British Library

ISBN 0 7619 5603 4
ISBN 0 7619 5604 2 (pbk)

Library of Congress catalog card number is available

Typeset by Mayhew Typesetting, Rhayader, Powys
Printed in Great Britain by Redwood Books,
Trowbridge, Wiltshire

CONTENTS

ACKNOWLEDGEMENTS

We thank all those who contributed towards the preparation of this book, especially Louis Chauvel, Gloriane Depondt, Laurence Duboys-Fresney, Marie-Odile Lebeaux, Henri Mendras, Lise Mounier and Douglas R. White. We also thank the journals *Clés* and *L'Année Sociologique* for kind permission to reproduce excerpts from certain articles.

INTRODUCTION: THE PARADIGM OF STRUCTURAL ANALYSIS

Social structure has long been an important concept in sociology. Network analysis is a recent set of methods for the systematic study of social structures. The sophistication of these methods now lifts them beyond the level of mere descriptive tools in the sociologist's toolkit. The decision to use this approach implies adopting a specific methodology but, at the very least, network analysis offers a new standpoint from which to judge social structures, and a look at its main features is now in order.

Categories and Relations

Most sociologists will allow that individual behaviour and opinions are rooted in the structures to which people belong. However, most researchers handling empirical data will ignore this reality. They will construct categories *a priori* by aggregating individuals according to sex, age, socioeconomic class or other attributes. Such breakdowns will enjoy the advantage of conforming to conventional wisdom. The next step is to determine the relevance and significance of these descriptive categories to the variables under investigation (e.g. age and religion). The massive development of research techniques opens the door to increasingly sophisticated interpretations (simple correlation analysis is now a needle in a haystack of multicriteria analyses) of links and their absence; but all these interpretations depend on how you group arrangements of independent events.

Indeed, any survey assumes that respondents are there for reasons which are structurally independent of one another. The opposite would amount to bias. Under such conditions, it becomes arduous to return to the starting point, that is, elucidation of the social structure and its effects on behaviour. Because these analyses treat the individual as a structural unit by definition, they will reasonably focus on the attributes of aggregates of individuals. So we end up studying relations between variables rather than individuals – not always the easiest of endeavours.

Since variables are based upon *a priori* categorizations, the study of links often boils down to verifying that categorizations are truly meaningful. For example, a researcher is classifying individuals into social categories and discovers one of her variables has no effect on religious practice. She still cannot definitively conclude her variable does not affect religious practice. After all, the grouping she performed (e.g. occupational status) may simply not 'work'. Other groupings might show significant effect. On the other hand, if the researcher does not go back to structure, she ends up with an accumulation of descriptions which will most likely offer no efficacious explanatory material *per se*. This gives the impression that we have massive accumulations of empirical research of this type that do not go beyond the stage of what Baechler (1992) calls 'sociography of the contemporary world'. Additional hypotheses are needed to overcome this limitation.

First, structure can be seen as a mere collection of individual attributes where individuals sharing the same attributes are structurally close. Each category would then correspond to a certain structural reality. But the investigative apparatus precludes any verification whatsoever of these hypotheses because any knowledge of relations between the units of analysis was precluded at the outset. So reference to or classification in a category does not determine action. No one ever says, 'I am young or I am a worker, therefore I do not go to mass.' Some researchers forget this while others emphasize they never study correlations alone; in plain English, they mean they can't explain their correlations from the data. Moreover, other explanatory frameworks have to be accepted as valid, e.g. that social behaviour is normatively oriented. Since individuals in the same category share the same norms, they act according to these internalized norms. Actually, this is only a generalization, with many exceptions, and one which encourages the belief that anyone who deviates from the average is a fringe member of society, although the fringe may only be a byproduct of inept category design. Not only has the problem shifted ground, but it is also obscured. Any tool that assumes independent units of analysis will very logically end up with pseudo-psychological explanations, e.g. individuals who behave the same way share the same norms or have the same collective conscience, which impels them to act the same way. In short, norms become causes.

Structural analysis opposes this view. Norms arise from the structural position of individuals or groups, because this position is sufficient to determine the opportunities and constraints which influence the allocation of resources and to explain the behavioural regularities observed. And this is so not because of an abstract relation to the whole, but because of concrete relations between individuals which shape the structure and explain why some have easier access to certain resources than others. Thus we are freed from resorting to explanations in which actors are driven by forces (internalized norms, collective forces or the more recent notion of *habitus*) or, finally, to an abstract causality synonymous with what Comte calls a metaphysical stage.

Network analysis assumes there is no way of knowing in advance how groups or social positions come about, i.e. how combinations of relations are formed. Network analysis analyses *overall relations* in an inductive attempt to identify behaviour patterns and the groups or social strata that correlate with those patterns. Then it sorts out the pertinent groups *a posteriori* and *identifies the concrete constraints of structure on behaviour at the same time as it uncovers constraints on structure from group interactions.*

Thus far, we have spoken of individuals for convenience and because the relations between individuals constitute the prime target of most network studies. But obviously, married couples, families or corporations are all candidate units of analysis. The main point is that the primary focus of study should be relations or links between units, effective or potential.

Focusing on relations does not mean that the dyadic relation of interaction between two people becomes a totally restrictive limit. Individuals cannot be studied independently of their relations to others, nor can dyads be isolated from their affiliated structures. The structural position of a dyad necessarily impacts its form, content and function; dyads become meaningless when detached from links to other dyads in the network. For example, we cannot study a group of three and settle for knowing only that A interacts with B and C. We need to know if B and C share a link too. A relation (or lack of one) necessarily requires a context or position within a structure for proper study.

Actual relations will vary sharply with the problem at hand. Ethnologists have taken an interest in the exchange of women in traditional tribal societies; social psychologists examine (dis)likings among actors in small groups; and organizational sociologists investigate power relations in firms or government agencies. The network need not only be a collection of informal relations. Network analysis goes beyond the study of sociability between friends, relatives or neighbours, although it offers no shortage of studies on this theme. Moreover, sociology is not alone in network thinking (Parrochia, 1993). Cousin disciplines with a growing tendency to think in terms of networks include geography (transport networks), ecology and the latest theories of free market economics. More distant disciplines include computer science (neural networks) and even crystallography. More dialogue among such specialists stands to reap handsome methodological returns, but the sociologist's main concern will of course remain social networks on a scale running from small groups to entire societies.

Structure, Constraint and Emerging Effect

Structure is considered here both as a network of relations and as a 'constraint'. From one standpoint, networks operate as a constraint on the personal preferences, behaviour patterns, opinions and so on of member individuals. Network analysis is therefore no end in itself. It is the means toward a structural analysis, which aims to explain phenomena in terms of the network's form. We consider the example of two networks A and B (Klovdahl et al., 1992) as shown in the figure on p. 4. These two networks share the same *density* of relations (see definition in Chapter 3). The number of effective relations divided by the number of potential relations is $9/28 = 0.32$ in both. And yet their forms are very different. Network A is

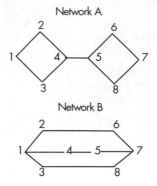

set up as two groups linked by a bridge, while B consists of a single group. Another structural difference is the average distance between individuals. The distance is 2.29 in A and 1.93 in B. In B, the members stand closer to each other than in A. New ideas, job tips or epidemics will thus have every chance of permeating B more rapidly. Moreover, a comparison of individuals labelled with the same numbers shows their structural positions differ too. We shall now compare individuals 4 and 5 in terms of contagion risk, since epidemics spread in predictable patterns. In A, 4 and 5 are cutpoints. Any exchange must pass through them. If 1 falls ill and infects 2, the disease cannot reach the entire population if 4 is vaccinated. In B, however, the virus that has infected 1 is an instant threat to everyone regardless of 4's vaccination status. This example underscores the major impact of a network's form on the process of contagion, communication or any other type of exchange. It is essential to know the complete form of the network if its relations are to be properly understood and its structural features correctly described.

On the one hand, structure has every chance of affecting exchanges; on the other hand, it is also the product of elementary interactions (i.e. dyadic relations in this case). For example, the interaction between 4 and 5 is a fundamental feature of network A, as is the absence of relations between 2 and 6 or 3 and 8, whose existence would cripple the importance of the 4–5 link. Structural analysis considers this circularity essential, since it constitutes the living framework of a structure which both determines and is determined by interaction. With regard to the great paradigms of sociological analysis, this line of research gives structural analysis an original position which requires precise definition.

The Position of Structural Analysis

There is a generally recognized schism between individualism and holism in the social sciences. However, each school has room for two different paradigms which need explicit definition for a proper understanding of structural analysis.

It is broadly agreed that individuals act to achieve goals, and to do that they choose between options selected according to their interests. However, methodological individualism starts by determining the features of these individual interests and goes on to reconstruct the structure from the effects of relational interactions, while holism asserts that reconstruction is of marginal interest because structures determine individual action. In the latter context, Granovetter (1985) writes of 'over-socializing' theory and Ronald Burt (1982) of 'normative' theory because actors' interests are determined endogenously (through a member's dependence on his group). Whatever the adjective preferred, holism can be summed up broadly in the following three propositions:

(a) Structure takes precedence over the individual.
(b) Structure cannot be reduced to the sum of individual actions.
(c) Structure exerts absolute constraint on individual actions.

These statements are however open to several interpretations. In its voluntaristic version, holism assumes individual actions are completely governed by the internalized norms of a group which the individual acquires in the process of socialization. Individuals become mere puppets of the structure, which acts on them such that it is the group which is acting in pursuit of self-seeking and self-contradicting goals all its own. When the group achieves those goals, it becomes dominant or hegemonic. Much criticism has been levelled at the reification toward which this doctrine leads but, by adopting a global approach, holism can consistently identify groups that can be held responsible for any given social evil and this achievement has won over a large following.

There is a second, more methodological interpretation, however. It emphasizes the implicit determinism the statements contain, i.e. that structure exerts all-powerful control over action. Durkheim is usually considered the founder of this school of strong determinism since he affirms that a social fact can be recognized by the constraint that it exerts on the individual; the idea itself implies a process of social differentiation which has caused us to pass from societies of mechanical solidarity, in which the individual is a non-existent concept in the structure, to societies of organic solidarity, in which the individual is a fundamental concept. That the individual comes into being because of this process (based on increasing division of labour) proves that the individual comes second; but actually also because his existence is decreed by the state of the collective conscience. Durkheim undeniably upholds strong determinism when, for instance, he explains that rural emigration is the result of a collective force which compels people into the cities.

This theory has paved the way for a paradigm also found in economics. Hoping to avoid the dangers of utilitarianism, some economists have tried to factor the effect of social relations into their equations but the results look too mechanical: they assume perfect socialization of the individual and condense complete determination of an actor's behaviour into his social class or his segment of the job market (Piore, 1975). Social influence acts as an external force that creeps into individuals' minds and changes the decisions that they would take if they were not mere agents of equilibrium. As Granovetter (1985) notes: 'Once we know in just what way an individual has been affected, ongoing social relations and structures are irrelevant. Social influences are all contained inside an individual's head, so, in actual decision situations, he or she can be atomized as any *Homo economicus*, though perhaps with different rules for decisions.' Even when economists take social interactions more seriously (Becker, 1976), they still have an invariable tendency to consider individuals separately from their structure and history. Interpersonal links are either extremely stylized or reduced to a mean. Actors conform to role stereotypes (e.g. husband and wife) which define the entire content of actions. According to Granovetter,

> This procedure is exactly what structural sociologists have criticized in Parsonian sociology – the relegation of the specifics of individual relations to a minor role in the overall conceptual scheme, epiphenomenal in comparison with enduring structures of normative role prescriptions deriving from ultimate value orienta- tions. In economic models, this treatment of social relations has the paradoxical effect of preserving atomized decision making even when decisions are seen to involve more than one individual.

Strong determinism (voluntaristic or methodological) is incompatible with structural analysis for two reasons. First, it leads to an *a priori* identification of structures which, as we have already seen, involves establishing an abstract causality between structures and individuals, i.e. actual social relations are disregarded. Second, as Granovetter shows, it does not necessarily avoid the atomization of individuals, which contradicts the relational principle stated at the outset.

However, there is another way of coming to grips with determinism and it borrows from Durkheim's own ideas, e.g. his explanation that suicide results from weak integration. Here we have a case of weak determinism grounded in only two propositions of methodological holism, i.e.:

(a)   Structure cannot be reduced to a sum of individual actions.
(b)   Structural constraint is merely formal, leaving the individual free to act but effectively closing off some of her options.

We know that the meaning of a dyadic relation extends beyond the two persons involved. This is more important to psychologists than socio- logists, for we cannot isolate it from structural context. The earlier example of two networks demonstrates that sociological meaning arises from con- text, i.e. the network as a whole. In other words, the function of a relation depends upon its structural position, as it does for a given actor's role and status. It is therefore clear that a network cannot be reduced to a simple sum of relations and that network form exerts constraints on each relation.

So these two propositions amount to acknowledging the concept of weak determinism, which therefore constitutes an element of structural theory without, as we shall see, summarizing it.

We are certainly not asserting that a network acts through the individual and her relation to others or that it determines individual choices. Structural constraint is only formal, not absolute. Network analysis starts with the idea that relations do not arise at random (there are sophisticated tools to check this) because the network is at stake, and tries to explain why 'birds of a feather flock together' strictly in terms of the network.

For instance, many studies show that most marriages remain homogamous in industrialized societies. But this is only a statistic with no power over individual behaviour: superior social standing is not in itself a prerequisite or guarantee of marriage to an eligible mate of comparable standing. We only have a macrosocial probability that is useless for any microsocial conclusions. Network analysis offers a concrete explanation that does not resort to statistical probabilities or overdetermination of the individual by the intentions of his group. All network analysis needs to do is point out that most people meet each other through personal networks and examine if and how the form of these networks favours homogamy.

Yet accepting weak determinism could still let us believe that social structures are essentially pre-existent to relations. Of course, an individual enters a pre-established network whenever joining a club, accepting a job or moving into a neighbourhood, but the relations that arise (*and do not arise*) will affect the structure in turn. Structure is also a dynamic response to individual interactions.

This brings us to the second major school of sociology: methodological individualism, and the two paradigms it accommodates. The first may be called atomistic (or intentional) and the second structural individualism.

Individualism relies heavily on actor goals to explain social action. It starts by determining the motives of all individuals in a given group and shows that the aggregate generates combinations that individuals had not expected. It holds that these combinations arise strictly out of interdependence or interaction among the actors themselves, not external constraints. To determine the individual motives, individualism assumes rational pursuit of self-interest by all individuals. However, results diverge by a wide margin if the study focuses on discrete actors or on actors linked to others by definition (see Weber and Simmel respectively).

Atomism is consistent with Weber's standpoint. In a letter quoted by Boudon (1988), Weber writes (our italics): 'Sociology itself can only proceed from the actions of one or more *separate* individuals. That is why it must adopt strictly "individualist" methods.' Simmel (1918) disputes Weber here and launches the interactionist tradition in the opposite direction (our italics):

> Yet if we examine 'individuals' more closely, we realize that they are by no means such ultimate elements or 'atoms' of the human world. For the unit denoted by the concept 'individual' (and which, as a matter of fact, perhaps is

insoluble, as we shall see later) is not an object of cognition at all but only of experience . . . As it develops gradually, society always means individuals connected by determinations and influences that are *reciprocally* experienced.

According to the above, sociology consists of nothing more than studying the forms of this reciprocal action. But if we ignore social relations and adopt 'separate' actors as the basic assumption, we are left with an 'under-socializing' theory of the individual, as Granovetter (1985) shows.

Historically, the 'under-socialized' or 'atomized' individual (Burt, 1982) is primarily the offspring of liberal or neoliberal utilitarian economics. She is a rational creature who acts out of self-interest and follows the path of decisions that allows her to maximize her utility, i.e. increase her return on effort. Her decisions are logical in the Paretian sense because reason is their only guide. She is totally rational. At the same time, her self-interest, which is objective by definition, is inevitably exogenous and her decisions are taken in a sort of social vacuum. This is radically at odds with the principle of structural analysis which says that individuals do not take decisions as social atoms (i.e. under-socialization) and do not blindly act out roles assigned by membership in a given category (i.e. over-socialization).

But where are the incompatibilities? Structural analysis says the principle of rational choice does not necessarily induce atomization, which is but a consequence of the absolute rationality in the utilitarian *Homo economicus*. Today, economics has a model with a *relatively* rational *Homo economicus*. This new and less restrictive model does not exclude endogenously determined interests and is therefore perfectly compatible with the inclusion of social relations. It is indeed another paradigm which we and Wippler (1978) call 'structural individualism' or 'structural interactionism'.

One major difference between structural individualism and atomism is that actors can still be considered rational even when they do not make the best possible choice, as judged by an impartial observer with full information. It suffices for an actor to follow self-interest as best he perceives it and according to his goals. Actors are guided not only by objective self-interest, but by subjective self-interest as well, i.e. interests pegged to a *relation* with the constraints of interdependence or to the actor's position with respect to her full set of relations.

So rational behaviour is more than action driven by self-centred bean counting. The current model of *Homo economicus* is capable of altruism. He may also opt to mimic his neighbours down to the last detail. Total conformism is a rational option for anyone eager not to be noticed. 'Tis better to be wrong together than to be right all alone', as the adage goes. He may also pay more than the lowest price for a product because he will not always have full information at the time of purchase. It is perfectly rational of him to decide at some point that he has enough information to buy and not systematically canvass all sources for every single purchase he makes. As Becker (1971) notes, rational behaviour only assumes the actor operates from a predetermined list of preferences and optimizes her choices according to the means at her disposal. This strategy applies to anything rare such as goods, power and prestige as well as our special domain of social relations. Whatever the case, modern rational choice theory can be summarized in three propositions:

(a) Individuals act to achieve goals they set themselves as a function of their personal preferences.
(b) Constraints interfere with action by influencing the probability of achieving some of these goals; the constraints are structural or institutional.
(c) Structural constraints induce individuals to act in the manner most consistent with their preferences and thereby lead them toward their goals.

None of these principles imply any absolute rationality. They imply not that people actually act on cold consideration of costs and benefits, but that they act as if this were indeed the case. In other words, these principles describe neither a cognitive process nor actor goals. It is up to the socio-logist to figure out the goals empirically or theoretically. The current model for *Homo economicus* is therefore no more 'realistic' than its predecessor: the actor in question is still a *model*. However, the theory gains in gener-ality. The epistemological status of the principle of rationality is to permit explanatory models of behaviour and interaction.

Without this principle, social networks would be 'black boxes'. We could not explain how an actor in a pre-established structure elects to enter into one relation rather than another. To enter into a relation is to make a choice, and Coleman (1990) gives a perfect demonstration that relational choices cannot be understood without a grasp of how the actor compares benefits with drawbacks before selecting the course of action she thinks will best satisfy her self-interests. To this end, it is sufficient to retain the hypothesis of an order of preferences. We shall illustrate this by returning to the example of homogamous marriages.

It is perfectly arguable that a homogamous marriage is 'more economical' than a heterogamous one. Structural analysis acknowledges the influence of the social environment, but differently than does strong determinism. We only assert here that the individual wants to get married regardless of the future spouse's social origin. The social environment does play an effective role because the marriage seeker evolves in a network of existing relations. If the network is homogeneous (this can be verified), a homogamous partner is a rational and more economical choice because his or her personal network generates most of the personal introductions to eligible partners. The network does not determine homogamy: its features simply combine with the actor's rationality to make heterogamous marriage less economical, i.e. more improbable. This translates into the following:

(a) Structure affects action formally via weak determinism: highly homo-geneous structures induce homogamy through the type of contacts they offer.

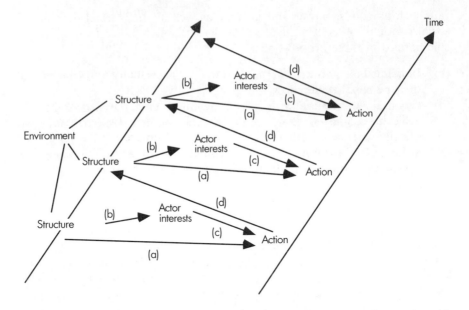

(b)   Structure affects perception of self-interest: any individual who wants
      to marry will perceive an eligible partner of his or her own social
      status as the most economical choice.
(c)   Rationality principle: rational individuals make decisions as a function
      of self-interest (i.e. along a scale of preferences) and this effectively
      induces them into homogamous marriage.
(d)   Structure is the emerging effect of interactions: every homogamous
      marriage reinforces structural homogeneity, which is but the sum total
      of all of homogamous choices.

We can now chart the sequence of these different propositions (a), (b), (c)
and (d), each of which is essential to the model. The schema shown above
is that which Burt (1982) uses to summarize the structural theory of action,
to which Leydesdorff (1991) has added the temporal dimension. The
circularity described earlier stands out nicely, illustrating that structure is
both a formal constraint and an effect of action. Always remember that,
for all practical purposes, any structure is always embedded in a larger
structure which consists of all the influences that escape the model.
    The homogamous marriage example contains two features which require
special attention if we are to avoid a misconception. Here the ongoing
effect of interaction is the result of an aggregate of elements that amount to
a maintenance process. Structures consolidate homogeneity every step of
the way. It goes without saying that structural interactionism is not limited
to the study of homogenization, just as structural change may be one effect
of interaction. Moreover, the addition of a new relation in a network is less
significant than its structural position. In the example of network A earlier,

we pointed this out when discussing the link between cutpoints (4 and 5). The importance of that link is that the two groups are now communicating; the resulting change in network density takes second place. In other words, the global layout of a structure is more important than the addition of an extra link. This is why network studies usually rely heavily on combinational rather than on purely aggregative logic.

One feature of combinational logic is that it shows how structure influences an actor's self-interest (proposition (b) above). Indeed, many network analyses conclude that actors evaluate self-interest in terms of how fellow actors, perceived as socially similar or structurally equivalent, evaluate their self-interest. If action is indeed guided by self-interest in this way, then action is also linked with what could be seen as structural self-interest and it becomes insufficient to compare individual utility *sensu stricto*. Information about the networks must not be neglected.

Guidelines

This rapid methodological presentation underscores that the structural analysis of networks is already a true paradigm, or at least well along that road. It does not attempt an impossible synthesis between holism and individualism since structural analysis clearly subscribes to structural interactionism or structural individualism. The original contribution of this approach stems from the fact that it acknowledges weak determinism, thus setting up a bridge between the two schools of sociological analysis while avoiding, because of this very fact, the drawbacks of each. We openly agree with Burt's (1982) statement that 'The structural perspective is deductively superior to normative action since its use of network models provides a rigorous algebraic representation of system stratification from which hypotheses can be derived. It is descriptively superior to atomistic action since it explicitly takes into account the social context within which actors make evaluations.'

North American sociology usually calls this approach 'neostructuralist' but in France we prefer 'structural interactionism'. The French term *structuralisme* covers too wide and motley a range of disciplines whose methodological and epistemological axioms often bear scant relation to the concepts we have just described, including a very focused school of ethnology with which we have little in common.

Not every researcher using 'network tools' subscribes to the principles of structural analysis. This manual concentrates on structural analysis in order to achieve greater coherence at the expense of exhaustiveness. It attempts to put structural analysis into perspective rather than plunge into details readily available from numerous studies in the literature. Nor shall we discuss studies that merely use network analysis as a tool or simply mention 'networks' metaphorically. It is common to see references to 'network analysis' that use no real network tools. Some such titles look promising at first glance, but their contributions are slight and scattered. The network analysis in this book has a clearly defined position that is both positive and cumulative. Structural analysis and the authors we cite consider that a concept only becomes valuable once it promises a yardstick that can serve as a basis for further serious debate and analysis.

The quantification of results usually means recourse to the language of mathematics. And such is indeed the case because we need this language for reasons which include the precise expression of data; detailed discussion of authors' calculations; a firmer grasp of the concepts we are handling; bedrock study content; statistical comparisons and the differences of approach they reveal; and what a given study is adding or correcting. We have not relegated methods to the Appendix. In some studies, methodology goes straight to the Appendix, but not in network analysis. Most network analysts put methods at the heart of the analysis. Moreover, most of the mathematics involved is based on graph theory, which has the virtues of internal coherence and simplicity. Our introduction to graph theory only takes one short chapter.

Actually, the main difficulty is not mathematics, but the cumulative nature of the studies. Each study belongs to a tradition and adds yet another specific contribution to it. The foundations of these traditions generally date back to between the 1930s and the 1960s (with a few turn-of-the-century mavericks such as Bouglé or Simmel). The 1960s and 1970s saw a boom in research that tightened up the methodology and fieldwork. The last two decades have been a period where researchers have been fine-tuning methodology and boosting its sophistication, but also pioneering new lines of research. Today structural analysis research is into the third generation. The book aims for a complete review of research to date.[1]

We have deliberately chosen to illustrate our tools and concepts with a maximum of actual field data and a minimum of abstract examples. The doggedly empirical attitude behind this presentation does not mean we play down theoretical issues and discussion, for network analysis also induces a theory of social structures.

This book offers readers a sound platform from which to appreciate the contribution of network analysis to the description and understanding of social structures. It positions readers to proceed confidently into the literature itself and design their own studies.

Notes

1   Knoke and Kuklinski (1982), Scott (1991) and Wasserman and Faust (1994) are three handbooks on the methods of network analysis. Leinhardt (1977) offers a compilation of the main texts.

1 SOCIAL RELATIONSHIPS AND NETWORKS

It is not unusual to see a wry smile and hear the quip that structural analysts see networks absolutely everywhere. Social structures are indeed networked. But any idea backfires beyond a certain point. The first issue is to inject real content into a concept that is expected to describe and explain a wide spectrum of social phenomena including kinship, power, communication, exchanges, economic markets, organizations, rural and urban communities, sociability and social support. In order to preserve a tight focus, we should begin by staking out our territory. That is far from obvious.

We shall start this chapter with Milgram's experiment, which shows that social relations are transitive, but in ways that generate different and complex answers to a simple question like 'How many people do you know?' The problem comes from the fact that a social network has no natural frontiers. Methodologically, we must therefore begin by deciding where to draw the boundaries that will yield network data of the highest grade. As we shall see, there are two main schools. One operates with personal networks, and the other with total networks. The latter school is more pertinent to the structural subjects of this book, but we dare not disregard the former, one of the linchpins of relational sociology.

The Small World Problem

Everyone has probably already met a stranger, only to discover one or more mutual acquaintances and sigh 'Gee, what a small world!' Some sociologists have gone on to wonder how this actually works out in the field. The first studies date back to the 1960s and we now know a good deal about the small world problem. We shall briefly sketch out the formal aspects (Kochen, 1989) and proceed directly to a few empirical results.

There are several strategies with which to tackle the problem of chance encounter. One angle is to start by asking: 'To what *degree* does every member of a given group know every other member?' It is conceivable that, although every member will not have met every other directly, they are nonetheless all linked to one another by chains of acquaintanceship with varying numbers of intermediaries. The average number of intermediaries between two people indicates the degree to which everyone knows everyone else. Person-to-person chains (see Chapter 3) must exist that will eventually link up absolutely any two individuals, except of course for members of totally isolated groups who know zero non-members. If *a* and *z* are any two individuals, a chain of intermediaries exists somewhere out there such that we obtain $a-b-c \ldots x-y-z$. This reformulates the small world problem to read: given two individuals chosen at random in any population, what is the probability that 0, 1, 2 or *k* is the minimum number of intermediaries required to connect them?

In order to collect empirical data for an answer to that question on the scale of societies like France or the United States, we need a tool of investigation. Stanley Milgram was one of the first to design and apply this sort of interviewing tool in the field and his works have become classics (Milgram, 1967). We shall describe the results from a study he conducted with Jeffrey Travers (Travers and Milgram, 1969). They sum up their procedure as follows:

> An arbitrary 'target person' and a group of 'starting persons' were selected, and an attempt was made to generate an acquaintance chain from each starter to the target. Each starter was provided with a document and asked to begin moving it by mail toward the target. The document described the study, named the target, and asked the recipient to become a participant by sending the document on. It was stipulated that the document could be sent only to a first-name acquaintance of the sender. The sender was urged to choose the recipient in such a way as to advance the progress of the document toward the target; several items of information about the target were provided to guide each new sender in his choice of recipient. Thus, each document made its way along a chain of acquaintances of indefinite length, a chain which would end only when it reached the target or when someone along the way declined to participate. Certain basic information, such as age, sex and occupation, was collected for each participant.

Documents operated just like biological markers.

All starters were told the target was a stockbroker living in Boston. They were divided into the following three populations:

(a) a random sample of Boston residents ($n = 100$)
(b) a random sample from all Nebraska residents ($n = 96$)
(c) a sample of share-owning Nebraska residents ($n = 100$).

The three samples were designed to reveal whether living nearer the target or having some business connection to him affected the number of intermediaries needed to reach him. In addition to the token document, each starter received a set of instructions that included, for example:

> If you know the target person on a personal basis, mail this folder directly to him. Do this only if you have previously met the target person and know each other on a first name basis. If you do not know the target person on a personal basis, do not try to contact him directly. Instead, mail this folder to a personal acquaintance who is more likely than you to know the target person. You may send the booklet on to a friend, relative or acquaintance, but it must be someone you know personally.

To prevent a document from looping back to someone who had already seen and relayed it, a roster was attached for signature by each sender. Thus all senders had a list of everyone who had already handled the

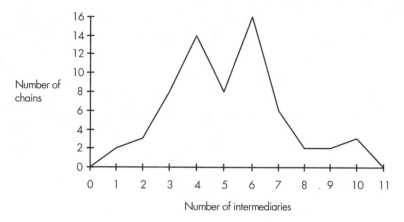

Figure 1.1   Length of completed communication chains (Travers and Milgram, 1969)

packet. The last attachment was a questionnaire about the sender and his or her relations.

Of the 296 persons in the three starting samples, 217 actually moved their documents. The target eventually received 64. The rest were classified as 'incomplete chains' because they were mislaid or forgotten along the way. Milgram and Travers point out that the proportion of incomplete chains diminished with the number of intermediaries. In other words, the chances of putting through the document *increased with* the number of intermediaries. Rosters must therefore have been a motivating factor. Nonetheless, not all relations proved transitive.

Among those that were transitive, 86% of participants sent the document to friends or acquaintances and 14% to kin. The distribution curve in Figure 1.1 shows the lengths of the 64 'complete' chains that reached the target. Chain length is the number of intermediaries needed to connect a starter in a random sample to the target. The mean in this study was 5.2. With due regard for the dangers of generalizing, the Milgram and Travers study demonstrates it only takes an average of five people to connect any two people in a country of over 250 million inhabitants.

This same graph also shows that chain length distribution is bimodal. The Mann–Whitney test confirms a significant difference between the two peaks flanking the trough near the median. Further investigation revealed they reflect two types of complete chains. Complete chains that reached the target person by exploiting knowledge of his address averaged 6.1 intermediaries, while chains exploiting knowledge of the target's job averaged only 4.6. This explains the bimodal distribution. Documents which exploited address to reach the target reached Boston quickly, but floundered for some time before final arrival. On the other hand, documents routed with the help of job knowledge reached the target's employer more quickly and contact followed immediately thereafter. Nonetheless, complete chains with random starters in Boston often proved shorter than similar chains out of Nebraska and the difference is significant (4.4 versus 5.7 intermediaries respectively).

The chains show overlap as they converge on the target. In other words, some intermediaries appear in several chains and this phenomenon increases the closer one comes to the target. The 64 copies of the packet were finally handed to him by only 26 people. The target received 16 documents from one neighbour alone, 10 from the same work colleague and five from a second colleague (the rest were scattered among the 23 other individuals). In the end, these three penultimate intermediaries accounted for 48% of completed chains. This convergence in communication chains on certain people is an important feature of small world networks.

Milgram's experiment made a breakthrough in the small world problem when he established that the average distance between two individuals was about five people in a mass society. Later studies (Kochen, 1989) confirm that this value is relatively stable, even with substantial variations in starter selection criteria. So it is important to remember the figure and to know it is stable.

Computer simulations on a planetary model claim that 'no more than 10 or 12 links are required to go from any person to any other person via the relationship "knows", where "knows" is defined as can recognize and be recognized by face and name' (Rapoport and Yuan, 1989). Small world research has a wide range of applications including epidemiology and biased samples in statistics.

How Many People Do You Know?

We have just discussed chains of acquaintances as if the definition were self-evident. But what exactly does it mean to *know* someone? We 'know' a state governor or a film star because we have a name and lots of information about her. With that definition, anybody can list huge numbers of people she 'knows' but yield no faithful picture of her network. So 'know' needs to mean 'know personally'. But we need an even more restrictive definition if we are to design useful studies and obtain intelligible results.

Granovetter (1976) was the first of many authors to insist that the question 'how many people do you know?' as such has little sociological meaning. Questions become meaningful in a study only if they yield results whose quality can be evaluated, i.e. the questions conform to an interview methodology and to a reliable sampling process. In short, the question 'how many people do you know?' becomes meaningless if detached from the method used to obtain a list of names from respondents. But the first issue is the exact meaning of 'how many people have you personally met or established direct contact with?'

Ithiel de Sola Pool (1978) once ran a little personal experiment. Every day he listed every contact with everyone he had already met. It lasted 100 days. Over time he witnessed a decline in the number of new people on his daily lists that never reached zero. He then extrapolated this curve to estimate how many acquaintances he would have totalled after keeping the list for 20 years. The answer is 3,500. In an older but still famous study, no doubt because it was the first of its kind, Epstein (1969) followed a single respondent around on all his weekend trips to list all his contacts. He was trying to prove that an African villager was not necessarily isolated in the city. He too found healthy numbers of contacts.

In another study, Sola Pool started by memorizing family names out of a phone book. He chose the Chicago and Manhattan directories, selected 30 pages at random from each and read them. Every time he saw a name that reminded him of an acquaintance, he jotted down the acquaintance's name. For a total estimate, he multiplied the average number of acquaintances per page by the total number of pages. His totals were 3,100 for the Chicago directory and 4,250 for the Manhattan directory. The difference is significant and raises questions about the effects of non-random name distribution in phone books. Some common names in the 30 page samples were more common than others, while rare names were missed.

Freeman and Thompson (1989) undercut this bias by taking chance phone book readings of names, not pages. They used the Orange County, California phone book and sampled students at the Irvine campus of the University of California. A computer selected 305 of the 112,147 listings and 247 students were asked to read the short list and report anyone they knew with the same family name. They were then asked for the reported person's first name and the type of relation (e.g. friend, cousin). The 305 names elicited respondent lists containing 0 to 58 names and averaging 15. They extrapolated the average to estimate that scrutiny of the entire phone book would have averaged 5,520 acquaintances per respondent (confidence interval 4,707 to 6,333). Distribution is clearly asymmetrical and networks of under 2,000 prevail. One network ran to about 20,000. Results clearly vary with methods. They do however converge strongly towards average sizes of about 5,000. There is significant scattering, probably due to social status. It is also probable that Irvine student networks of less than 2,000 will beef up once they enter the job market and settle down.

These results confirm Sola Pool's and give a good idea of the size of the average adult's personal network. Note that Sola Pool's experiment is easily reproducible. All you need is a good phone book. A 'good' directory is a list of names which is representative of the population in which the respondent has lived and fairly reflects all national and ethnic origins. Freeman's precaution of checking for representative distribution on the lists he gave his respondents is extremely important if results are to be meaningful.

Estimating a person's total number of acquaintances in a limited population, such as that of a city, is a somewhat different matter. Some authors have used the list questionnaires developed by Granovetter, which are discussed in the Appendix. For the moment, we need only know that list questionnaires consist of a random sample of names drawn from the entire population of the survey city. They ask respondents to indicate who they know or do not know on the list. The underlying principle differs here. Granovetter's method asks respondents to recognize specific persons while Sola Pool and Freeman only used names to trigger recall. The latter explores everyone a respondent knows: the scope is wide indeed. List questionnaire studies focus more on active links, even if contact is infrequent. They report networks of a few hundred people at most. But figures obviously vary with the size of the total population sampled.

Alternatively, some researchers limit an individual's network to those people who will do him a favour. This leads to another way of generating name lists. The technique consists of giving respondents a list of potential targets, telling them there is an important undelivered message, and asking 'How would you reach this person through your acquaintances?' All names are fake but carefully designed with built-in ethnic clues and rounded out with home addresses, job titles or other suggestive titbits. This sort of study merely aims to identify the first link that respondents would choose to reach their targets. In their first study, Killworth and Bernard (1978) submitted a list of 1,267 targets to 40 respondents, who volunteered an average of 210 names. A subsequent study (Killworth et al., 1984) with 40 respondents and 500 targets reports an average of 135 acquaintances per respondent.

All these approaches focus on virtual links. No respondent receives a deadline and an instruction to actually establish contact. Nor is anyone asked about the nature of links to the people they cite. The study simply seeks out the longest possible lists of people who meet the 'personally know' criterion. Imagination is any researcher's best friend and there is always room for new approaches, but this type of questioning will not teach us any more about personal relations.

The name generator is one tool to study both virtual and real links in a personal network, or only the latter. We shall see how it performs on a family. The researcher focuses on one family member who lists father, mother, spouse, parents-in-law and children. Scope can optionally be extended to siblings, siblings-in-law, cousins and beyond. Family is a strong structure and the researcher need only frame a clear definition of kinship for respondents to reel off the right names. The interview can then delve into the details for each name cited and the links to the respondent. The sociologist operates like an electronics technician checking current flow between pairs of points on a circuit board. Family is doubtless the most 'natural' example of structure, but virtual networks can also be defined in terms of spatial proximity. In this case, the virtual network is constructed around the respondent at the centre. All coworkers or job contacts also constitute virtual links, forming a platform to explore for friendship and other personal links.

It thus appears that the distinction between virtual links and real links refers not to the presence or absence of contacts but to the fact that a cognitive principle is operative among people. Family ties, spatial proximity, common employers and previous contacts are all no less than cognitive principles to which the researcher refers in order to map out the virtual links on which she bases interviewing. Questions may cover the content, form and frequency of interactions. Thus name generators carry a simple imperative: the cognitive principle underpinning the study must be explicitly stated and as unequivocal as possible.

Personal address books are a real temptation. The researcher just asks respondents to flip them out, asks questions about each entry and fills up interview forms with lots of answers. His wisely designed questions will probably cover personal information about the contact and the nature of relations to the respondent. But unfortunately such a researcher is rashly assuming that address books are a meaningful cognitive principle and some people fail to update them regularly.

Some name generators work backwards. Instead of starting with a list of virtual links to see which are active and how, they infer the cognitive principle at work after interviewing active links.

One hallmark of active links is contact. Here the researcher tries to enumerate who the respondent has contacted over a given period. But point-blank questions are tricky. Too many studies have tried this, only to discover how many contacts respondents had forgotten – and the forgetfulness obeys a pattern. Frequent contacts and people involved in important events are more memorable than others. The diary is a handy way around this problem. Every respondent is issued with a pocket notebook and instructions to write down every contact in the study timeframe (Granovetter ran one such study for 100 days). As an example, we shall now review the *contact entre les personnes* (interpersonal contacts) study carried out from May 1982 to May 1983 by INSEE, the French national statistical institute.

It surveyed a representative sample of 5,900 French households in eight phases to detect seasonal variations. One household member was singled out as prime respondent. It is ill-advised to question one person, even another family member, about someone else's relations. Researchers issued diaries for one week. Respondents were instructed to write up every direct contact they made once daily, including names, circumstances and personal data about the contact. At the second interview, researchers rounded out the data with any follow-up questions needed. In particular, they classified contacts into 10 broad categories (kin, friends, neighbours, coworkers, shopkeepers, club comembers, practical/total strangers, indirect relations, others, and difficult to classify).

Diaries are invaluable. They distinctly outperform unsupported questionnaires. They minimize bias due to memory lapse and respondent rationalizations *a posteriori*. Paradoxically, they also pick up weak links and rare contacts better than any other method. Offhand, you would expect a diary used over a short timespan to do this very poorly. But rare contacts turn up at a frequency approaching the actual rate for the entire population when the sample is correctly sized. Diaries record weak links that are fit for evaluation with greater statistical reliability than direct interviews which risk masking them. The downside is that some people hate to write. The INSEE study registered a 19% dropout rate, which rose to 30% for respondents without a high school diploma.

Diaries serve as name generators. They are excellent triggers to help respondents recall contacts. They also help to review the entire range of a respondent's areas of daily life, with circumstances and places of contact. But what about the results?

François Héran (1988b) summarizes that: 'The average adult sees seven kin per month, in-laws included. He has three or four friends, does one favour per year for one or two neighbouring households and belongs to one civic organization. That sums up the social life of the average individual aged 18+ years living at home, i.e. in any non-institutional environment.' The INSEE study also reports that the typical French citizen has an average of two strictly non-business conversations with each of 17 people per week, e.g. family, friends, neighbours and coworkers (range 0 to 80 people).

We also have the case of Claude Fisher's (1948) sociability study on 1,050 respondents, which resulted in a total of 19,417 names. He investigated the following types of sociability:

1 who would care for their home if they went out of town – water plants, pick up the mail, etc.
2 (if the respondents worked) with whom they talked about decisions at work
3 who had help with household tasks in the past three months
4 with whom they had recently engaged in social activities (such as having over for dinner, or going to a movie)
5 with whom they had discussed common spare-time interests
6 (if the respondents were unmarried) who were their fiancé(e)s or 'best friends' they were dating
7 with whom they discussed personal worries
8 whose advice they considered in making important decisions
9 from whom they would or could borrow a large sum of money
10 who over 15 years lived in the same household (obtained from enumeration of the household).

In North America, the 1985 *General Social Survey* (GSS) is frequently cited as the first to explore personal networks. It asked a representative sample of 1,500 US residents with whom they discussed issues of personal importance. Results averaged three confidants per person. Alexis Ferrand (1991) interviewed a similar sample of 200 French persons for a study on sexual and emotional confidants. He too finds about three per person.

Therefore, the size of someone's social sphere varies with how the question is framed and what aspect of an ego network is being explored. A personal network is a set of concentric circles centred on the individual.

Acquaintances form the largest, a virtual network that includes everyone the respondent has ever met. The average for this outermost circle is about 5,000 people. The circle of immediate contacts is far smaller. The average respondent has only 100 to 200 people he can contact to link himself up to a target stranger. She has regular talks with fewer than 20 people per week, subject to variation with age, sex, education and other sociodemographic criteria. Again, real confidants average only three.

Actually, researchers show little interest in outermost circles. The most important studies focus on who respondents meet more or less regularly. This overview of name generators also illustrates the wide range of interview techniques available, but the sampling methods themselves are standard. More details on these surveys are in the Appendix.

Stars and Zones

The studies presented above seek to measure the size of personal networks that a given name generator will cover. Mostly based on representative samples, they belong to the first type of network analysis. Their output is called a personal network or an ego network. It readily submits to all manner of routine statistical processing to obtain inferences about networks on the scale of entire populations.

At a minimum, these studies either observe respondents over a certain timeframe or ask them to identify relations meeting a predetermined criterion. This gives us a star for each ego, but stars selected at random in the general population share no connection with each other. Nonetheless, you can still obtain a mean volume of relations, a standard deviation for distribution curves and more. But investigation must probe more deeply for representative structural data. Unfortunately, costs quickly become prohibitive and impose tradeoffs.

Studies can aim beyond the number of alters per ego and consider several types of relations (e.g. friends, relatives and neighbours) to obtain representative data on multiplexity in networks. We obtain frequency by observing the number of contacts over time or asking the ego for estimated figures. We interview every member of the ego's star about links among themselves to obtain an indicator for social density. Most often, density is reckoned from a random sample off a list of names supplied by the ego or selected by virtue of special relevance (e.g. kin and close friends in Bonvalet et al., 1993). With a medium-sized random sample of 10,000 persons for a single relation type and a density sample of five names per respondent, we instantly find ourselves saddled with an additional 50,000 interviews to perform. Plainly, few density studies get past this staggering point. One arguable solution is to ask the ego herself for data about relations among her alters. But this can be criticized on two counts. First, studies have shown that respondents are not necessarily well informed of all relations afoot within their network. Second, the data harvested differ from those between the ego and her direct relations. Direct relations are grounded in fact, whereas relations between alters belong to the realm of represented images; yet both will suffer processing as if they were homogeneous. Adding apples and oranges is hazardous.

As a rule, the best of personal network studies only capture a very rough structural picture of volume, frequency, multiplexity or density, and the statistical gain is a structural loss. For better results, structural analysis needs to operate on total networks.

This shifts us into the second type of network analysis, where the total network comes into being. The prime handicap of this approach is the time and expense of data collection on populations that range into the thousands. The approach is only feasible for smaller populations unrepresentative of mass society.

Moreover, researchers must design the right partitions into their study before the fieldwork. The two basic judgements concern the best population breakdown and which relations to study. As with personal networks, partitioning will always be somewhat arbitrary. No network has 'natural' frontiers; researchers impose them. Kinship networks can be vast but we usually draw the line at close living relatives. Organizations do have clear-cut institutional frontiers but they also have organic links to the outside world that need a cutoff at some point. Towns have legal borders but townfolk entertain relations further afield, which will usually be ruled out. A study of interneighbour relations in one housing project will exclude relations with individuals in the project down the street. Partitions are unavoidable because the innate transitivity of relations quickly mushrooms into unmanageable quantities of data. Because partitions are always somewhat arbitrary, we must ever bear in mind that there is always something *tentative* about network analysis data. For example, we study a smallish town and learn that townsman A has a relation to C but only through B. So we pencil in an indirect relation between A and B. Then we learn C lives in the next town and is disqualified for our study. So we take out the eraser and record both A and B as isolated individuals!

Obviously, researchers do their best to approximate ideal groups with clear identities such as high school class, company or township, but our vision always remains vulnerable to blind spots about partitioning anything except hermetically sealed communities.

Moreover, we are often dealing in asymmetrical relations. Ask a given villager to name his friends and compare the list with other villagers' lists. The chances of symmetry are slim: A names B and C, and C names A, but B may very well name neither, as shown in the following graph:

This asymmetry may feel peculiar at first glance but it proceeds from the question asked. Symmetry improves markedly if we only ask for lists of best friends, but it would still be imperfect because A may consider B as her best friend, but B may see his best friend in D, and D in A. This graphs differently:

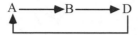

The odds of finding perfect symmetry in exchange networks are equally slim, if only from the standpoint of the value of the commodities they trade. But sometimes vice turns to virtue and a wealth of network analysis methods exploit asymmetry to churn out more thought-provoking results than symmetrical graphs will allow.

The total network approach dates back to 1934 and the publication of Jacob L. Moreno's key study *Who Shall Survive*. But his taste for formal analysis of social groups is older still: the preface he wrote for the French translation gives 1923 for his first total network studies (*Fondements de la sociométrie*, 1954). In 1937, the review *Sociometry* was founded and the discipline started winning a following in the 1940s. The first French studies came out in 1950. More recently, Pierre Parlebas (1992) reviewed the field and presented a special chapter on the application of total networks to the world of sports.

The sociogram is a sociometric tool used to build a record of relations among members of a group, but we should bear in mind Moreno's maxim that sociometry is a science of action that turns passive respondents into active researchers who participate in both the experiment and data evaluation.

Moreno's study on affinities between schoolchildren relies heavily on sociograms. To create real rapport, he turned the children into actors by walking into a classroom and announcing:

> You are seated now according to directions your teacher has given you. The neighbour who sits beside you is not chosen by you. You are now given the opportunity to choose the boy or girl whom you would like to have sit on either side of you. Write down whom you like best; then, whom you like second best. Look around you and make up your mind. Remember that next term the friends you choose now may sit beside you.

The children had a full minute's thinking time before being asked to write down the names. Here is a researcher who took pains to establish real personal contact with respondents and to impress them with the importance of their decisions.

One of Moreno's sociograms is given in Figure 1.2 as an example. It shows the results of this grade school experiment. Square and circle represent boy and girl respectively. Arrows show choices and unarrowed lines indicate reciprocal choices. We immediately notice that boys and girls

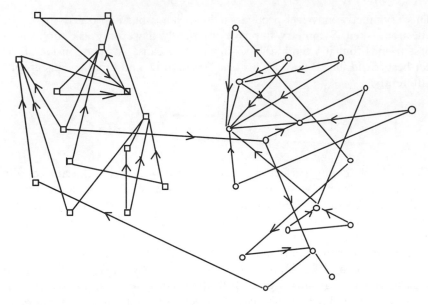

Figure 1.2   Grade school sociogram (based on Moreno, 1934)

rarely choose each other. The groups are disconnected except for two one-way choices.

Moreno went on to conduct a wealth of such sociometric studies and developed a theory of interaction that drew extensively on data from a sexual maturity study of children. He notes:

> From the first grade the group develops a more differentiated organization; the number of unchosen decreases, the number of pairs increases; from about the third grade on, chains and triangles appear . . . From the fourth grade on, the percentage of heterosexual attractions drops very low. There is indicated the beginning of a *sexual cleavage* which characterizes the organization from then on up to the eighth grade. Parallel with this, the number of pairs and of other social structures increases rapidly. It appears as if the sexual cleavage is accelerating the process of socialization, deepening the emotional bonds between the members of the two groups of boys and girls into which the class is now broken up.

More generally, he distinguishes the following stages:

1   first heterosexual phase up to 6–8 years of age
2   first homosexual phase at 8–13 years
3   second heterosexual phase at 13–15 years
4   second homosexual phase at 13–17 years.

The sociogram in Figure 1.2 can also be pictured as a group of overlapping sociometric stars. The person at the centre of each star is the ego and the person at the end of each arrow is an alter, someone the ego has selected. A sociometric questionnaire serves to sort relations into three types: positive choice (e.g. friends), negative choice (e.g. enemies) and indifference (neither). This serves to constellate the stars. The next step is to interview everyone in the population that is in the sociogram, e.g. a grade school class in the example above. Sociograms are standard tools today. The output data are sociometric choices, which add up to a *total* picture of an ego's network of binary relations: for each person, there is a choice by the ego and thus the presence of an ego/alter relation, or a non-choice by the ego and so the absence of an ego/alter relation. Later we shall see how sociograms, which express a network in its most primitive form, offer a basis not only for mapping out relations but also for setting up matrices that can be processed in many statistically valuable ways. Returning to sociometric choices, we shall only be referring to positive choices of an affinitive nature.

In France, the national demographic survey institute (INED) once attempted a sociogram for an entire village. Daniel Courgeau (1972) selected the village of Nolay and neighbouring villages in Burgundy. Ideally, he wanted to recruit every inhabitant. Out of a total of 1,394 permanent dwellings, he managed to interview 459 households (33%). Interviewing 260 out of the 500 households in Nolay proper, he scored 52%. Notation for respondents was as follows:

c_1 child living with the respondent
c_2 child no longer living with the respondent
r_1 relative seen at least once a month
r_2 relative seen less than once a month but with phone/mail contact at least once a month
r_3 relative seen less than once a month or unspecified contact frequency
f_1 friend seen at least once a month
f_2 friend seen less than once a month but with phone/mail contact at least once a month
f_3 friend seen less than once a month or unspecified contact frequency.

The average number of relations by type in Nolay is as follows:

c_1	c_2	r_1	r_2	r_3	f_1	f_2	f_3	Total
1.2	0.8	2.4	0.7	2.9	1.8	0.3	1.7	11.8

In reality, total and personal networks are complementary. The socio-graphy of large populations needs the personal network approach, and structural sociology needs the total network approach. In any case, nothing stops us from switching back and forth. When reconstructing a total network, respondents may be interviewed in any order, or we can start from the ego and use his responses as a basis for subsequent interviews. We have a star in the strict sense of the term when there are no cross-linking data on alters, but we shall speak of an ego zone (Barnes, 1972) whenever we have those data. Once the ego names A, B and C, we interview A, B and C to constitute the ego zone (Figure 1.3). However, each of the three is also an ego who will name new alters α, β, γ and δ; these configure into a

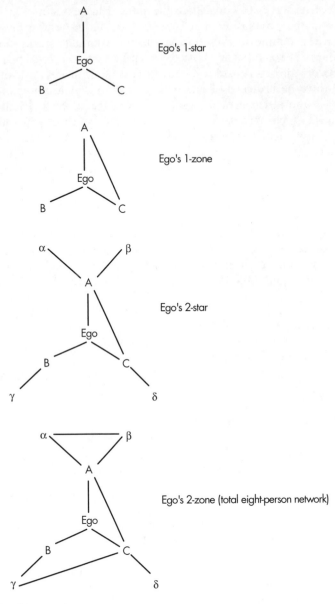

Ego's 1-star

Ego's 1-zone

Ego's 2-star

Ego's 2-zone (total eight-person network)

Figure 1.3　Stars and zones

2-star from the standpoint of the first ego, but a 1-star for egos A, B or C. We need only to repeat the process until we have pinned down every member of the survey population. Or we can settle for a snowball sample by restricting in advance how many times we iterate the naming process. A total network is no more than the sum of interconnecting stars or personal networks.

Snowball samples link up the total and personal network approaches, but the complexity involved quickly spirals out of control (Snijders, 1992). However this method is useful and justified to detect rare or hidden populations (Spreen, 1992).

By now, moderately alert readers will have understood that our focus is on total networks. Nonetheless we shall toggle over into personal network data whenever they offer better insight into sociability or into certain elementary features of structure.

2 PERSONAL NETWORKS AND LOCAL CIRCLES

Sociability studies are a sort of kickoff point for structural analysis. First, we can stick to describing personal networks in terms of behaviour patterns such as filmgoing, club meetings and social evenings. These patterns are the platform on which we base an understanding of the relations that make up the structures. We then enrich the stars with density and other zone data for structural insight. We can also adopt a more global viewpoint by looking at how relations weave the fabric of a local society. Researchers tend to think in terms either of a community, which expresses at least some degree of unification at the local level, or of a circle, which generalizes the idea of interpersonal links.

Before going into the various sociological definitions of sociability, we first need to strip the word of its psychological connotations. Sociology says sociability should be understood not as a person's intrinsic trait or ability to 'mix' but simply as a set of relations that an individual or group maintains with others, including their forms.

In the early twentieth century, Simmel (1911) became the first to raise the issue of sociability as a sociological concept. 'I thus designate sociability as the *play-form of association*,' he asserts, adding that 'Its character is determined by . . . amiability, refinement, cordiality and many other sources of attraction' that affect content. This opened the floodgates for numerous other researchers. Neighbourhood studies (McKenzie, 1921) began focusing on social disintegration in the city (Park and Burgess, 1925) and this line of research evolved into the Chicago school of sociology. The American school of interactionism gradually came to emphasize the importance of the exchange ritual (Goffman, 1967) and its symbology (Goffman, 1959). Community studies based its interpretation of how communities function on sociability (Lynd and Lynd, 1937; Caplow and Forman, 1950; Young and Willmott, 1957; Gans, 1962; 1967). Organizational sociology uses on-the-job sociability (Sainsaulieu, 1977) as one way of understanding how some organizations function or malfunction. The list goes on because sociability is so broadly defined that several specializations of sociology have found the concept appealing in one way or another. The Frenchman Gurvitch (1950) even wanted to raise sociability into a 'total social phenomenon' that would become a field apart and explain all manner of social woes.

We are restricting ourselves to network-oriented research, i.e. research that homes in on sociability proper. In France, qualitative and quantitative studies of this ilk fall into the following categories:

1 ethnographic or sociographic local network studies that most often disregard the workplace (Bozon, 1984 and Forsé, 1981b respectively)
2 on- versus off-the job sociability studies (Bidart, 1997; Bozon and Lemel, 1990)
3 localized or delocalized milieu studies (e.g. working class sociability) (Dubar et al., 1982; Pinçon, 1986)
4 statistical studies of personal networks.[1]

Regardless of category, sociability studies focus on the form, function and content of relations. Content has become a field in its own right and has spawned its own assortment of focused studies. One type of content study investigates transactions or exchanges in information, services, goods, people and even emotions. A second sort stresses the influence of status and the process of identification or differentiation which results from the respective positions of actors in a network. A third reports on control over relations within a group. A final set of studies examines how a network's image affects actor relations and strategies (Guilbot, 1979). All or any of these aspects can be studied simultaneously, of course. One interesting possibility is to investigate how transactions and social status affect links. Another is the interplay between relational form and function. Each of these studies offers its own brand of insight toward a finer understanding of sociability.

Forms of Sociability

Sociability is either formal or informal. This usually means it is either organized or spontaneous. However, 'spontaneous' does not mean 'uninhibited' since the game of sociability is always played by rules and norms. In practice, the real distinction is that formal sociability operates within an organization or institution such as a school or company while the informal thrives around an unestablished setup like a coffee table or bar counter. Obviously, there are examples between these extremes, such as when a political party canvasses support from prominent citizens, or when social circles crystallize ire into an action committee against an organization. Still, informal sociability most often correlates with a lower degree of role specialization, but a shift of perspective can make 'formal' look 'informal' or vice versa. A company will chart formal links into an organization table but there will be an underlying network of informal relations beneath it. A group of friends may reach critical mass and found a club or society. They write up articles of incorporation that stake out frontiers with the outside world and elect officers to formalize internal relations. Yet all these formal links still allow the informal network to continue operating after business hours.

Sociability can also be either collective or individual. The distinction lies in whether or not the relation continues to exist outside the group or specific supportive context, i.e. whether other relations are vital to its existence or the relation is strictly interpersonal. For example, a Friday night poker party is collective, but the sociability becomes individual when two players go fishing together on Saturday morning. Some relations do not survive the disappearance of the collective context of their practice. A teenage gang generally has strong relations but most dyadic relations dissolve once the gang breaks up. Family ethnologists report that brothers see each other frequently until the death of their common ancestors, at which point frequency tends to nosedive. At the other extreme, veterans may pursue sociability well into old age regardless of the chasms that build up over the years.

Sociability is also either of weak or of strong intensity, ranging from passing acquaintances through to best friends. And the final distinction is between elective and affinitive relations. One's choice of workmates is restricted. Family member relations allow some leeway for choice and are semi-elective. The choice of a lover is based on pure affinity. You are free to love whom you will, but the relation will still obey norms and sociological patterns. And with that paradox, we shall move on.

Affinitive Relations

In qualitative studies, respondents stress certain essential traits when asked to define friendship. It is egalitarian and therefore rules out authority or hierarchy but not influence. It is reciprocal, with expectations of some sort of two-way flow. It is contracted freely and rejects constraint or coercion. There is but little leeway on these definitions, and we would add that, in industrialized societies, we prefer something 'uninstitutional' about our friendships. Friendship norms are also more flexible than other norms. But there is fact and fancy in friendship too.

Ethnologists have long known that friendship means very different things from one society to the next. Robert Brain (1976) ran one comparative study that equated the friendship link with the marriage link in agrarian or rural societies. Just as the prime function of marriage is to establish an alliance between two kinships by swapping women, friendship establishes bonds between the groups to which principals belong. Like marriage, it is ritualized and institutionalized. In many societies, the inner hunger for a counterpart finds expression in myths about twins. The myths depict man as a dual being torn in half and doomed to tarry in a bid to recover his other self. When he eventually finds that lost love or friend, he seals the alliance, thereby contributing to restoring order in a universe of chaos.

Friendship rituals underscore the permanence of the alliance. Everybody institutionalizes friendship. Brain notes that blood brothers were common in the early Middle Ages of Europe. He writes: 'Initially the Church itself had sanctioned this rite, the priest offering up a prayer in which he dwelt on the duties of the two comrades who wished to become blood brothers. He then witnessed the declaration of a solemn oath between the two friends, who kissed and then scratched each other's arms, mixing a few drops of blood with wine, which they drank.' The Church later condemned this ritual but continued to sanctify other forms of friendship. Baptism is one rite where priests seal links among godfathers, godmothers and the child's parents. An institution called *compadrazgo* still exists in many communities. Brain translates this bond as 'co-godparenthood' and defines it as

> the relation between the parents and godparents of a child christened in church; through their participation in the ceremony, godfathers, godmothers, the parents of the child, and sometimes the priest who baptized the child, become ritually related. Having replaced the 'pagan' institution of blood brotherhood, *compadrazgo* became common all over Europe and still exists in parts of Greece, Italy, Russia, Serbia and Spain. In England, co-godparents were known as godsibs (that is 'siblings in God'); here, however, the relationship did not endure as an institution and went through the vicissitudes of social change which the etymology of the word – from godsib to gossip – indicates.

Links are even institutionalized before God between cousins-in-law in Hispanic countries, from where the word originates.

The Church thus consecrates both friendship and marriage as unique and permanent. Myth consecrates the twins as unique too. They are 'given unto us', not chosen by us, and they are irreplaceable. Industrialized societies retain key features of this myth: the term 'best friend' infers a relation more durable than others of the same nature.

The need for the superlative shows that friendship is a weaker link than it used to be. Godparenthoods still exists but today it is honorary rather than an institution. Marriage has changed from bond to lease and 'friends' change with a new job or house move. Today, bonds and links can be mixed, matched and replaced. Mythically speaking, we live in a cosmos of 'interchangeable twins'. The idealization of 'my one and only' or 'best friend' is less a feature of resistance to this trend than one of compensation. It has ballooned as quickly as relations have become increasingly inter-changeable. In Western societies, the Vatican alone seems to be sticking to tradition. So we have a gap between affinitive ideal and practical reality, because ideals tend to hover near traditional symbology.

Qualitative inquiries on this subject (Allan, 1979) define friendship between two people as being of two kinds. With some leeway, some see friendship as a link that is instrumental, while others see it as expressive of solidarity (Allan, 1989). In the first case, a friend is someone to count on to face a problem, i.e. 'A friend in need is a friend indeed.' For others, a friend is whom you tell secrets to. The definitions are not necessarily mutually exclusive, but working class men favour the first attitude and middle/ upper class women prefer the second (Bidart, 1997). In both cases, friend-ship assumes reciprocity, i.e. solidarity. It expects you to 'keep the ball rolling'. Traditionally, of course, affinitive relations have always operated by establishing links of mutual obligation between two people or groups. This is nothing new. What is new is their weakening.

Interchangeable affinitive relations do not suffer strong institutionalization, but will cope to some degree. We still attend weddings that preserve traditional attributes but most couples are now 'living together' with commitments they do not consider readily breakable. Longer lifespans mean godparents are unlikely to need to give effect to their commitment to become foster parents in the event of parental death. Today children get only one token godmother and godfather apiece and links to the godchild may be quite loose. Nonetheless, devout godparents still take the responsibility seriously. Friendship rites are of more variable geometry nowadays too. Rights and duties are more flexible and implicit. But, beyond the categorical imperative of reciprocity, ancient customs are surviving remarkably well. Having friends over for dinner is an update of ancient rituals, with gifts of food going both ways as tokens of trust and friendship. In most societies, friends and lovers still maintain, more or less loosely, the ritual of exchanging gifts and services (e.g. birthday presents, which perpetuate a cyclic perception of time).

We shall take a tangent here to explain the quite similar treatment we have given to friends and lovers. Language itself incarnates the ambiguity. English calls lovers boy*friend* and girl*friend*, while the French equivalent translates as 'little *friend*' and Swedish just says '*friend*'. Obvious distinctions between the two are of course in order. Commerce functions differently on the friendship and marriage markets. Friendship implies no duty of sexual reproduction. But that said, other absolute distinctions are hard to find. Most general features are common to both, with a few exceptions. One such exception is that most friendships are same-sex while heterosexual marriage prevails. But majority is not the only yardstick. On this point, Brain speaks of African tribes that allow wealthy women to marry a woman and establish their own *patriarchal* lineage. They become honorary *fathers* (yes, there *are* also examples of man-to-man marriage, so to speak). But if we set aside the exceptions, relations between friends and lovers obey specific patterns that operate much the same way. The main point subsists: the function of both relations is to establish links of reciprocal solidarity between individuals and groups. Leaving this tangent, we return to the characteristics of the affinitive exchange. We have seen that it assumes relating on an equal footing, whatever the degree of ritualization or institutionalization. Representation and reality concur on this point.

Homogamy and Homophily

The data confirm that 'birds of feather flock together', and homophily is a key feature of affinitive relations. Homophily between spouses or lovers is referred to as homogamy, but they are essentially one and the same. In industrialized societies, like attracts like in love and friendship despite

Table 2.1   Homogamy coefficients by spouses' social origin

Husbands	Wives			
	Farmers	Lower class	Middle class	Upper class
Farmers	2.56	0.62	0.59	0.30
Lower class	0.61	1.38	0.86	0.45
Middle class	0.58	0.89	1.37	1.32
Upper class	0.34	0.43	1.42	4.92

In each cell the observed number of couples is divided by the number expected if there was complete independence between spouses' social origins. Values greater than 1 indicate a preferential choice.

Source: INSEE Emploi survey, 1989, authors' computations

freedom of choice. Moreover, homophily and homogamy share certain criteria. Friends and lovers tend to be of roughly the same age, family background, social and job categories. They share similar levels of education and live in the same neighbourhood. Personal networks owe precious little to random sampling: they are the product of homophilic bias.

One example is given in Table 2.1, which summarizes the data on ascribed status homogamy computed from the 1989 INSEE *Emploi* labour force survey. Social origin of spouses is judged by fathers' occupations classified into four main categories. The fundamental trend is towards homogamy, regardless of social origin (Boudon's homogamy index is 0.51).[2] However, Michel Forsé and Louis Chauvel (1995) have shown that, all other things equal, homogamy declined between the previous and the present generations if we look at social origin, although it remains practically stable in terms of level of education. So change is possible. As other studies also show, achieved status (e.g. educational level) tends to outweigh ascribed status (e.g. social origin) in contemporary societies. All these changes notwithstanding, homogamy is the name of the game.

The conclusions for homophily are comparable, according to two studies on three 100-respondent samples each of corporate factory workers, office workers and executives by Jean Maisonneuve (Maisonneuve, 1966; Maisonneuve and Lamy, 1993). Table 2.2 suggests the following conclusions:

(a)   Homophily based on occupation shows an overall decline (the index drops from 0.50 to 0.40) but affinities between professional categories remain strong and unchanged. Office workers, technicians and middle managers act as intermediaries. Extremes socialize little and prefer to communicate by establishing relations with intermediaries who operate as bridges despite their own homophily.

(b)   Homophily based on economic resources is moving the other way and comes out strengthened.

(c)   Educational homophily is fairly stable on the whole, despite a slight dip; it is stable among executives, declining among workers and rising among office workers.

Table 2.2   Homophily evolution by occupation, education and income (%)

Have friends who are/have:	Workers 1960	Workers 1990	Clerks 1960	Clerks 1990	Engineers 1960	Engineers 1990	Average 1960	Average 1990
Production workers	50	40	15	5	2	2	22	16
Technicians	6	14	2.5	13	3	11	4	13
Craftsmen, shopkeepers	7	9	6	10	5	6	6	8
Clerks	17	19	53	41	8	8	26	23
Middle managers	4	8	8	17	9	18	7	14
Upper managers	1.5	5	4	5	45	41	17	17
Professionals	1	1.5	1.5	3	8	8	3	4
Rural inhabitants	2	0	2.5	2	1	2	2	2
Inactive and others	11.5	3.5	7.5	3	19	4	13	3
Same income	71	91	67	72	73	76	70	79
Greater income	25	9	27	23	14	5	22	11
Lower income	4	0	6	5	13	19	8	10
Same level of education	74	60	52	61	64	62	64	61
Greater level of education	14	26	20	13	3	6	11	14
Lower level of education	12	14	28	26	33	32	25	25

For each of the three groups of row variables, the columns total 100%.

Source: Maisonneuve and Lamy, 1993

The overall picture is roughly the same as for homogamy. Despite some slippage over the past 30 years, homophily remains significantly more probable than heterophily. We can reasonably presume this is mostly due to the tighter weave of today's professional networks. On the other hand, educational homophily holds its ground, tending to confirm that cultural stratification is stronger than occupational stratification. However, these conclusions are strictly tentative since Maisonneuve points out he used unadjusted data for his statistical analysis.

There is no shortage of hypotheses to account for homophily. First, individuals will readily see a peer in someone whose lifestyle and standard of living are broadly similar to their own. Peers stand a higher than average chance of sharing common personal tastes, opinions and values which make it easier to establish affinitive relations. This tendency is reinforced by objective lifestyle features. For example, people of similar social backgrounds tend to live in the same neighbourhoods, thus generating homophilic synergy. People tend to select friends from among those in their own social environment where most introductions to other people occur. Friends also tend to live not too far apart, making frequent contact more convenient. One study of medium-sized US towns by Merton (1954) showed that 56% of men and 75% of women selected friends from among their neighbours. A 1979 study on best friends in the working class Malakoff suburb of Paris by Christian Baudelot and the ENSAE national school of statistics and economic administration confirms women see best friends more often than men because, in 24% of cases, as compared with 14% of men, they lived in the same community. The relative social homogeneity of neighbourhoods is thus closely bound with homophily based on status within a network.

Other contributing factors include the division of labour, which encourages contacts between equals and restricts contacts with more senior and junior levels, different occupations or personnel in other departments, companies and industries. In addition, marriages stand a higher chance of being homogamous than heterogamous because of homophily and the fact that networks generate most personal introductions to potential spouses (Girard, 1964; Bozon and Héran, 1987). Homogamous marriages then go on to foster homophily since the combined networks of the couple will most probably show strong sociodemographic overlap.

Thus numerous factors combine to explain why structural position and sociability relations show broad correlation. Given the social and economic barriers to socializing, two people need a good number of common traits to stand any chance of establishing a relation. People who are structurally remote from one another will tend to have mismatched traits and simply find few opportunities to mix. So it is; and statistical studies have unearthed other patterns pertinent to personal networks.

Sociability Relations

Statisticians have focused their skills on sociability as on any other domain. Numerous studies of large representative samples are available to estimate the prevalence of certain social patterns and how they correlate with a broad spectrum of sociodemographic variables.

The INSEE *Loisirs* leisure survey was the first investigation into French sociability. It defined sociability by activities. Yannick Lemel and Catherine Paradeise (1976) performed a secondary analysis on data for sports, evenings on the town (e.g. movie, restaurant), civic organization meetings, dinner parties at home, dinner parties out, cafés, card games and dancing. Forsé (1981a) ran two other such analyses: one was of the 1975 INSEE *Environnement de l'habitat survey*, which covers the same range of activities, and the other of the 1979 INSEE *Emploi du temps* (time budget) survey, which yields data on whom people share activities with. Finally, we also have secondary analyses for the 1982 INSEE *Contacts entre les personnes* survey, mentioned in Chapter 1, and the 1988 INSEE *Modes de vie* survey, which gives specific data on mutual help between households and brings in the personal network dimension. All this research has turned up a wealth of consistent behaviour patterns (all samples exceed 4,000 respondents).

The first salient conclusion is that sociability generally decreases with age. The number of contacts and conversations decline over the years, especially after 40. Contacts with coworkers all but disappear between the ages of 60 and 70, and contacts with friends wane too. Relations with neighbours or service suppliers (e.g. doctors or shopkeepers) fare better. Kin account for 20% of all contacts at age 20 but surge past 50% by age 80.

Second, the higher the social status, the greater is sociability with job contacts, friends and acquaintances. As shown in Figure 2.1 (Héran, 1988b),

Kinship relations

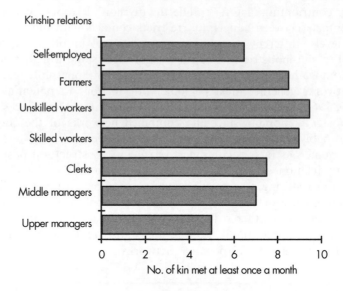

Friendship relations

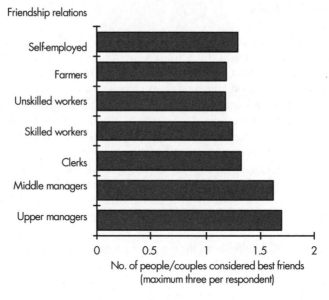

Figure 2.1   Kinship and friendship relations (Héran, 1988b)

salaried professions show a strong hierarchy. Executives and the liberal professions show the greatest proportions of friend contacts and the lowest levels of kin contact. The opposite holds for blue-collar workers. Farmers and self-employed workers are a special case.

The third big finding was that the French blue-collar workers' reputation for intense sociability as a strong subculture does not stand up to scrutiny.

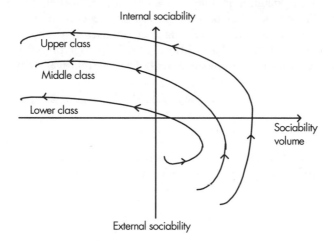

Figure 2.2   Sociability, age and social status (Forsé, 1981a)

Paradeise (1980) was the first to show this. Sociability is far less developed among factory workers than among executives, even if well-developed forms of sociability do exist, e.g. 'working class comradeship' or going to cafés (Hoggart, 1957; Sansot, 1991).

The fourth finding is based on an indicator of internal or external sociability. This indicator expresses physical or symbolic distance to the household (Forsé, 1981a). Young people tend to seek out external relations, e.g. clubs and sports teams. Sociability patterns shift toward the internal when they set up their own homes with a mate, and especially after the birth of a child. Sports and exercise now drop off and more evenings are spent in the privacy of the home. Sociability focuses on dinner parties in one home or another, the odd dinner at a restaurant, and membership of appropriate clubs. In old age, sociability shrinks to religious associations, kin and the local neighbourhood. Forsé summarizes the trends as in Figure 2.2. This graph summarizes the main trends detected by a principal component analysis. The abscissa shows the volume of contacts, increasing from left to right, while the ordinate gives sociability by type. It contrasts internal sociability with external sociability. Arrows indicate the direction of increasing age. Each curve plots a social stratum by age. So sociability goes through an initial upward swing toward the outside world in youth and flips over in a gradual decline before closing in on kin in old age. This broadly sums up the results of the different studies.

This overview offers an insight into how sociability functions in practice and into pertinent sociodemographic variables. Before going into details about links, we stress that our standpoint only claims to apply to *urban populations in industrialized societies*. Rural society networks show far more overlap between social circles (see Chapter 8) because everyone knows everyone and a neighbour may also be kin, coworker, friend and/or employer. The dissociation of these circles is the consequence of urbanization and industrialization, creating metropolises that sharply diminish relational overlap. Thus we have different types of sociability to analyse. In the big city, coworkers are not necessarily friends, relatives or neighbours.

Neighbours

François Héran (1987) based a sociability study on neighbours on four levels of contacts which are given in Table 2.3.

Table 2.3   Neighbourhood relations (%)

No contact	8.7
Small talk and coffee	18.8
Exchange of favours	44.8
Close ties	27.7

Source: Héran, 1987

Relations between neighbours are far more vulnerable to urbanization than any other form of sociability. Figure 2.3 shows that rural and small town populations enjoy above-average relation levels, while those in medium to large urban areas have below average levels. These 1990 data are stable: data from the 1970s plot out almost identically (Forsé, 1981a).

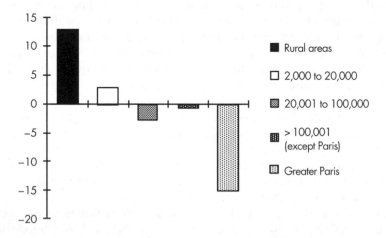

Figure 2.3   Neighbourhood relations and city sizes (deviations from the mean, %) (Forsé, 1993b)

Fun and Recreation

There is no shortage of excuses to go out. Standard French reasons include new films, cosy restaurants and soccer matches. Olivier Choquet's (1988) study on interpersonal contacts enumerates the average number of out-of-home activities per year including non-household members.[3] By specifying the involvement of non-members of the household, we increase the values obtained for workers and decrease those for executives and middle management, resulting in 89 per year for executives and skilled workers and 70 for unskilled workers (overall average = 73). This design somewhat attenuates the conclusions on worker sociability mentioned above.

The number of times people go out varies widely according to type of household and lifestyle. Extremes are 320 per year for an unmarried male in the 18–35 age range, and 16 for a married woman aged 60+ (Table 2.4). Women go out less than men across the board, but living as a couple is the biggest single reason for suddenly going out much less often. These differences apply to all age groups. The greater the age, the stronger the tendency to stay at home.

Table 2.4   Average number of out-of-home activities per year with non-household members, by age group and type of household

	18–35		36–60		60+	
	Men	Women	Men	Women	Men	Women
Single	320	220	168	72	51	21
Couple	107	57	63	32	33	16

Source: Choquet, 1988

About 55% of respondents go on hikes and car trips with friends and 45% take these with family. Over 70% of film, theatre and dance outings are between friends. Some 50% to 70% of sports and athletics events are shared with coworkers or neighbours or are in an athletic association. So there are distinct correlations between leisure activities and partner choices. Choquet's data are illustrated nicely in Figure 2.4.[4]

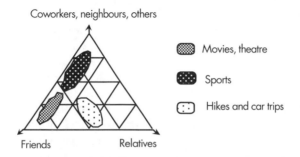

Figure 2.4   Leisure activities and partner choices (based on Choquet, 1988)

Studies also find that personal income affects attendance at football games, theatres and other paid entertainment (Forsé, 1993b). The number of available attractions varies with the size of a town, which influences attendance. The bigger the town, the more there is to do. And Paris is the crowning experience. All things equal, the effects remain stable.

Friends and Relatives

People visit family far more often than they go out. Forsé (1993b) analysed a 1990 survey on a quota sample of 2,000 adults aged 18+ by the BVA polling service. Over 41% of respondents called on family at least once a week and 42% less than once a week but more than once a month. Another 15% see family less often, and 2% never.

Family visiting frequency shows no gender difference. Marital status exerts significant but unspectacular influence. Married couples see relatives slightly more than singles, but divorcees of both sexes see them much more (50% visited family at least once a week). This ties in with another result. Divorce has become an accepted matrimonial pattern that now operates to reunite people with family rather than to isolate them. Thus, the family's traditional role as a haven of emotional and material support seems to weather the times quite successfully.

This positive effect of divorce applies across the entire social spectrum with no gender gap (in a similar way, celibacy undercuts family sociability). Unlike marriage and widowhood, divorce reconnects people to family regardless of class, education and other social variables.

The number of children has little significance. One can only argue the slightest correlation between more children and more family visits. As the 25–34 age group tend to visit family less, we might suggest that children's ages are more important than their number. Kin visits become more frequent with the birth of the first child. Any subsequent children carry no extra impact *per se*. Family visits slacken slightly as children mature. Therefore the life cycle has an effect on family sociability, but events such as divorce tend to intensify sociability while the birth of a second child and other events do not.

This profile applies to all social categories, but the frequency of family visits shows variations according to social class at each stage of life. The higher a person's occupational status, the less she is likely to socialize regularly with family: 57% of unskilled workers see family at least once a week as against 29% of executives. Visiting rates for self-employed urban-ites are about average but, among the unemployed, full-time housewives call on family most. Given the above, it is unsurprising to find that family sociability falls as income and social status rise. If we disregard lower educational levels, it is interesting to note that this inverse relationship divides people of identical occupational status, e.g. an office worker with an associate degree will see relatives less often than a coworker with a high school diploma. Whether profession itself exerts an impact is less clear and, all other things equal, the relationship is seen in blue- and white-collar workers but is insignificant in other social categories.

These results cast new light on our data. Family sociability is common to all social strata, but our data describe it better in workers than in the upper strata where relations of friendship are more highly developed, as we shall see. But the preceding studies did not point up the specific effect of job category on sociability.[5] The effect of occupational status on sociability becomes quite complex once we go beyond the working class. For example, low family sociability in the middle and upper strata results from more than the mere fact of being an executive. The data show that educational level has greater impact than job level on family sociability. In short, usually well-educated executives and middle managers socialize with relatives less frequently than usually less well-educated office and factory workers, but it is only among workers that the effect of low education combines with socioeconomic status to yield a high sociability with relatives.

The figures for sociability with friends are comparable to those for relatives: 40% see friends at least once a week, 43% less than once a week but at least once a month, 14% more rarely and 3% never.

Childless unmarried individuals see friends most. Frequency decreases until age 50 when it picks up slightly. Unlike kin sociability, higher education correlates with seeing friends more frequently. As with kin sociability, educational level explains frequency better than occupational status. Since friendship is the primary concern of Parisians up to age 35 with a higher education, high socializers are likely to be unmarried individuals, childless couples or executives.[6]

If the data are correct and the frequency of friendship relations rises as kin relations fall, this does not suggest that friends replace kin outright. Indeed, the under-35 age group do not neglect family visits despite an inclination to see friends frequently. Their probability of seeing kin only takes a plunge after film going and other activities come into effect. If kin and friend sociability do not compare point by point, it is because several types of sociability are at work simultaneously and any distinctions result from their combined impact in varying proportions.

Civic Organization Membership

After long stagnation, the French started joining civic organizations in larger numbers in the 1970s (Passaris and Raffi, 1984). Judging from official sources, the number of new not-for-profit organizations rose by 20% from 1977 to 1982. It grew by another 30% by 1987, which saw 51,327 new organizations. In 1992, 61,887 were founded, but the growth rate had fallen back to 20% (Forsé, 1984; 1993a). However, net variation is impossible to deduce because we do not know how many have folded.

Table 2.5   Voluntary association memberships and number of members

Type of non-profit organization	Membership (thousands)	(%)	Active members (thousands)
Athletic	9,350	27.6	8,280
Labour unions, professional societies	4,430	13.1	3,990
Educational/musical	3,040	9.0	2,780
Veterans	2,330	6.9	2,190
PTA	2,320	6.9	2,230
Charitable	2,230	6.6	1,900
Senior citizens	2,100	6.2	2,040
Tenants' residents	1,930	5.7	1,870
Religious	1,610	4.7	1,550
Alumni	1,030	3.0	1,000
Political	800	2.4	800
Corporate alumni	500	1.5	490
Ethnic	340	1.0	330
Consumer rights	340	1.0	330
Rotary and Lions clubs	250	0.7	250
Others	1,260	3.7	1,230
Total	33,860	100.0	20,030

Source: Héran, 1988a

Nonetheless, membership numbers confirm this trend. About one in two Frenchmen belongs to some voluntary association, as does one French-woman in three. The 1967 figures were 38% of men and 20% of women (Lemel and Paradeise, 1974). So we are talking about an important increase. Table 2.5 (Héran, 1988a) gives the overall breakdown of membership according to type of non-profit organization.

Multiple memberships are shown in this table via the difference between the number of active members and memberships. This distinction is common in most bodies, but not in political parties, Rotary clubs and the like.

Actual attendance at organization meetings is less frequent than visits to kin or friends: 13% attend at least once a week, 20% less than once a week but at least once a month, 26% more rarely and 41% never. There is also a significant gender difference: 36% of men attend meetings at least once a month as against 30% for women. This gap is narrower than in earlier studies and is close to insignificant, all other things equal. So the strong gender gap reported in older studies (Lemel and Paradeise, 1974) has probably shrunk.

Marriage affects attendance with only slight significance, but age is important. Attendance rises through to age 50 and then turns into mild decline. After 20 years of modest increases, senior citizens now score highest for weekly attendance and overperform in monthly attendance.[7] So pensioners are overcoming their reluctance and investing a significant share of their considerable free time in civic organizations. Yet the under-35 age group find civic organizations less attractive. Their attendance undershoots the national average and 50% report zero attendance. True, their rate of zero attendance is the same as that of the 60+ age group, but the other half of the latter show much higher attendance than the former.

The effect of education is only significant (with both raw and adjusted data) because of the gap between educational extremes. The highly educated are the keenest joiners. Behaviour patterns among other educational groups show change but differ less clearly. Trained technicians join more than secondary school graduates. Having a university degree still predisposes holders to join civic organizations, but at a gentler rate of increase than before and with variations according to type of degree.

Occupation is also significant. Although upper occupational categories show higher attendance than middle categories, the gap has been narrowing. When it comes to monthly attendance, executives underperform farmers but outperform pensioners and housewives. Attendance continues to slip through middle managers and office or factory workers. University students show low attendance, confirming general apathy by all youth towards civic organizations. However, the data confirm the strong commitment of pensioners. Self-employed non-farmers show the least commitment. For weekly meetings, middle managers and pensioners outperform executives. These two categories are the only ones to retain a net significant effect.

The above demonstrates that occupational categories do not suffice to explain involvement in civic organizations. Pensioners and middle management are catching up with executives and upsetting the familiar hierarchy that would have attendance and social status increase side by side.

Weekly meeting attendance rises with increasing urbanization, except for Paris where it remains minimal. Here again, it is difficult to establish a clear hierarchy, mostly because the positive impact of urbanization only applies to rural communities and big cities, and not to Paris where the impact is significantly negative.

On the whole, age is the only clearly significant factor that cuts across all categories. But the effect of age has been changing and we can expect pensioners to join civic organizations in even greater numbers in the future.

Several examples have already shown that different social categories are converging toward common patterns of sociability. But the data do not point to any upset on a mass scale. We repeat our main findings. Most film/theatregoers are under 35. Neighbour relations predominate in towns with fewer than 20,000 inhabitants. Executives are the strongest joiners of civic organizations. Sociability is not an area of spectacular change, but gradual change has been afoot and more is expected. Broadly speaking, the traditional distinctions began to blur between the 1960s and the 1990s, but remain generally relevant. However this does not imply the extinction of distinct types of sociability; it suggests only that individuals choose one type or another in a more haphazard fashion. Sociability is more diversified while the gaps between types have become more subtle and tenuous. Moreover, the slight decline of homophily and homogamy augurs greater overlap among networks in the future. On all these points, education remains a stratifying factor while occupations stratify less than before. Education now seems to play a greater role than occupation in determining the composition of personal networks and the types of sociability that prevail there.

Mutual Help

Up to now we have described relations in terms of volume, type and frequency. The next focus is on the transactional content of personal networks. We shall use the 1988 INSEE *Modes de vie* survey on French lifestyles based on a table respondents were asked to complete. It listed 18 different favours that households are likely to exchange. They were listed on a card submitted to respondents. Each column indicates one couple from a different housing unit with whom the respondent has already had at least one exchange. The instructions said: 'Using this card, mark down any work, favours or other assistance that have been exchanged between your household and other households in the past year (include close relatives, distant relatives, friends and neighbours). We want to know all kinds of help, however trivial, rare or commonplace.' Coding distinguished help received by respondents, help they provided and help operating both ways at once.

Alain Degenne and Marie-Odile Lebeaux (1991) were immediately struck by the fact that couples reported giving more help of almost all kinds than they received. The discrepancy is large for services like baby-sitting or driving someone somewhere (23.6% of couples had asked someone to baby-sit for them as against 37.2% who had baby-sat for others; 24.9% had asked someone for a ride and 40% had driven someone somewhere). The figures for minor household repairs and improvements tally more closely (20.6% and 20.4% for help received and given). The number of households with a baby to sit is lower than the number of potential baby-sitters, especially in the 50+ age group who baby-sit often but need no baby-sitters themselves. The same imbalance applies to most favours traded in the course of a day. Younger and older couples tend to receive most help while middle-aged couples with established households mostly tend to provide it. On the other hand, furniture moving, home improvements and physical labour are examples of help that entitles the provider to something in return. Here mutual backscratching is the rule and discrepancies are minimal or non-existent.

In another connection, kin are a more likely source of help and favours than unrelated couples. Again, discrepancies vary with type of help but two-thirds of all help comes from kin, as shown in Table 2.6.

The age of the head of household has an impact on help (Table 2.7). Babysitting is an obvious case where young couples receive help. Although they may baby-sit for others on occasion, this is help they will mostly receive and grandparents will mostly provide.

Table 2.6   Informal help from kin or non-kin couples

	Help from kin couples		Help from unrelated couples	
	Total	%	Total	%
Baby-sitting	3,336	70.4	1,405	29.6
General help	5,613	57.7	4,124	42.3
Country kitchen	3,780	81.8	844	18.2
Plants and pets	2,572	57.5	1,902	42.5
Odd jobs	4,382	62.3	2,650	37.7

The data are based on reported help received. The statistical unit is not the couple but a favour traded between the respondent couple and another couple.

Baby-sitting: individual baby-sitting sessions.
General help: personal care, transport, errands, housework and help with government forms.
Country kitchen: preserving fruit and vegetables, sewing and knitting.
Plants and pets: watering plants and feeding animals.
Odd jobs: washing cars, painting, decorating, major repairs and heavy physical labour.

Source: Degenne and Lebeaux, 1991

Table 2.7   Help according to the age of the head of household

	Age of head of household											
	Under 30		30-39		40-49		50-59		60-69		70+	
	Total	%	Total	%	Total	%	Total	%	Total	%	Total	%
Help received	268	34.0	821	54.5	217	19.7	49	5.0	17	1.9	9	1.6
Help given	292	37.1	623	41.4	367	33.2	379	38.5	410	44.8	107	19.4
No. in age group	707		1,506		1,104		984		916		552	

Source: Degenne and Lebeaux, 1991

Mutual help is a complex form of sociability. It is supposed to meet a recipient's need. However, the highest proportion of couples who receive no help are found in the lowest income brackets. For all manner of help, the middle and upper brackets stand out as leading recipients. Mutual help does not attenuate social inequalities; rather it reinforces them.

Density and Multiplexity

So far we have analysed sociability in terms of a star but we also need data about direct links among the people the ego cites. Two identical stars become radically different structures depending on whether everyone knows everyone or hardly knows anyone. For this reason, some studies incorporate data on ego zones and use it to measure density. Other studies focus on the specialization of existing links, usually by obtaining an indicator of multiplexity.

Broadly speaking, the density of a network is the proportion of existing to maximum possible links. In the following graph, all links are undirected and therefore a maximum of six are possible, as given by $n(n-1)/2$ where n is the total number of persons. Since three links exist, the density is 3/6 = 0.5.

With a personal network, the notion of density only becomes meaningful once it maps out the links between members that do not go through the ego. The next example shows six partners with a potential to set up 15 links (assuming the graph is undirected). The density calculation disregards links to the ego for two reasons: first, the ego/partner and partner/partner links are of different natures (full versus broken lines); and second, ego/alter links all exist by construction.

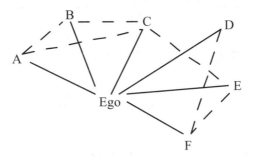

Multiplexity is explored by surveying several types of relations in a network. One such study asked couples to list what they exchanged with whom. Any single relation is multiplex if it transacts several kinds of exchange concurrently. A couple's total network is all the more multiplex as the ratio of exchanges to partners increases. In this case, multiplexity is given by $m = n/p$, where n is the total number of exchanges and p is the number of couples effecting at least one exchange. The indicator gives overall multiplexity which covers an entire personal network but does not reflect differing levels of multiplexity. A good indicator should also give some idea of variance for each link, thus bringing us into standard statistical methods. Now that we have the concepts in hand, we can proceed to the applications.

Elisabeth Bott (1957) starts from the principle that the household is a relational system of links among household members and to the outside world. She set out to understand the relation between these two sets of links through an in-depth survey of 20 London families. She concluded that: 'The degree of segregation in the role relationship of husband and wife varies directly with the connectedness of the family's social network.' She went on to describe husband/wife and parent/child exchanges. For a straightforward definition of family, she only recruited two-parent families with children living at home. She also classified the husband/wife interaction into three types of arrangements she called complementary, independent and joint organization.

> In complementary organization the activities of husband and wife are different and separate but fitted together to form a whole. In independent organization activities are carried out separately by husband and wife without reference to each other, in so far as this is possible. In joint organization activities are carried out by husband and wife together, or the same activity is carried out by either partner at different times.

All families practised each of the three arrangements. Elisabeth Bott differentiates between two relational systems: 'segregated conjugal role relationship', where complementary and independent organization predominate (i.e. each spouse has assigned duties with strict division of labour, each has separate interests and spends individual time with their own friends out of the home); and 'joint conjugal role relationship', where joint organization predominates (i.e. spouses swap duties and share as many tasks and as much leisure together as possible).[8]

Bott goes on to classify couples according to density of relations to the outside world. She developed a hypothesis that was consistent with her observation that the families with the densest networks, and in which kinship links played a key role, were those who had been living in the same place for a long time or had never moved at all. Spouses who continue to keep up individual friendship links established before marriage are less emotionally dependent on each other than those with few such links. Wives with premarital friends can always find a helping hand for cleaning and childcare. This makes it easier to preserve traditional sex roles in a couple. On the other hand, couples who move out of their original environment, or consist of two migrants, will have sparse individual networks. Moreover, neither can fall back on a network reflecting a shared value system. Their best strategy is to face the outside world as a team and they will tend to develop a joint personal network. So segregated conjugal roles correlate with families who stay put and have dense networks with traditional, clearly assigned sex roles. On the other hand, joint conjugal roles correlate with low-density networks due to a change of residence or social status.

Degenne and Lebeaux (1993) used Table 2.8 to correlate conjugal roles with type of mutual assistance network. The table lends itself to analysis by sex roles since the breakdown specifies which spouse usually does which household chore. This led them to consider a couple traditional if both

Table 2.8   Distribution of chores in contemporary
couples (as % of all couples)

	Proportion of households in which chores are mostly done by	
	Husband	Wife
Traditional duty of wife		
Mending	4	81
Cleaning floors	8	87
Washing windows	10	84
Making beds	8	90
Cooking	10	89
Laundering	3	95
Ironing	3	93
Dishwashing	10	87
Dishdrying	12	77
Traditional duty of husband		
Cleaning house exterior	51	22
Minor repairs	73	5
Car washing	64	14
Cleaning inside car	59	22

Source: INSEE *Modes de vie* survey, 1988; Degenne and Lebeaux, 1993

spouses performed over 60% of chores for their own traditional sex role, and non-traditional where both spouses performed over 40% of chores belonging to the opposite sex role.

Our distinction between the two types of couples is based solely on network data about mutual help, but they suffice for two hypotheses. The first relies on lifestyle differences and assumes that husband/wife relations obey the same principle as their relations to the world at large. Couples operating large mutual help networks might use household chores as a pretext for exchanges of sociability. Thus husband and wife might share household chores for the same reason. And indeed, non-traditional couples frequently have large networks (Table 2.9).

Table 2.9   Division of domestic tasks according to network size

Network size	Non-traditional couples (%)	Traditional couples (%)
Less than 2	25	46
2-5	39	37
Greater than 5	36	17
Total number	380	1,708

Source: INSEE *Modes de vie* survey, 1988; Degenne and Lebeaux, 1993

Likewise, couples who exploit mutual help as a major form of sociability should not have reason to specialize the chores they share with other couples. Thus mutual help networks of non-traditional couples should

Table 2.10   Division of domestic tasks according to network specialization

Network specialization	Non-traditional couples (%)	Traditional couples (%)
1 or 2 different kinds of help per relation	46	58
3 and over	54	42
Total number	380	1,708

Source: INSEE Modes de vie survey, 1988; Degenne and Lebeaux, 1993

multiplex more than those of traditional couples. And indeed, the data confirm such multiplexity but the statistical significance is unimpressive.

The second hypothesis assumes rational behaviour. It says couples should allocate some chores to themselves and farm out the rest (Table 2.10). Furthermore, traditional couples should farm out according to competence and productivity, given that gender specialization tends to sharpen skills. So they should ask for favours better done by others and develop highly specialized networks (i.e. weak multiplexity). Against this, non-traditional couples share chores and are less demanding about skill levels. They would therefore farm out anything the network will carry (i.e. strong multiplexity). Both hypotheses prove compatible with the data.

Researchers working on social support also reason in terms of density and multiplexity. Relational support assumes everybody needs satisfactory social integration. If the network is too limited or its architecture inadequate, there is a threat to physical welfare and perhaps even individual mental health. But the issue is what makes up a 'good' network.

The idea that satisfactory social integration is a prerequisite of overall welfare has inspired a great number of studies, especially investigations to see if traditional rural communities offer better platforms than urban or urbanized social systems. Simmel launched this trend. He classified social relations in terms of degree of personal involvement. His *Philosophy of Money* (1900) shows how money operates as a principle of personal disinvolvement. Under royal government in France, the feudal duty to repair roads gradually began giving way to a road tax. Conscription required citizens to sacrifice time (and perhaps life) for God and country, but the law allowed conscripts to avoid induction by paying someone to serve in their stead (this holds for the US Civil War too).

Simmel says urbanization operates to make such abstract relations mundane, i.e. it promotes personal decommitment. Money cuts the urbanite's dependence on others, thus giving her more personal freedom, but not necessarily greater happiness. He notes that men were 'free' in feudal times once they came under common law, i.e. the norms of the largest social circle, but the serf's rights were grounded in the feudal unit, i.e. the smallest social circle. Likewise, today's urbanite is 'free' of the petty prejudices that regulate people in small towns.

Simmel (1903), Robert Ezra Park (Park and Burgess, 1925) and Chicago sociology kept coming back to the theme of destructured city life. Their ideal was the small rural community of frequent exchanges where everyone knew everyone (Mendras, 1976) and role specialization was low. But everyone also watches everyone else. The norms are clear-cut but constrictive. Metropolitan lifestyles are different. Park and Burgess (1925) note that transportation and communication

> have multiplied the opportunities of the individual man for contact and for association with his fellows, but they have made these contacts and associations more transitory and less stable. A very large part of the populations of great cities, including those who make their homes in tenements and apartment houses, live much as people do in some great hotel, meeting but not knowing one another. The effect of this is to substitute fortuitous and casual relationship for the more intimate and permanent associations of the smaller community. Under these circumstances the individual's status is determined to a considerable degree by conventional signs – by fashion and 'front' – and the art of life is largely reduced to skating on thin surfaces and a scrupulous study of styles and manners . . . This makes it possible for individuals to pass easily and quickly from one moral milieu to another, and encourages the fascinating but dangerous experiment of living at the same time in several different contiguous, but otherwise widely separated, worlds.

So the city stands for personal freedom. Anyone is free to go from one moral world to another, navigate between different sets of norms and establish her own private world and identity. Formal superficial relations to others serve to keep trespassers at bay. Close interdependence with others gives way to formal, highly encoded relations that keep commitments to a minimum. But this autonomy has a downside: loneliness and little of the real emotional support that comes from belonging to a focused community with shared values. This makes the city morally hazardous and a threat to the sanity of its population.

This grim portrait of city life has been taken to extremes that surpass Park or his contemporaries, but spawns the simple idea that the greater the number and density of someone's personal relations, the better his chances of preserving sound mental health. In this sense, any relation that provides emotional and material support is invaluable.

Fisher's (1948) study tries to substantiate doubts about this last hypothesis. Indeed, he suspects that traditional communities and dense networks may also subvert mental health. If they offer support, they may well cause anxiety too. He quotes respondents who complain some relations are pure poison rather than supportive. Cities are more heterogeneous than communities and offer a wealth of different subcultures. The city is a mosaic of small worlds. But if all this is true, urbanites should be suffering no shortage of personal relations.

Fisher used a name generator for this study, i.e. a list of opportunities to contact people. For each person in a relationship with the subject, he noted sex, how they first met, the strength of links, and if they lived less than 5 or over 60 minutes away by car. He then sought additional information from a maximum of five people he considered closest to the subject. He asked them who knew whom to gauge density. Fisher then asked the following questions:

1 In how many different ways is an individual linked to someone else? Why is this considered important?
2 Who has dense or multiplex relations?
3 Does this have psychological consequences?

The most generally admitted hypothesis suggests that the nearer one's lifestyle is to the traditional rural model, the denser and more multiplexed personal networks should be. Indeed, personal networks stand every chance of being very dense among people who live in a confined community with little occasion to migrate and meet new people. Likewise, multiplexity should also be high because of the limited number of persons in the network.

But Fisher found the multiplexity data more complex. In practice, people with large networks have more multiplex links than people with small networks. Small networks do show higher *average* multiplexity, but large networks show *stronger* multiplexity. Fisher explains this result by affirming that the more active a person is, the greater her chances of multiplexing her links.

Density submits to other readings too. It all depends on the variety of the network's ambient contexts. Network density falls as the number of social contexts rises. Networks confined to a single context average a density of 0.84 but fall to 0.65 if they span two contexts. Three contexts ease density to 0.49 and four shave it to 0.38. But the number of contexts varies with urbanization. The density of a given person's network also depends on the density of her contacts' networks. Figure 2.5 charts Fisher's results.

Fisher also drew up an index of personal satisfaction about sociability. He wanted to know if people with low-density networks suffered a lack of emotional support and longed to enrich their networks. He generally found that the denser the network, the less respondents report an urge for new links and the greater the tendency to report high personal satisfaction.

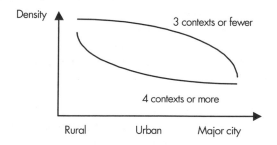

Figure 2.5   Density of personal networks

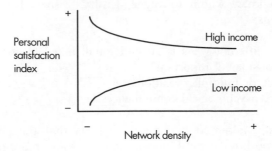

Figure 2.6   Personal satisfaction about sociability

However, the overall results mask differences related to social status. There again, those who have the means of managing a wide relational network stand aloof from those who cannot. This maps out nicely in Figure 2.6.

It is therefore unwise to use density and multiplexity indicators as simple acid tests. Their meaningfulness depends on the context. In 1977, Charles Kadushin (1982) studied the relation between network density and emotional stress by adding combat duty as a explanatory variable. He sampled 380 males, of whom half were Vietnam veterans and half were non-veterans; half were over 29 years of age, half were younger; half were blacks, half were whites; and half were college educated, half were not. He then asked about the following:

1   three best friends at age 18
2   three best 'buddies' during active duty (or equivalent timeframe for non-veterans)
3   person who found the respondent his present job
4   person living with the respondent (usually a spouse)
5   four current friends
6   three veteran friends (for veteran respondents only).

This gives a theoretical ceiling of 15 names per respondent. In fact, 9 names were obtained at most and the average was 5.3. Respondents were then asked to put a cross in a matrix for each person who knew another on his list. This served to calculate density.

Kadushin measured stress with a standard stress scale questionnaire of 30 questions used to evaluate post-traumatic stress. He then used path analysis to evaluate the data and obtained the coefficients in Figure 2.7 (each measures the influence of the variable from which the arrow starts on the variable at which it finishes).

His approach routinely treats social density like any other variable. Under these conditions, Kadushin observes a negative correlation between stress and density.

Hugues Lagrange (1992) and Sebastien Roché (1993) have studied fear for physical safety in France. Multiplexity was one of their variables. A

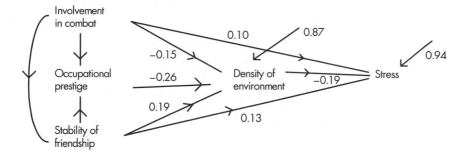

Figure 2.7   Network density and emotional stress

survey was undertaken in the city of Grenoble in 1986 and another in the
town of Tullins in 1987. Both studies evaluated networks in terms of six
spheres of sociability, i.e. friends, family, neighbours, coworkers, comembers in civic organizations and coparticipants in leisure activities. Two
indexes were used. A patent fear index was used to reflect perceived threat
at home, reluctance to go out alone after sunset, and door locking before
8:30 p.m. A latent fear index was based on attitudes to re-establishing
capital punishment, tougher law enforcement and municipal voting rights
for resident aliens.

In the Grenoble survey, fear shows positive correlation with network
multiplexity that stays positive when matched with age, sex or socioeconomic category. The same is true of latent fear. The difficulty is the
opposite results of the Tullins study. Here, low-multiplexity networks did
not correlate with lower fear levels. So we cannot generalize about the
impact of multiplexity.

Highly multiplexed rural people belong to dense networks that preserve
high levels of norm enforcement. Latent fear scores reflect strong support
for law and order. However, a strong sense of belonging to a network
keeps patent fear low. Uniplexing urbanites are characterized by greater
personal freedom but uniplex networks assume managing a mixed bag of
relations. Failure to master this form of social integration leads to patent
and latent fear over law and order. Lagrange concludes: 'Analysis shows
that multiplex villagers (type I) and uniplex urbanites (type IV) could be
the two extremes of a sliding scale of judgemental coherence. The former
would have the least relational autonomy while the latter would have the
most. Uniplex villagers (type II) and multiplex urbanites (type III) would
be intermediary types of comparable behavioural autonomy' (Figure 2.8).

Barry Wellman's (Hall and Wellman, 1985) study of East York, Canada
in 1968 also reports that dense networks of tightly integrated links do not
necessarily assuage safety fears.[9] In fact, he reports the effect of these links
is positive or negative according to circumstances. Too much emotional
support and closeness contributes to destabilizing personality. Finally, the

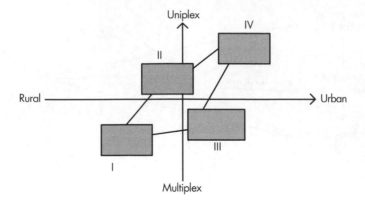

Figure 2.8   Types of behavioural autonomy (Lagrange, 1992)

Wellman team (Wellman and Leighton, 1981) consider that urbanization has not completely wiped out smaller communities. But it does not safe-guard them either. This team affirms that the narrow networks they found fulfil the same function communities once did, i.e. they offer personal recognition, a sense of belonging, emotional support, small favours and social control. But they are personal (not physical) communities.

Thus, the studies refute the idea that bigger is necessarily better in personal networks. The metropolis does not reproduce traditional rural sociability patterns but offers new patterns that allow greater personal freedom. This assertion becomes meaningful if we go on to recognize that a relation only takes on meaning when situated within its *total* relational environment. The next issue is how to identify this total system for a given locality if the concept of the traditional community has become inadequate.

Social Circles and the Community

Wellman returned to East York in 1978 to answer this last question. He interviewed 33 respondents from his original sample about their relations (Wellman et al., 1988). He starts by rating relations as intimate or non-intimate, and routine or non-routine. He then constructs the 'typical ideal' network shown in Table 2.11.

Non-intimate and non-routine ties prevail in the ideal network of 11 persons. Most intimate links are kin, and neighbours prevail as routine non-intimate links. Friends are mostly intimate non-routine contacts. Cow-orkers and fellow members of civic organizations are seldom intimates. But the main finding is that few links are autonomous: 81% are embedded in larger groups. This percentage is even higher for neighbours and coworkers. Thus, Wellman concludes that links mainly operate within circles and that these circles are too small to appear immediately upon analysis.

Table 2.11

	Routine links	Non-routine links	Total
Actives and intimates	2	2	4
Only actives	1	6	7
Total	3	8	11

The ways in which most ties are structurally embedded in clusters and cliques greatly facilitate group support and social control. The fact that so many ties are structural in origin – and some not even sources of individual satisfaction – calls into question the social psychological assumptions that community ties are formed and maintained through 'interpersonal attraction' between parties . . . Many East Yorkers are tied to persons with whom they have to deal in their neighbourhoods, kinship groups, or on the job – whether they are attracted to them or not. Such ties are maintained by general social networks, or formal organizations that constrain network members to be parties to relationships. In these situations, interpersonal attraction may sometimes affect the intensity of ties, the frequency of contact, and the number of strands in the relationship, but not the existence of these ties themselves . . . Certainly these ties exist and are well structured. But they exist in small clusters – through meetings in private homes and on the telephone – and not in large, palpable bodies gathering in public squares, cafés, and meeting halls. Indeed, the very privacy of their operation may help to account for the stability of these networks. It is quite difficult for East Yorkers to meet many new persons unless they change homes, jobs, or spouses. (Wellman et al., 1988)

Of course, this is a North American study and sociability may take other forms in Barcelona or Paris. But despite such variations, we hold that the notion of embedded circles and their power to shape the development of interpersonal relations is a key concept of general validity.

Actually, this idea is not new and Simmel was among the first to use circles as key units of a sociological model. Analysing the impact of urbanization on sociability, he notes that big cities offer a plethora of social circles which provide individuals with a framework to engage in specific pursuits without giving up personal freedom. A wide assortment of circles allows individuals to tailor sociability to order. Simmel's concept of the social circle includes groups of varying degrees of organization where individuals meet around a common interest. This applies from informal groups all the way to civic organizations.

At about the same time, Frenchman Célestin Bouglé analysed the circle concept with explicit references to Simmel. Bouglé based his own sociological model on him. In the article 'What is sociology?' (1897) he dreams up a small town called Saint-Pol and wonders how an observer would recognize and classify the inhabitants:

Let me recapitulate the people I saw go by in the street today and the labels I gave them. Two men in shirtsleeves, hands white with plaster: 'workers'. Then a man dressed in blue and red with copper buttons and white gloves, looking both idle and worried: I dubbed him 'soldier'. Then a 'gentleman' with a top hat: 'man of the world'. Two old women in black, speaking quietly and walking silently:

'pious old ladies', I thought. Then a glimpse of someone with a rounded back and on wheels: 'cyclist'. Then a noisy group of people blowing into copper instruments, a velvet banner in their midst: 'musicians'. Band members, cyclists, pious ladies, man of the world, soldiers, workers, all thrown together in the middle of the street: these are the labels that I gave my fellow citizens. What do they mean? That I classify individuals into so many societies. I separated these people from each other by assimilating them to persons united by very different ties: work or appearance, duties or pleasures, practices or tastes. So there, before my eyes, were some of the countless circles that intersect within the narrow circle of Saint-Pol.

That these individuals I classified were not only specimens of these classes, that the attribute of soldier or cyclist did not exhaust all their attributes, is a matter of course. They do not belong to one social circle but to several which overlap: a cyclist can be, if not a member of a band, a man of the world: long ago it was said that a soldier is nonetheless a man. It is rare for an individual to belong only to one society. . . .

As with infinity, this rapid survey shows us the infinite diversity of societies. There are ephemeral ones, like those that gather travellers around a restaurant table, and there are secular ones, older than cathedrals where believers gather; there are limited ones like that of the Saint-Pol band, and there are broad ones, uniting working classes or scholars across mountains and beyond the seas. Immense or tiny circles, rigid or flexible circles, circles of smoke that vanish as soon as they are formed, circles of stone sealed by priestly hands, circles of iron forged by warriors' hands, circles of flowers woven by poets' hands, in our eyes social links will be clad in greatly varied dress.

The greater part of our behaviour has thus no *raison d'être* except in and for society. The people in my street would not dress, walk, feel or think as they do think, feel, walk and dress if they were not workers or band members, men of the world or soldiers. That is to say, in order to understand their attributes, outer or inner, I had to ask myself what relations they maintained with other individuals. Whether in church or club, family or army, these relations prove, by the changes they impose on individuals, their own reality.

Bouglé sees circles as more than mere focal points of sociability. He includes job, religion and other groups that influence a person's behaviour. Moreover, he uses 'circle' and 'society' synonymously.

More recently, Kadushin (1966) has advanced a classification system for social groups that includes a category called the circle, much like Simmel does. His typology varies with both degree of institutionalization and forms of interaction inside the group (Table 2.12).

However, Kadushin calls his table 'Typology of social circles', which suggests that 'circle' can cover both any grouping the researcher so designates and a specific class of groups. Peter Blau (Blau and Schwartz, 1984) also uses 'social circle' to designate any group that results from interaction between individuals. Thus circles should be considered as the pertinent framework to study the genesis of behaviour patterns.

The idea of studying sociability by looking at the local circles where it happens also owes much to anthropology. Anthropologists have always looked for normative cultural systems which prescribe behaviour patterns for the internal exchanges that set the group apart. In 1940, Radcliffe-Brown introduced the concept of network to describe the structure of these

Table 2.12   Classification of social groups

		Density of interaction: High				Moderate
		Indirect chain of interaction		Direct chain of interaction		
		Basis for interaction:				
Formally instituted relations	Formality of leadership	Propinquity	Interest	Propinquity	Interest	
Moderate	Informal		Social set or circle	Crowd	Salon	Mass society
	Formal		Membership of voluntary organizations, fans	Cliques, gang	Demonstrations, picket lines, protest	Mass media audience
High	Informal	Community	Market	Neighbourhood	Marketplace	Mass society
	Formal	Tribe	Formal organization	Family	Live entertainment	Nation-state

relations: 'Direct observation does reveal to us that . . . human beings are connected by a complex network of social relations. I use the term "social structure" to denote this network of actually existing relations.' But the concept was still too broad and metaphorical. In the 1950s, Barnes (1954), Bott (1957), Nadel (1957) and Firth (1954) advanced tighter definitions of real operational impact on later studies. All led to an attack on culturalism which they accused of paying insufficient attention to relations that run through or beyond the group borders staked out by ethnology. In short, they were clamouring for sociology to take account of problems we now call intersecting and systemic. Nadel is clear on this point: 'By "network" . . . I do not merely wish to indicate the "links" between persons; this is adequately done by the word "relationship". Rather, I wish to indicate the further linkage of the "links" themselves and the important consequence that what happens between one pair of "knots", so to speak, must affect what happens between other adjacent ones.' It looks quite like Nadel is talking about a social circle without actually naming it.

   Barnes's (1954) ethnological study of Bremmes Island, Norway underscores the importance of intersecting relations to sociability. He divides social relations into the following three types:

1 territorial systems with permanent boundaries and stable relations (e.g. family, parish, county, club)
2 industrial systems with numerous relatively autonomous units and hierarchical relations but, unlike for territorial systems, with unstructured relations to the outside world
3 diffuse systems with no unity, hierarchy or boundaries and unstable relations (e.g. friends and acquaintances).

Now these last systems, which are the island's informal sociability networks, have the particular quality of intersecting the other two. Diffuse systems reunite and separate actors from industrial and territorial systems. Barnes notes that a network with a high degree of overall intersection improves its mediation capabilities. Without formally analysing network density, his study points a finger at the importance of local circles. In the 1960s, similar studies specifically targeted urban contexts (Mitchell, 1969).

In the 1970s, France launched a major sociological research programme, whose goals included exploring the local circle as a concept and living entity, entitled Observation du Changement Social et Culturel. In the first phase, about 100 researchers produced monographs on 60 different places. The main results of this phase were presented in *L'Esprit des lieux* (OCS, 1986). The second phase yielded a study of representative samples from seven places. We would like to present its findings on local sociability.

The hypothesis of the study is that local circles explain the forms of sociability they encapsulate. It does not imply that the sociability circles will annihilate social or occupational differences but it does imply that certain forms of sociability may be circle-specific and cut across social strata. To confirm this, we need to set up indicators of sociability.[10] The first monographs identified complex forms of sociability that were place-specific. The places were rural communities, towns, metropolitan districts and satellite cities.

The boundaries of rural communities are apparent. They still have 'natural' outlines and local sociability is easily recognized. Some cases are tricky, however. As residential areas expand into rural areas, we see situations that elude the traditional village model of an isolated entity in which the village organizes all communal life. Nevertheless, rural communities remain the simplest to stake out. Towns are more of a problem. Complete uniformity becomes impossible in an urban entity of over 20,000 inhabitants and it becomes difficult to detect what types of sociability exist there. But the boundaries are still fairly obvious. Difficulties increase with metropolitan districts and suburbs. Sometimes a researcher's knowledge of the district will help her determine the boundaries but in other cases they will appear almost arbitrary.

Operationally, the hypothesis to prove is that sociability at the local level (sometimes) seeks out a special location, i.e. sociability needs a private turf to flourish in its own way and rise above the sum total of individual effects and features. If this is so, we would expect to find a strong locality effect in every case, regardless of the variable(s) being studied. It then follows that a given type of sociability will resist sociodemographic analysis the more it is typical to, and entrenched in, a small number of places. On the other hand, more diffuse and atypical forms of sociability should prove easy to study with sociodemographic variables. Seven localities were selected to investigate the hypothesis, all chosen to ensure the greatest possible diversity of communities (Figure 2.9).

Figure 2.9   Localities for sociability analyses

The first is a rural community in Brittany. The second is Saint-Jean, a traditional part of Bordeaux. The third is the Mirail district of Toulouse, recently renewed to avant-garde standards of urbanism. The fourth is a group of townhouses in Menucourt, next to a Paris satellite city. The fifth is a working class suburb of Lyons. The sixth is the middle class residential town of Manosque in south-western France. The last is the medium-sized working class town of Condé-sur-Noireau in Normandy.

The first type of sociability is grassroots. It appears in a population's attachment to local festivals, dances and athletic events and in an interest in local news. Grassroots sociability is most common to localities unswamped by urbanization or migrations. It implies everybody knows everybody. It also assumes a long history of local residence. Grassroots sociability was most conspicuous in the rural community in Brittany.

The second type of sociability is neoconvivial. It describes local integration that operates through civic organizations. Members use such bodies to acquire positions that give them an active role in the community and even a chance to amass power. Organizations are platforms of formal sociability, but they do have the virtue of transforming mere consumers of

Table 2.13   Sociability indices (%)

(a) Grassroots sociability index

| Index | Locality[1] | | | | | | |
	1	2	3	4	5	6	7
0	2	18	27	9	17	16	7
1	15	47	34	22	41	28	26
2	38	28	25	38	29	36	37
3	29	5	12	24	10	17	25
4	15	2	1	6	2	3	5
Sample size (no.)	116	137	122	148	106	122	123

(b) Neoconvivial sociability index

| Index | Locality[1] | | | | | | |
	1	2	3	4	5	6	7
0	8	17	20	18	18	2	7
1	24	29	27	28	25	7	15
2	55	49	41	43	48	54	50
3	13	4	12	11	8	37	28
Sample size (no.)	116	137	122	148	106	122	123

[1] 1, rural Brittany; 2, traditional Bordeaux; 3, renovated Toulouse; 4, townhouse Menucourt; 5, working class Lyons suburb; 6, residential Manosque; 7, working class Condé.

Source: OCS survey, authors' calculations

local goods and services into active citizens with responsibilities to their community. This sociability is most visible in middle class residential Manosque.

The third type of sociability is low-key traditional. It appears by not appearing, i.e. by the absence of direct interpersonal exchange in particular circumstances (something that eludes questionnaires about practices). Everyone says hello and scurries off to keep to themselves. But everybody keeps tabs on everybody else and judges their behaviour. It is a system of control and adjustment to a local norm which operates and thrives in silence. This sociability prevailed in a Parisian district with a large proportion of pensioners. We never found a satisfactory index for this type of sociability, so we shall restrict ourselves to the first two types.

The index for grassroots sociability runs from 0 to 4 and the one for neoconvivial sociability goes from 0 to 3. Table 2.13a shows up the differences found from one locality to the next. Grassroots sociability scores of 3 or 4 prevailed in the rural community (1), the townhouse project (4) and the working class town (7). Values of 0 or 2 were scored in traditional Bordeaux (2), the renovated district of Toulouse (3) and the working class Lyons suburb (5), while middle-class residential Manosque (6) falls in between.

Neoconviviality presents quite another picture (Table 2.13b). Only the two medium-sized towns (localities 6 and 7), attain 3, the top score. All others rate 1 or 2.

It remained to be seen whether this variation is better explained by socio-demographic variables or the locality itself. We answered this question with a procedure called segmentation.[11] We use variables known to affect local sociability, i.e. age, length of local residence, young children in the family, education, geographic mobility and occupational status. Of course, each locality is a specific variable.

For grassroots sociability, segmentation allows the mean value of the index to vary from 1.5 to 2.6. Locality is the most discriminant criterion, followed by length of residence, mobility and small children. Age and education do not weigh heavily in this index. The lowest mean value (1.5) was noted for groups of newly arrived inhabitants to the localities of traditional Bordeaux (2), the renovated Toulouse district (3) and the working class Lyons suburb (5) (total 146 people). The highest value (2.6) was scored in the rural community of Brittany (1) by a group of 78 people with personal histories of geographic mobility.

For neoconvivial sociability, locality is the dominant variable although education is important too. The weakest mean value (1.7) went to a group of 172 undereducated persons from one of the first five communities. The strongest relates to a group of 35 people of average age living in residential Manosque or working class Condé-sur-Noireau. The importance of education to sociability is a familiar finding and locality stands out as the main variable.

These results confirm the idea that circles coalesce in specific places. In the course of time, they take on novel forms of sociability that defy explanation merely in terms of the sociodemographic composition of the local population. The actor is first 'inserted' into these circles. But of course circles are never just local.

In fact, every actor belongs to a good number of social circles, each with its own mix of resources and constraints, roles and functions, rules and rituals. We shall return to this topic in more theoretical detail in the last chapter when we study crisscrossing memberships and their consequences. For the moment, we stress that it necessarily follows from the above that structural sociology cannot settle for conceiving networks as simple aggregates of dual relations. Social circles are constituent elements of networks. Of course, the circles are invisible and their existence must be inferred from individual interactions.

Our treatment of personal networks throughout this chapter shows how interaction has become a standard object of extensive studies. However, standard studies only sift out structures and circles in an indirect and rather rudimentary manner. We need a systematic approach if we are to understand network structure properly. Circles, groups, statuses and links must be deduced from investigation of the *entire* relational network. In other words we restate our basic position that the researcher has to look at the total network for a full structural perspective. The following chapters will go into greater detail. The methods are all based on graph theory and we shall begin with a review of that subject.

Notes

1 Full bibliographic references are given later in the detailed discussion of this subject and only a few examples are given here. Interested readers should also look up 'sociability' under 'history', e.g. Agulhon et al. (1982), Dujardin (1988) or Valade (1990).

2 Boudon rates homogamy with the ratio: (observed homogamy – minimal homogamy)/ (maximal homogamy – minimal homogamy).

3 Out-of-home activities include paid entertainment (e.g. opera, football), outdoor pursuits (e.g. hunting, biking and picnicking), commercial socializing (e.g. drinks or dinner in public establishments, clubbing and gambling) or the practice of any athletics. Choquet makes a distinction between active and passive out-of-home commitments (e.g. mountain climbing versus tagging along for drinks with coworkers) but our figures lump them together.

4 The closer an activity to a vertex of the triangle, the greater the tendency to share it with the type of person indicated. French horserace betting occurs with friends in 42% of cases and family in 23%, the remaining 35% being with coworkers, neighbours and others.

5 We used the logit model to judge the influence of a variable and its modalities with all other factors held constant. Readers interested in details of this type of statistical analysis should consult Jobson (1992).

6 All things not equal, the effect of income is expressed through professional status, i.e. more money makes it easier to socialize.

7 For more details of civic organizations in France, via the INSEE enquiries, see Lemel and Paradeise (1974) on *Loisirs* (1967); Forsé (1985) on *Environnement de l'habitat* (1973) and Héran (1988a) on *Contacts entre les personnes* (1983).

8 Bott researched 'only' 20 families but did it thoroughly. Her team interviewed each couple eight to 19 times (average 13) to obtain the fullest possible picture of family life. In addition, she held private 'clinical' interviews at the research centre on sex and other subjects too sensitive to discuss in front of other family members.

9 This quiet, homogeneous, residential Toronto suburb is populated by middle class British Canadians. The study covered the relations of 845 adults.

10 The indices used are simple aggregates of indicators of behaviour reported on questionnaires. Therefore, they reflect *individual* data. Even if we are theoretically dealing with traits that are the expression of a locality, our tools allow us to compare the explanation in terms of standard variables with the one that assumes a community effect.

11 We take the index and a set of criteria and then divide the population into two groups for each criterion. Next we calculate how well each classification explains the variance. Now we retain the one which gives the better result. Two subpopulations result. We repeat this operation on each of these subpopulations. This gives four groups. The operation is again repeated, which creates eight groups, and so forth. In each operation, we use the most efficient variable for the group considered. The algorithm stops when the size of one of the constituted groups falls below a preset threshold, or when no variable yields any further contribution to explain variance. If the method is efficacious, the average values of the index in each of the groups obtained by the operation should differ appreciably.

3   GRAPH THEORY

Graphs are invaluable to a formal description of social networks. Graph theory is a branch of mathematics (Berge, 1967; 1970; 1987) that the social sciences proved quick to welcome into their toolkits (Flament, 1963; Harary et al., 1965; Bertin, 1967).

Basic Graph Theory

Basically, a *graph* consists of finite set of points x_1, x_2, . . ., x_n plus the set of arrows that connect them. Each point is termed a *node* and each arrow is an *arc*. If the total number of arcs directed one way from x_i to x_j cannot exceed p, we have a *p-graph*. The set of nodes in a given graph G is usually called X and its set of arcs is U. An arc running from node x_i to x_j is denoted (x_i, x_j). More formally, a graph $G = (X, U)$ consists of the following:

1   node set $X = (x_1, x_2, . . ., x_n)$
2   arc set $U = (u_1, u_2, . . ., u_n)$, elements of the Cartesian product $X \times X = \{(x, y)/x \in X, y \in X\}$.

The total number of nodes in G is called its *order*. Most graphs are *directed*, as implicitly supposed when speaking of arcs. An edge is a line connecting two nodes in an undirected graph.[1] Every arc (x, y) starts at x and ends at y; x is the predecessor of y and y is the successor of x. The number of arcs converging on a given node is called its *indegree* while the number of outbound arcs is the *outdegree*. Indegree and outdegree add up to the *degree*.

A graph is *complete* if, for any pair of nodes (x, y), there exists at least one arc (x, y) or (y, x). A 1-graph is complete only if $(x, y) \notin U \Rightarrow (y, x) \in U$. A *clique* is the set of nodes of a complete subgraph of G.

The *density* is the ratio of the number of arcs in a graph to that of the arcs in a complete graph with the same number of nodes. If K is the number of elements in U, and N is the number of elements in X, the density is $K/[N(N-1)]$.

A *chain* of length q is a sequence of q arcs such that each arc in the chain shares one terminus with its preceding arc, the other with its succeeding arc. The chain is *elementary* if it does not pass twice through the same node. It is *simple* if it does not pass twice through the same arc. A *cycle* is a simple chain that ends at the starting node.

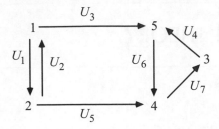

In the graph shown,

$L = \{U_1, U_5, U_6\}$ is a chain
$C = \{U_2, U_3, U_6, U_5\}$ is a cycle

A *path* is a sequence of arcs going in the same direction. A *circuit* is a simple path that starts and ends at the same node. Thus, in the same graph,

$L = \{U_2, U_3, U_6, U_7\}$ is a path
$C = \{U_6, U_7, U_4\}$ is a circuit

The path length (or distance between two nodes) equals the number of arcs connecting them. Between nodes 2 and 5 in the graph, we have a path of length 2 through node 1 but also another of length 3 through nodes 3 and 4. The *geodesic distance* is the length of the shortest path between two nodes, i.e. 2 between nodes 2 and 5 in this example.

A *loop* is an arc in graph G whose contour is (x, x). In the literature, 'loop' sometimes refers to a circuit of two arcs, e.g. circuit $\{U_1, U_2\}$ in the graph shown, but we shall restrict ourselves to the first definition.

A graph is *connected* if it has a chain from x to y for every x–y dyad. Nonetheless, unconnected graphs may have components. Thus, each connected component is a maximal connected graph.

A graph is *strongly connected* when every x–y dyad has a path between x and y. In the previous graph, (1, 2) and (3, 4, 5) show strong connection.

In a connected or strongly connected graph, a *cutpoint* is a node whose removal would increase the number of (strongly) connected components in the graph. The previous graph above presents (1, 2) and (3, 4, 5) as strongly connected components. For example, A and B are cutpoints in the following graph but not C because its removal would still leave only one connected component.

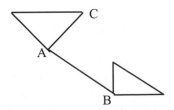

If $G = (X, U)$ is a 1-graph (with or without loops), it can be described in an *adjacency matrix*. In this matrix M, each line corresponds to a node of G; the same holds true for the columns, assuming the nodes are taken in the same order as for the lines. Then m_{ij} is an element of M, where:

$m_{ij} = 1$ if $(i, j) \in U$
$m_{ij} = 0$ if $(i, j) \notin U$

The matrix is symmetrical if the graph is undirected. This is not necessarily the case with directed graphs. The matrix is square, binary and of order n. Convention dictates that a 1 where row i intersects column j designates i as the predecessor of j. For example, for the graph

the adjacency matrix is found as follows:

$m_{11} = 0 \qquad m_{12} = 1 \qquad m_{13} = 0$
$m_{21} = 0 \qquad m_{22} = 0 \qquad m_{23} = 1$
$m_{31} = 1 \qquad m_{32} = 0 \qquad m_{33} = 0$

$$M = \begin{pmatrix} 0 & 1 & 0 \\ 0 & 0 & 1 \\ 1 & 0 & 0 \end{pmatrix}$$

This type of matrix describes what network analysis calls sociometric choices, which merely depict the presence or absence of a given type of relation. But data obviously sometimes take a different form. Sometimes the goal is to study several types of relations within the same body of people. We now move into the multigraph, or more accurately, if multiple types of relations are involved, a p-graph with p relationship choice matrices. For example, we need two binary matrices to represent relations of kinship and neighbourliness among n individuals.

Some network analyses offer weighted data that will, for example, give the frequency of relations between two individuals or the volume of contacts. Such a graph is said to be *valued*. Each arc carries a number that expresses the weighting for each relation. Numbers in adjacency matrices indicate weightings. But you can always revert to a binary approach, where 1 expresses relations above a certain threshold and 0 otherwise.

Where a relation is marked plus or minus to indicate positive (friendly) or negative (hostile), we have a *signed graph*. Cells in the adjacency matrix are coded with 0 (no links), +1 or −1.

A *block* is a subset of contiguous rows and columns in matrix M. A 1-block is a block full of 1s; a 0-block contains only 0s. In

$$M = \begin{pmatrix} 1 & 1 & 0 & 1 \\ 1 & 1 & 0 & 0 \\ 0 & 0 & 1 & 1 \\ 0 & 0 & 0 & 1 \end{pmatrix}$$

you can distinguish the block consisting of rows 1 and 2 from the block consisting of rows 3 and 4. This is expressed as

$$M_{B(2)} = \quad \begin{array}{cc|cc} 1 & 1 & 0 & 1 \\ 1 & 1 & 0 & 0 \\ \hline 0 & 0 & 1 & 1 \\ 0 & 0 & 0 & 1 \end{array}$$

The initial matrix is of order 4 while the blocked matrix is order 2. It is summarized by

$$B = \begin{pmatrix} 1 & 1 \\ 0 & 1 \end{pmatrix}$$

We put a 0 in the block matrix that corresponds to M_B if every value is 0. Otherwise we insert a 1. Other conventions for block matrices are possible, e.g. 1 for relations beyond a certain density within the block (or 0 for less) or 1 only if all M_B values equal 1.

A *square matrix* has an equal number of rows and columns. A *triangular matrix* is a square matrix with a triangle of cells full of 0s. A *diagonal matrix* is a square matrix where all terms except those on the diagonal are 0. So, matrix B above is a triangular matrix, and

$$M = \begin{pmatrix} 1 & 0 & 0 \\ 0 & 1 & 0 \\ 0 & 0 & 1 \end{pmatrix}$$

is a diagonal matrix of order 3. From here, we can go on to speak of diagonal and triangular block matrices:

$$M = \quad \begin{array}{cc|cc|cc} 1 & 1 & 0 & 0 & 0 & 0 \\ 0 & 1 & 0 & 0 & 0 & 0 \\ \hline 0 & 0 & 1 & 1 & 0 & 0 \\ 0 & 0 & 1 & 1 & 0 & 0 \\ \hline 0 & 0 & 0 & 0 & 1 & 1 \\ 0 & 0 & 0 & 0 & 0 & 1 \end{array}$$

is a diagonal block matrix, and

$$M = \begin{array}{|cc|c|} \hline 1 & 1 & 1 \\ 1 & 1 & 0 \\ \hline 0 & 0 & 1 \\ \hline \end{array}$$

is a triangular block matrix.

A *permutation matrix* is a binary square matrix where each row or column contains only one 1. Entering 1 at the intersection of row i and column j of P expresses an exchange in matrix M of the same order between rows i and j (matrix PM) as between columns i and j (matrix MP):

$$P = \begin{pmatrix} 1 & 0 & 0 \\ 0 & 0 & 1 \\ 0 & 1 & 0 \end{pmatrix}$$

$$M = \begin{array}{c|ccc} & 1 & 2 & 3 \\ \hline 1 & 0 & 0 & 1 \\ 2 & 1 & 0 & 1 \\ 3 & 1 & 0 & 0 \end{array}$$

The matrix product $PMP = M_\text{p}$ yields

$$M_\text{p} = \begin{array}{c|ccc} & 1 & 3 & 2 \\ \hline 1 & 0 & 1 & 0 \\ 3 & 1 & 0 & 0 \\ 2 & 1 & 1 & 0 \end{array}$$

Mathematical operations that can be effected on matrices are given in the Appendix. The graphs associated with M and M_p are obviously identical. Permutation can obtain a triangular or a diagonal block matrix. Thus, M will not render as a triangular block matrix, but M_p will:

$$M_\text{p} = \begin{array}{c|cc|c} & 1 & 3 & 2 \\ \hline 1 & 0 & 1 & 0 \\ 3 & 1 & 0 & 0 \\ \hline 2 & 1 & 1 & 0 \\ \end{array}$$

$$B = \begin{pmatrix} 1 & 0 \\ 1 & 0 \end{pmatrix}$$

Thus, a triangular block matrix corresponds to a hierarchic or recursive graph. Such a graph has no circuits, i.e. the adjacency matrix is triangular. Otherwise, the graph is said to be interdependent. Diagonal block matrices help point up the strongly connected components of a graph.

Graphs show up the following three types of link between nodes:

Direct links

These are indicated by a 1 in the adjacency matrix.

Indirect links

If x and y connect through a path of length k, the link appears by raising the adjacency matrix to the power k. If m_{ij}^2 is an element of M^2, then:

1   If $m_{ij}^2 = 0$, there is no path of length 2 between i and j.
2   If $m_{ij}^2 \neq 0$, there is at least one path of length 2 between i and j.

As a rule, matrix M is raised to the power k to establish if i and j enjoy a link of length k. Either of the following two types of arithmetic operation may apply to matrix multiplication:

1   Standard arithmetic, where $1+1 = 2$.
2   Pseudo-Boolean arithmetic, which comprises the rules of standard arithmetic except that $1+1 = 1$ (the matrices are binary). Thus we also express $a + b = \max(a, b)$ and $a \times b = \min(a, b)$, where $a, b \in \{0, 1\}$.

With pseudo-Boolean arithmetic, m_{ij}^k indicates there is at least one path of length k between i and j. In standard arithmetic, the paths indicated by m_{ij}^k are not necessarily elementary. The same holds true for the number of circuits of length k given by m_{ii}^k. This number may include non-simple circuits, and circuits may be counted more than once.

Basic links

These are arcs (x, y) whose *removal* cuts off all paths from x to y. In the following graph, $(1, 3)$ and $(3, 2)$ are basic links but $(1, 2)$ is not, because path $(1, 3, 2)$ remains available.

Building on binary or sociometric data, many methods of index calculation require prior transformations. Burt (1982) in particular transforms the matrix of observed sociometric choices O into matrix Z where z_{ij} indicates the strength of the relation between nodes i and j respectively. The resulting matrix is then subjected to various mathematical operations and algorithms. We shall demonstrate this with a simple example where O is a matrix reflecting the following sociometric choices:

$$O = \begin{pmatrix} 0 & 1 & 0 \\ 1 & 0 & 1 \\ 1 & 0 & 0 \end{pmatrix}$$

First we calculate the geodesic distance matrix G:

$$G = \begin{pmatrix} 0 & 1 & 2 \\ 1 & 0 & 1 \\ 1 & 2 & 0 \end{pmatrix}$$

Then, matrix Z and element z_{ij} are obtained by:

$$z_{ij} = \begin{cases} 0 & \text{if there is no path between } i \text{ and } j \\ 1 & \text{if } i = j \\ 1 - \dfrac{f_{ij}}{n_i} & \text{otherwise} \end{cases}$$

In this formula, n_i is the number of people i can contact, including himself, and f_{ij} is the number of people who are at the same distance as j to i or closer. This transformation is noteworthy for attributing more importance to infrequent relations even with several intermediaries while minimizing direct links which are infrequent. In this way, the relation between i and j is established as a function of its position with respect to all other relations. In our example, this yields:

$$Z = \begin{pmatrix} 1.000 & 0.667 & 0.333 \\ 0.333 & 1.000 & 0.333 \\ 0.667 & 0.333 & 1.000 \end{pmatrix}$$

This enables us to build a matrix D of Euclidean distances between nodes using the following standard formula:

$$d_{ij} = \left[(z_{ij} - z_{ji})^2 + \sum_q (z_{iq} - z_{jq})^2 + \sum_q (z_{qi} - z_{qj})^2 \right]^{\frac{1}{2}}, \quad q \neq i, j$$

For example, we calculate d_{12} as follows:

$$d_{12} = \left[(z_{12} - z_{21})^2 + (z_{13} - z_{23})^2 + (z_{31} - z_{32})^2 \right]^{\frac{1}{2}}$$

$$= \left[(0.334)^2 + 0 + (0.334)^2 \right]^{\frac{1}{2}}$$

$$= \sqrt{0.222}$$

$$= 0.471$$

This operation is repeated for the other distances to yield the following symmetrical matrix (all distances only happen to be equal in our example):

$$D = \begin{pmatrix} 0.000 & & \\ 0.471 & 0.000 & \\ 0.471 & 0.471 & 0.000 \end{pmatrix}$$

As will be shown, the shorter the Euclidean distance between two actors, the more they tend towards 'statistical' equivalence. Zero distance indicates strict equivalence. It does not occur in our example.

Connectedness and Hierarchy

Reduced Graphs

We have seen how a directed relation allows us to conceptualize a path as a series of arcs that can be travelled in a given direction. This implies something is in circulation, e.g. consumer goods or information. But direction may also represent a social relation such as hierarchy or dependency. Here, a path stands for order, with someone first and someone last.

In the graph in Figure 3.1, we can start at node 3 and move through 4, 5 and 6 before returning to 3. As already stated, this is a circuit. Other circuits include 1 and 2 as well as 7, 8 and 9, because you can reach 8 from 7 via 9 and return the same way.

In the graph, every node can be reached from every other node in the same circuit. Now let us bundle together all nodes in a given circuit into clusters. However, this presents a difficulty. Nodes 3 and 4 fall into the same cluster because they belong to the same circuit. But this circuit is itself part of the larger circuit 3, 4, 5, 6. And this larger circuit is maximal because it belongs to no even larger circuit. We cannot bundle 3 and 4 into a cluster without including 5 and 6. So clusters arise from maximal circuits.

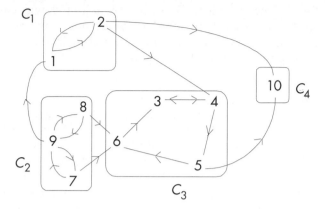

Figure 3.1 Strongly connected components

Note that clusters are considered strongly connected components. We shall label them C_1, C_2, C_3 and C_4.

Now consider arcs that span elements between clusters, e.g. the arc between node 8 in C_2 and node 6 in C_3 or from 7 to 6 between the same two clusters. If a given arc goes from a node in C_2 to another in C_3, all arcs from C_2 to C_3 share the same direction, i.e. from a C_2 element to a C_3 element. In effect, if the relation operated in both directions, it would build a circuit encompassing all C_2 and C_3 elements, but our example assumes maximal circuits.

Thus, all arcs that move from one cluster to another share the same direction. This allows us to build a reduced graph with nodes that stand for clusters, i.e. strongly connected components. Arcs are drawn between clusters whenever at least one arc connects a component of one cluster to that of another. In our example (Harary et al., 1965), the following obtains:

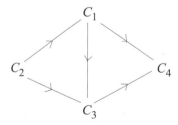

As a rule, reduced graphs have no circuits. If, indeed, any circuit were found to exist in a reduced graph, there would be a circuit in the original graph that would encompass several circuits used to build the clusters, but which our examples assume are maximal.

Having no circuits, our reduced graph lays out a hierarchy of the clusters, i.e. of the strongly connected components from the original graph. It has at least one first component and one last. The order in our example is C_1–C_2–C_3–C_4. The order is total in that the nodes follow one another in single file. Order is partial when some nodes are not comparable. And of course you can also have a single equivalence class in the presence of a graph that is strongly connected throughout.

Transitive Closure

Transitivity is the search for individuals with a relation of length 2 or more. Strictly speaking, a relation is transitive if x has a link to z through y which has separate bilateral links to x and z. Here, transitivity is imposed by indirect links, i.e. paths of length greater than 1. So we have a transitive closure of the relational graph once all the indirect links have been filled in. This graph is based on a pseudo-Boolean consideration of the matrix $A* = A + A^2 + \ldots + A^{(n-1)}$ and by inserting an arc between nodes i and j if the corresponding cell in the matrix is not null. Thus, the matrix for this transitive closure is completed by filling in a 1 in the cell where row i intersects column j if a path of any length exists between i and j. The following matrix represents the graph for the preceding example:

	1	2	3	4	5	6	7	8	9	10
1	0	1	0	0	0	0	0	0	0	0
2	1	0	0	1	0	0	0	0	0	1
3	0	0	0	1	0	0	0	0	0	0
4	0	0	1	0	1	0	0	0	0	0
5	0	0	0	0	0	1	0	0	0	1
6	0	0	1	0	0	0	0	0	0	0
7	0	0	0	0	0	1	0	0	1	0
8	0	0	0	0	0	1	0	0	1	0
9	1	0	0	0	0	0	1	1	0	0
10	0	0	0	0	0	0	0	0	0	0

Readers will easily confirm that the transitive closure matrix is as follows:

	1	2	3	4	5	6	7	8	9	10
1	1	1	1	1	1	1	0	0	0	1
2	1	1	1	1	1	1	0	0	0	1
3	0	0	1	1	1	1	0	0	0	1
4	0	0	1	1	1	1	0	0	0	1
5	0	0	1	1	1	1	0	0	0	1
6	0	0	1	1	1	1	0	0	0	1
7	1	1	1	1	1	1	1	1	1	1
8	1	1	1	1	1	1	1	1	1	1
9	1	1	1	1	1	1	1	1	1	1
10	0	0	0	0	0	0	0	0	0	0

This shows diagonal blocks of 1s from top left to bottom right. This transitive closure for the initial graph is typical of cliques, i.e. sets of nodes all having dyadic links. There are three cliques: (1, 2), (3, 4, 5, 6) and (7, 8, 9). They are the strongly connected components. In the transitive closure, they become cliques. There is no outbound arc in node 10, so it does not register as a clique. Nonetheless, 10 is a strongly connected component.

For any given analysis, it may prove worthwhile to reshuffle rows and columns so as to bring out the diagonal blocks that characterize cliques. This is neatly accomplished simply by arranging nodes as a function of the number of 1s in the row that corresponds to the transitive closure matrix. Then we arrange them in order of decreasing number of links. In transitive closure, all elements in a clique are equivalent in the strictest sense of the term (see Chapter 4), i.e. they all enjoy precisely the same links with each other.

In our example, let us denote the set (1, 2) by C_1; (3, 4, 5, 6) by C_2; (7, 8, 9) by C_3; and 10 by C_4. They constitute the following matrix which characterizes the reduced graph. The cell where row C_3 intersects column C_2 has a 1 because there are 1s in the transitive closure matrix for all cells where a row C_3 element intersects a column C_2 element.

	C_1	C_2	C_3	C_4
C_1	1	1	0	1
C_2	0	1	0	1
C_3	1	1	1	1
C_4	0	0	0	0

Now let us reshuffle rows and columns to obtain a decreasing order for the number of 1s in each row. This gives C_3, C_1, C_2, C_4.

	C_3	C_1	C_2	C_4
C_3	1	1	1	1
C_1	0	1	1	1
C_2	0	0	1	1
C_4	0	0	0	0

The matrix now takes on the characteristic triangular form of the subjacent hierarchy in our example. As mentioned, the transitive closure graph has no circuits and the strongly connected components are therefore ordered. Matrix construction and calculations (i.e. raising matrices to successive powers, an operation that can readily be automated) thus prove a convenient way to discover a number of structural properties in a given graph.

Variations in Connectivity

The above leads into the value of distinguishing between different kinds of connectivity and the structures they represent. Apart from the weak

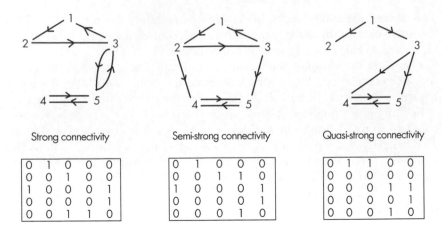

Figure 3.2   Types of connectivity

connectivity of an undirected graph, connectivity falls into the three types shown in Figure 3.2. Strong connectivity arises where nodes i and j always share a path in each direction. Semi-strong connectivity is where i and j always share a path in at least one direction at any time. Quasi-strong connectivity is where i and j merely share at least one common predecessor.

In the first case, the matrix has to be taken to the fourth power if all paths are to appear because it takes a path length of 4 to connect nodes 1 and 4. In the last two cases, a path length of 3 will suffice. This is the basis for the following matrices which give the shortest path lengths between two nodes.

3	1	2	4	3
2	3	1	3	2
1	2	2	2	1
3	4	2	2	2
2	3	1	1	2

3	1	2	2	3
2	3	1	1	2
1	2	3	2	1
#	#	#	2	1
#	#	#	1	2

#	1	1	2	2
#	#	#	#	#
#	#	#	1	1
#	#	#	2	1
#	#	#	1	2

Convention labels a cell with a 'sharp' (music) sign # if there is no path between nodes. In the first matrix, circulation is possible between any two nodes and we have strong connectivity. In the second, two blocks stand out. The first consists of nodes 1, 2 and 3; the second, of nodes 4 and 5. The subgraph for the first block is strongly connected because its corresponding submatrix contains no 0s. The same is true for the second block. You can go from the first block to the second, but not the other way. So there is a hierarchy between these blocks. In the third case, we have the block (4, 5); the others only have one node apiece. There is order, but only partial order. You cannot go from 2 to 3 or 3 to 2 and the nodes are said to be incomparable. Generally, this gives the following definitions:

1   Strong connectivity defines transitive closure that builds a single block.
2   Semi-strong connectivity defines transitive closure with total order.
3   Quasi-strong connectivity defines transitive closure with partial order.

But why make such distinctions? To give this all a more intuitive feel, let's assume we're describing dependency within an organization. And let's say an arc runs from *i* to *j*; *j* is dependent on *i* if the latter is the source of all his important information. Going further, *j* is dependent on *i* if there is a path from *i* to *j*. Indeed, *j* is dependent on *i* if such a path exists and he gets all his information from *i*, be it directly or through an intermediary.

In a strongly connected matrix, such as the first case, 4 and 5 are considered equivalent because they have an equal duty to share information that either may learn. The same holds for 3 and 5. But if 3 and 5 are equivalent, and so are 4 and 5, then 3 and 4 must be considered equivalent as well. Furthermore, 2 is dependent on 1 and so is 3 on 2, but 1 is dependent on 3. So these three nodes show no hierarchy and they too are equivalent. The bottom line is equivalence among all five nodes. In conclusion, all nodes are considered equivalent when a set of nodes in a graph forms a strongly connected subgraph. No hierarchy can be established from an investigation of relations.

In the case of semi-strong connectivity, 4 and 5 instantly stand out as equivalent, as do 1, 2 and 3. But there is no path from 4 or 5 to any of the three others. Thus, 4 and 5 are dependent on 1, 2 and 3. In other words, semi-strong connectivity brings out equivalent nodes and lays down the complete hierarchy for equivalence classes. The result is stratification, and Vincent Lemieux (1982) refers to a 'stratarchy' in this case.

Quasi-strong connectivity compares nodes less well. In the first two cases, the two nodes were comparable in that either they were equivalent or one was dependent on the other. In this case, they are incomparable. But they share a common predecessor despite their incomparability. Thus a global hierarchy does exist but it is incomplete. Nodes 2 and 4 are incomparable but both are dependent on node 1.[2]

In short, strong connectivity $\Rightarrow$ semi-strong connectivity $\Rightarrow$ quasi-strong connectivity.

Representing Relational Data

Network analysis is most often applied to sociometric data. If *X* stands for a population under investigation, observations will be entered directly on an $X \times X$ table or on a series of such tables if several types of interaction are involved. Occasionally, however, the matrix is derived from another table. Chapter 6 reviews connectivity studies in managerial bodies. The next analysis applies to intercompany links induced by the fact that some people sit on several boards of directors. In this case, the study starts from an $X \times Y$ table, where *X* are the companies and *Y* are the board members. This is often termed an actor–event matrix.

Companies X

1	0	1	1
0	1	1	0
1	1	1	0
1	0	1	1
0	1	1	1
0	1	1	0

Board members Y

This table will yield the next table, giving the number of people who sit on the boards of both company i and company j in the cell where row i intersects column j. We have entered the total number of board members for each company on the diagonal, but this is only another arbitrary convention. We may recast the diagonal after subsequent calculations.

Companies X

3	1	3	2
1	4	4	1
3	4	6	3
2	1	3	3

Companies X

The following $Y \times Y$ table can be deduced in the same fashion to identify board members and how many companies they meet at.

Board members Y

3	1	3	3	2	1
1	2	2	1	2	2
3	2	3	2	2	2
3	1	2	3	2	2
2	2	2	2	3	2
1	2	2	2	2	2

Board members Y

Representing data in table form is a convenient way to conceptualize links and set up data for direct calculations. It does however pointlessly take up a good deal of hard disk space, especially when tables are rich in 0s. This explains the widespread representation of graphs in the form of arc lists. The following shows a relation represented in three different ways:

Graph: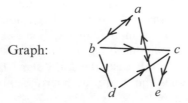

	a	b	c	d	e
a	0	1	0	0	1
b	1	0	1	1	0
c	0	0	0	0	1
d	0	0	1	0	0
e	1	0	0	0	0

Adjacency matrix:

Arc list: *ab, ae, ba, bc, bd, ce, dc, ea*

Notes

1 An undirected graph is a special kind of directed graph. As the latter happens to be more general, we shall simply use the term 'graph' to designate it. The term 'digraph' is not needed. If it has to be underscored that the direction of arcs is disregarded, we shall use the term 'undirected graph'.

2 If there is always a path from node i to j and another from j to i, then at least one path exists. Thus all strongly connected graphs are semi-strongly connected. If i and j have a path in at least one direction, the two nodes will always share a common predecessor: whichever of the two is at the start of the path. Thus, a graph of semi-strong connectivity enjoys quasi-strong connectivity.

4 EQUIVALENCE AND COHESION

We shall now apply graph analysis to seek out subsets in networks. The most intuitive approach is to look at existing relations and to distinguish groups according to their cohesion, i.e. the strength of the link density among subset members. There is a second criterion, however. Individuals sharing the same relations can be grouped even in the absence of shared links. This is called equivalence. Thus we have two basic principles.

Cohesion

The idea of using the cohesion principle is implicit throughout the work of Moreno, and his disciples went on to run numerous studies on cliques. But the idea was also common among the disciples of Radcliffe-Brown at Harvard in the 1930s. More specifically, Elton Mayo and Lloyd Warner developed an entire series of investigations into local communities and industrial organizations to which they tried to apply structural thinking.

Industrial sociology was born in the 1920s with Mayo's study of Chicago-based Western Electric's Hawthorne plant. The management wanted to understand the effect of modified working conditions on productivity. After a first modification had indeed reaped higher output, they were disconcerted to see output stagnate despite more changes to working conditions. Mayo was called in to discover why. He concluded that the determining factor behind the initial productivity surge was simply the inclusion of workers in the experiment itself: they perceived that management cared about them and this feeling carried over into a significant output boost. Productivity then simply had no further reason to continue climbing.

Mayo (1933) then ran an ethnographic study of the plant. His team picked up just about every kind of data but focused on informal coworker relations. They then drew up sociograms for informal worker relations, much like ethnologists would for kinship.

In their main report on Hawthorne, Roethlisberger and Dickson (1939) identify the cliques in the cable factory where the relational data had been collected. They explicitly used the term 'clique' but did not define it with formal criteria at the time. They only included subgroups cited by the workers themselves. Nonetheless, the data were good enough for later secondary analysis of effective cliques. At the time, the team settled for mapping out sociograms indicating the contours of cliques cited by the respondents themselves. Nonetheless, these pioneering investigations definitely made a strong contribution towards accrediting the idea that it is essential to study networks and identify subgroups from the standpoint of cohesion for a proper understanding of a social system.

In the same timeframe, Lloyd Warner was firmly applying this conviction to his studies too. He investigated a New England town in the early 1930s that he rechristened 'Yankee City'. The study laid the foundations for empirical analysis of social stratification. As stated, Warner was influenced by Radcliffe-Brown and perceived the organization of a social community, rural or urban, as a fabric of relations through which actors interact. In a modern city, however, he calls 'cliques' groups that take the form of clubs, parishes, etc. He defines cliques as informal groupings of people who share a feeling of belonging, some degree of intimacy and recognized norms of behaviour. He sees such informal links as more important to urban social integration than formal political or economic links. Somewhat as in Mayo's shopfloor studies, Yankee City cliques were identified by respondents themselves who cited the 'circles' to which they belonged.

When individuals belong to several overlapping cliques, those cliques form a network of integrating interrelations. In the end, cliques are the product of overlap between social circles. Warner and Lunt (1941; 1942) did an entire series of graphs to show up overlap in cliques. For Yankee City, they found 31 cliques and a scale of six social status levels. One such table plots cliques against status to show which stratum dominates which clique and to identify existing combinations (or structural positions) in the city.

Warner is remembered for his ideas on social stratification as expressed in a six-layer scale running from lower–lower to upper–upper, but we easily forget that stratification operates on a set of cliques and is not, according to Warner, to be separated from the structure of effective relations between members of a given community.

Allison Davis, a colleague of Warner's, picked up on the study of cliques as a crossroads of social circles in 'Old City' (Davis et al., 1941). He focused primarily on the internal structure of cliques and distinguished three structural levels: (1) a core of members sharing the most intimate links; (2) an inner circle of members that do not constitute a group but join core members in certain activities; and (3) an outer circle of low-participation members. The Davis team's study formulated a number of hypotheses about interclique relations. For example, it notes how high-status core members of one clique provide their own low-status outer circle members with access to high-status members of other cliques.

The Hawthorne, Old City and Yankee City studies are contemporary with the Moreno studies. However, they probably evolved independently. Funnily enough, the two founding schools of network analysis never 'linked up' at the outset.

The linkup finally came thanks to George Homans (1951), a researcher interested in small group interaction and anything that could affect its intensity, duration or other parameters. Moreno gave him the methodological framework to perform a secondary analysis on the Davis data. For example he took one of the Old City matrices on the participation of 18 women in 14 social events and became the first to show that it could be reprocessed to reveal groups of women sharing strong links, i.e. cliques that attend the same events.

The features of these cliques, and of those in the Hawthorne study he also reanalysed, led Homans to theorize on what he called internal systems, now known as informal relations networks. One of his hypotheses is that individuals who interact frequently tend to like each other, so cliques tend to foster self-reinforcing cohesion because mutual likings encourage greater intimacy and more frequent contacts.

Since these pioneering studies, graph theory has come along with more precise tools to investigate cohesion. As seen in Chapter 3, graph theory sees a clique as a set of completely interconnected nodes. In other words, it has a chain of length 1 between each pair of nodes. In a directed graph, every ordered node pair must be connected by a path of length 1 (strong clique). If the relational context so allows, we may soften this last criterion and ignore direction in a graph (weak clique). Graph theory also considers cliques as complete subgraphs. The adjacency matrix of a clique consists exclusively of 1s (except possibly on the diagonal, whose value is irrelevant here).

But the definition is still incomplete. Most often, the complete subgraphs should also be maximal, i.e. no clique should lie entirely within another clique having a greater number of nodes.

As an example, we shall take relations between civic organizations in a booming French suburb outside Grenoble. At the time of the study (Ferrand, 1982), the population of Meylan was just under 20,000. The study quotes census data reporting that population doubled in the timeframes 1954 to 1962, 1962 to 1968, and 1968 to 1975. Population growth affected the social makeup. Between 1962 and 1975, the proportion of farmers fell from 7% to under 1% while that of workers plunged from 30% to 15%. However, top executives rose from 11% to 31%, middle managers from 18% to 22% and office workers from 7% to 10%. Meylan attracts upper middle class homeseekers.

The local civic organizations reflect this trend. Harmonie, an old musical society, suddenly witnessed the foundation of Centre Musical, a municipally sponsored club that takes an upbeat, teaching-oriented approach to music. The town hall is proactive about civic organizations. It sponsored the APACH local events society and APEDI information centre while maintaining firm control over the MJC local youth centre. These four bodies absorb half the town's cultural budget. Harmonie has almost no links to the town hall; nor does Saint-Valentin, a local festival committee catering for the elderly. Revirée and Buclos are local shopkeepers' lobbies. Haut-Meylan, Eyminées and Grand Pré are neighbourhood societies.

The data cover people sitting on the boards of two civic organizations. Links in Figure 4.1 identify common board members. They were deduced

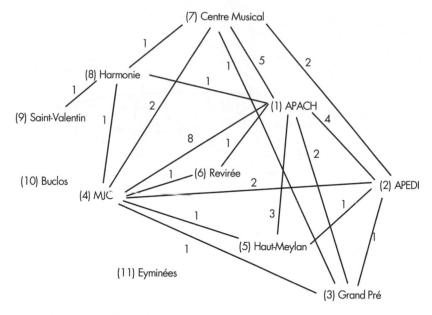

Figure 4.1 Relational graph for local civic organizations in Meylan

directly from membership lists. They are weighted but undirected, e.g. APACH and MJC share eight board members while APEDI and Grand Pré share only one.

We shall begin the search for cliques with two simplifications. First, we drop Buclos and Eyminées because they are isolated bodies that clearly share no clique memberships with the other bodies. Second, we merely note that a relation does or does not exist: either two boards have a common officer or they don't. In other words, we shift from a valued to an unvalued graph having the following matrix shown in Table 4.1.

Table 4.1 Sociomatrix for local civic organizations in Meylan

		(1)	(2)	(3)	(4)	(5)	(6)	(7)	(8)	(9)
APACH	(1)	0	1	1	1	1	1	1	1	0
APEDI	(2)	1	0	1	1	1	0	1	0	0
Grand Pré	(3)	1	1	0	1	0	0	1	0	0
MJC	(4)	1	1	1	0	1	1	1	1	0
Haut-Meylan	(5)	1	1	0	1	0	0	0	0	0
Revirée	(6)	1	0	0	1	0	0	0	0	0
Centre Musical	(7)	1	1	1	1	0	0	0	1	0
Harmonie	(8)	1	0	0	1	0	0	1	0	1
St-Valentin	(9)	0	0	0	0	0	0	0	1	0

This matrix readily submits to computer processing to locate the maximal cliques, and the following list gives all sets containing at least two nodes (node numbers given only):

82 INTRODUCING SOCIAL NETWORKS

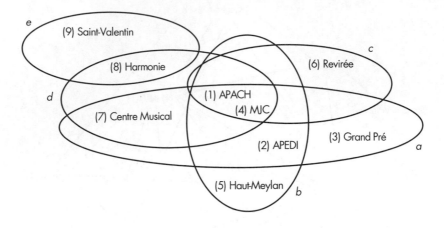

Figure 4.2   Maximal cliques and overlap for Meylan example

a   1, 2, 3, 4, 7
b   1, 2, 4, 5
c   1, 4, 6
d   1, 4, 7, 8
e   8, 9

This ensemble of cliques does not show firewalls between cliques; it identifies overlap. Cohesion maps out a graph of subsets with elements that share dyadic links. Figure 4.2 represents the Meylan data in a more straightforward form. APACH and MJC hold a central position on the graph because their officers belong to a majority of maximal cliques.

We perform clustering by building a matrix of cross-memberships for subjects and cliques under investigation (Table 4.2). In this matrix, the value in the cell where row *i* intersects column *j* gives the number of times nodes *i* and *j* fall in the same clique. The matrix now submits to hierarchical clustering (see Appendix) and yields Table 4.3. APACH (1) and

Table 4.2   Matrix of clique cross-memberships for Meylan example

		(1)	(2)	(3)	(4)	(5)	(6)	(7)	(8)	(9)
APACH	(1)	4	2	1	4	1	1	2	1	0
APEDI	(2)	2	2	1	2	1	0	1	0	0
Grand Pré	(3)	1	1	1	1	0	0	1	0	0
MJC	(4)	4	2	1	4	1	1	2	1	0
Haut-Meylan	(5)	1	1	0	1	1	0	0	0	0
Revirée	(6)	1	0	0	1	0	1	0	0	0
Centre Musical	(7)	2	1	1	2	0	0	2	1	0
Harmonie	(8)	1	0	0	1	0	0	1	2	1
St-Valentin	(9)	0	0	0	0	0	0	0	1	1

Table 4.3   Ascending hierarchy of clique cross-memberships for Meylan example

Level	Nodes								
	(3)	(5)	(6)	(2)	(1)	(4)	(7)	(8)	(9)
4	.	.	.	.	X	X	X	.	.
2	.	.	.	X	X	X	X	X	X	X	.	.
1	X	X	X	X	X	X	X	X	X	X	X	X	X	X	X	X	X	X

MJC (4) are the two bodies sharing the most cliques, which confirms their key position in terms of cohesion. APEDI (2) and Centre Musical (7) follow.

The Meylan graph happens to be fairly dense and this explains the presence of four-member cliques in a set of only nine elements, which is unusual. Three-member cliques are already rare enough. Nonetheless, our clique-building criterion is too severe and needs softening. There are several ways of doing this. The simplest is to include indirect links, but a few more definitions are needed first.

A 2-clique is a set of nodes on a graph where every dyad shares a path of length 1 or 2 (or chain in an undirected graph). Likewise, an n-clique is a clique with paths of length $\leq n$ between any two nodes. For example, the next figure is not a 1-clique but a 2-clique, because B and D enjoy a path of length 2.

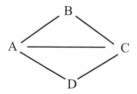

However, n-length paths prove tricky to interpret. Moreover, some intermediaries in an n-clique may be outsiders to the clique. Mokken (1979) resolves this problem by demanding inclusion of all and any paths between members of n-cliques. The result is an n-clan which is thus a subgraph with a maximal distance, or diameter, of $\leq n$ between two nodes.

The k-plex is another more flexible concept first advanced by Seidman and Foster (1978). This is a set of nodes such that each is adjacent to all except k others. In other words, for a k-plex containing n nodes, every node connects at least to $n - k$ nodes. K-plexes only record direct links and differ in this way from n-cliques and n-clans which incorporate indirect links.

Other methods of examining cliques are statistical. They apply to quasi-cliques or pseudo-cliques which are defined by certain minimum link ratios.

With a directed graph, we can elect to keep direction and bring out cliques with strong connectivity. Or we ignore arc directions to obtain cliques with weak connectivity. This is performed by transforming the elements o_{ij} in sociometric choice matrix O into matrix S such that either s_{ij} = min (o_{ij}, o_{ji}) if reciprocal relations alone are to be retained, or s_{ij} = max (o_{ij}, o_{ji}) if all relations are to be symmetrically aligned.

Next we apply Burt's method (Chapter 3) to transform the raw or symmetrical data into matrix Z, where z_{ij} gives the strength of the relation between any two nodes. As a rule, matrices are not symmetrical and must be made so. There are two ways to perform this:

1 Look for strong cohesion by considering that the strength of cohesion between two nodes, i and j, should not exceed the lowest strength of relations between them. Thus, matrix C of cohesion indices between nodes is given by c_{ij} = $min(z_{ij}, z_{ji})$. This amounts to acknowledging cohesion only in the presence of direct links between i and j.
2 If indirect links suffice, we can settle for weak cohesion and consider that cohesion strength is equal to the greatest relational strength between two nodes. In this case, we apply c_{ij} = $max(z_{ij}, z_{ji})$.

All that now remains is to select and apply an algorithm of ascending hierarchical order to matrix C containing cohesion indices c_{ij} (with values from 0 to 1) which obtains an indexed partition of individuals into cohesion clusters. In this model, clusters with the strongest cohesion are listed first and cohesion drops off as the clustering process goes on. We then determine the number of pseudo-cliques and need to decide where to set the cut off level of cohesion. As with earlier choices free of statistical imperatives, this level must be selected according to the relational context. Moreover, the results will probably vary depending on whether strong or weak connectivity has been retained and whether the cohesion option is strong or weak. Table 4.4 sums up the options.

Table 4.4

Connectivity	Cliques: strong cohesion, direct links	n-cliques: weak cohesion, indirect links
Strong	Complete directed subgraph	Complete directed subgraph; strong transitivity
Weak	Complete undirected subgraph	Complete undirected subgraph; weak transitivity

Do not confuse these clique- and pseudo-clique-building criteria with those of Alba and Kadushin (1976). They base cohesion on social circle overlap among members, an idea that occurred to Warner. Kadushin says the cohesion of a social circle should not be seen as a 1-clique that forces one-on-one encounters. His circles are the product of direct interaction but their boundaries are not always clear to members. If i has n_i relations (including himself) and j has n_j relations, i and j share n_{ij} relations. The degree of overlap between circles is thus $n_{ij}/(n_i+n_j-n_{ij})$.[1] This similarity

Table 4.5   Circle overlap for Meylan example

Cohesion level	(6)	(5)	(1)	(4)	(2)	(3)	(7)	(8)	(9)
1.000	.	.	X	X	X	.	.	.	.
0.833	.	.	X	X	X	.	X	X	X
0.833	.	.	X	X	X	X	X	X	X
0.750	.	.	X	X	X	X	X	X	X
0.667	.	X	X	X	X	X	X	X	X
0.571	.	X	X	X	X	X	X	X	X
0.400	.	X	X	X	X	X	X	X	X
0.375	X	X	X	X	X	X	X	X	X

index varies from 0, where i and j are excluded from each other's circles, to 1, where they are included or have the same contacts. These indices are called Jaccard indices and may be expressed in a matrix that can be processed to yield a hierarchy.

Applying this method to the unvalued Meylan graph, we see APACH and MJC have the same (i.e. direct) contacts (Table 4.5). Next come Grand Pré, Centre Musical and APEDI, which did not cluster at the preceding level. Grand Pré does not often belong to the same cliques as APEDI and Centre Musical but it does belong to circles that overlap with them.

Lastly, we can approximate cohesion with a k-core. In an undirected graph, a k-core is a maximal connected subgraph in which the degree of all nodes is $\geq k$ (Seidman, 1983). It must contain at least $k+1$ nodes. Therefore, a k-core is a part of a network in which each member connects to at least k others. So such a group has some degree of cohesion without necessarily qualifying as a clique.

For any degree k, there may exist one or more k-cores. The presence of several k-cores means we have identified groups with a certain amount of cohesion who share weaker links. If we have only one k-core, it is a part of a $k-1$ core, itself part of a $k-2$ core and so on (Doreian and Woodward, 1994). We have a sort of Russian doll configuration, i.e. a series of perimeters whose density increases as we approach the densest core. Such is the case in Meylan, because after processing relations among these civic bodies we obtain the clusters in Table 4.6.

Table 4.6   Partition into k-cores for Meylan example

Degrees	(1)	(2)	(3)	(4)	(7)	(5)	(8)	(6)	(9)	Density d
5	.	.	.	.	.	.	.	.	.	
4	X	X	X	X	X	.	.	.	.	1.00
3	X	X	X	X	X	X	X	.	.	0.76
2	X	X	X	X	X	X	X	X	.	0.64
1	X	X	X	X	X	X	X	X	X	0.53

Equivalence

Another way of distinguishing subsets in a network is to group individuals or social positions according to the relations they keep with others. This is called equivalence. We can illustrate this with a doctor/patient relationship. The interaction is basically asymmetrical. Patients need treatment and physicians provide it. The relation can be considered as directed from the doctor to the patient (the doctor is a health care 'provider') and from the patient to the doctor (the patient is a 'client'). If we now consider the set of all doctors, and that of all patients (actual or potential), a relation stands out that will lead us to put all doctors in one basket and all patients in another (of course, doctors get sick too and they form a special group). But we can also assume that these doctors do not know each other and have no relations. We assume as much for patients unless some extraordinary event pushes them into contact (although some links will exist). Such clustering into doctors and patients owes nothing to cohesion logic. We shall assume zero cohesion among doctors or patients. Nor are we using any status data about individuals. Indeed, the only justification for a category of doctors and another of patients is the relation that any individual in one category maintains with at least one member of the other category. Here we are dealing with what Ossowski (1963) calls correlative classes, i.e. classes that are defined not in terms of themselves, but in terms of the relations that connect their elements.

Equivalence is a cognitive operation that the sociologist performs to describe relations and social roles; the issue is how to actually construct them from the data. Most roles take on meaning in the context of daily living, e.g. father/son, employer/employee and shopkeeper/client. This is because of the institutionalized definition these roles enjoy. But other roles are fuzzier. 'Boss' and 'expert' mean very different things depending on the context.

Sociologists have made great progress in their thinking about the definition of classes based on individual roles. They have moved the focus beyond individual attributes for classification purposes. To this end, we now have a distinction between 'sex' and 'gender'. Sex is an attribute of biological classification while gender expresses the sociological concept of sex roles.

The Marxist concept of social class stresses economic equivalence in individual relations. But the vast body of literature this concept triggered shows that most researchers, including Marx, found the concept insufficient to describe relative positions. They also take into account class cohesion (or 'class consciousness'), individual attributes and various forms of mobility between classes.

In tackling these questions, the definitions of equivalence for purposes of social network analysis amount to going back and refining the logical basis for defining roles and classes (Nadel, 1957; Naville, 1982; Ossowski, 1963). The principles are as follows.

First, we assume that we are working on a single relation in a clearly defined population. This relation is shown in a graph or its associated matrix. Let us start with the following easy example:

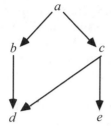

	a	b	c	d	e
a	0	1	1	0	0
b	0	0	0	1	0
c	0	0	0	1	1
d	0	0	0	0	0
e	0	0	0	0	0

Here we classify individuals, expressed as nodes, in a way that best expresses the major aspects of the structure. For example, let us bundle up [b, c], then [d, e], and isolate [a]. We now have classes I = [a], II = [b, c] and III = [d, e]. The only value of these classes is their potential to offer an image of interclass relations from the initial relations between individuals.

The first criterion is that we may draw an arc between two classes as soon as we have established that at least one arc exists in the initial relation between a member of the first class and another of the second.

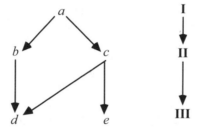

So we have an arc from class I to class II because the original graph shows an arc from a to b and another from a to c. We now add an arc from II to III because of the arcs between b and d, c and d, and c and e. We may not draw an arc from I to III because the original graph shows none between a and d or a and e. The same holds true between III and II as well as II and I. This is consistent with the principle of weak cohesion: you have an interclass relation whenever there is a relation between at least one element of the first class and another of the second. Note that this operation does not authorize any loss of information. Conversely, it adds none because an arc is drawn between two classes only if the arc already exists at the individual level. In fact we are using the block model principle (White et al., 1976).

Formally, if P is an initial population and R is the relation under investigation, classifying is the function f which makes class f(a) correspond to each element. If R' is the image relation between classes, the principle just stated becomes: regardless of a and b (any two elements of P), aRb implies $f(a)R'f(b)$ and $xR'y$ implies that there exist c and d in P such that $x = f(c)$, $y = f(d)$ and cRd.

This is the principle of homomorphism. From now on, we shall only be speaking of homomorphic classification. Homomorphism sets up relations of equivalence among all elements sharing the same image. Note that homomorphism is preserved by iterating the relation aRb and $bRc \Rightarrow aR^2c$. If f is a homomorphism, aRb leads to $f(a)R'f(b)$ and bRc leads to $f(b)R'f(c)$, and consequently $f(a)R'^2f(c)$. Thus $aR^2c \Rightarrow f(a)R'^2f(c)$. Ergo $aR^nb \Rightarrow f(a)R'^nf(c)$.

Returning to the previous example, we see that class I and II relations differ from those of II and III in that a has a link to b and c, i.e. all class I elements enjoy the same link to class II elements. However, c has a link to d and e while b only has a link to d. So we have an asymmetry. And this looks like a weakness if we are trying to put into one class all individuals sharing the same relations. Does this mean we are wrong to construct II and III?

Let us return to the concept of a role, our sociological object. If we are studying a relation where the individual at the origin of an arc teaches something to the receiving end, then d is receiving lectures from both b and c but e is only receiving them from c. The roles are perfectly defined and this is all very acceptable. We can now infer that b and c are professors lecturing to students d and e. There is no reason to claim that all professors teach all students or that all students are taught by all professors. Such a claim would fall foul of the role concept. However, why consider someone a student if he attends no courses and someone else a professor if he has no students? This question begs a second criterion to define regular equivalence.

A classification, or relation of equivalence, is considered *regular* on two conditions. First, it must be homomorphic. Second, an arc must always exist in the image relation between classes I and J wherever the initial relation shows at least one arc from each element in I to an element in J, with each element of J being at the end of at least one arc from an element I. In the binary matrix for the graph, blocks with rows representing elements from an equivalent class and columns that represent a different equivalent class must contain at least one 1 for each row and column, otherwise it must contain nothing but 0s.

We have just outlined two criteria for equivalence. A second example will highlight the difference between them. Let us imagine an army where subordinates show deference to superiors, and assume that we want to establish the hierarchy by observing behaviour. So we set about observing deference and classifying. Regular equivalence is clearly inadequate: if J is a class of servicemen subordinate to class I, all members of J show deference to all members of I. We have here equivalence in the strict sense of the term: two individuals are equivalent when they have exactly the same relation to everyone else. This is *structural* equivalence.

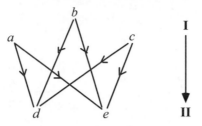

Structural equivalence is possible when the relation under observation obeys a rule, e.g. shopkeepers must serve all customers (except in very special cases), or all members of an army at war must automatically treat members of the opposing army as enemies.

When it is feasible to construct structural equivalence for a relation, there is either 1 or 0 in the blocks in the adjacency matrix whose rows correspond to elements of one class and whose columns correspond to those of the other class. Thus structural equivalence is *a fortiori* regular.

	a	b	c	d	e
a	0	0	0	1	1
b	0	0	0	1	1
c	0	0	0	1	1
d	0	0	0	0	0
e	0	0	0	0	0

The following figures illustrate the difference between these two forms of equivalence nicely:

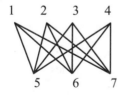

Structural
equivalence

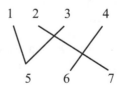

Regular
equivalence

In both definitions, we have insisted on links between individuals in different classes. Indeed, links among individuals in the same class create a problem. We shall consider the following example where non-regular equivalence prevails.

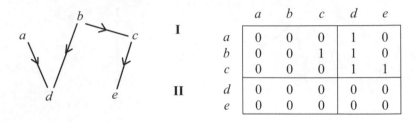

	a	b	c	d	e
a	0	0	0	1	0
b	0	0	1	1	0
c	0	0	0	1	1
d	0	0	0	0	0
e	0	0	0	0	0

Here, links between classes [a, b, c] and [d, e] fulfil all conditions. The upper right-hand block in the matrix contains at least one 1 per row and per column. However the arc between b and c induces a loop on the image graph within the same class. Because of this internal loop, regularity requires that every element in the class is at the origin and terminus of an arc, at least in the initial relation. This is not the case here. This restriction is important. Some professors may also be students. If roles are to be clarified properly, the criterion must apply to individuals within a class as much as it does to individuals between classes. More formal definitions for various forms of equivalence follow (see Reitz and White, 1989).

If X is a set and R is a dyadic relation in X, equivalence relation E is strong or automorphic if and only if, for every $a, b, c \in X$, aEb implies:

$aRb \Leftrightarrow bRa$　　and
$aRc \Leftrightarrow bRc$　　and
$cRa \Leftrightarrow cRb$

If X is a set and R is a dyadic relation in X, equivalence relation E is structural if and only if, for every $a, b, c \in X$ such that $a \neq c \neq b$, aEb implies:

$aRb \Leftrightarrow bRa$　　and
$aRc \Leftrightarrow bRc$　　and
$cRa \Leftrightarrow cRb$　　and
$aRa \Leftrightarrow aRb$

If X is a set and R is a dyadic relation in X, equivalence relation E is regular if and only if, for every $a, b, c \in X$, aEb implies:

$aRc \Rightarrow \exists\, d \in X: bRd$ and dEc　　and
$cRa \Rightarrow \exists\, d \in X: dRb$ and dEc

Returning to Meylan, we obtain the matrix in Table 4.7 after reconfiguring the rows and columns. APACH and MJC have exactly the same relations to the other organizations. When we merge them with APEDI and Centre Musical, we obtain regular equivalence. The only problem is the irregularity that arises when we come to Saint-Valentin which only relates to Harmonie. This sort of approximation is acceptable when classification respects

Table 4.7   Equivalence in Meylan example

		(1)	(4)	(7)	(2)	(6)	(5)	(3)	(8)	(9)
APACH	(1)	0	1	1	1	1	1	1	1	0
MJC	(4)	1	0	1	1	1	1	1	1	0
Centre Musical	(7)	1	1	0	1	0	0	1	1	0
APEDI	(2)	1	1	1	0	0	1	1	0	0
Revirée	(6)	1	1	0	0	0	0	0	0	0
Haut-Meylan	(5)	1	1	0	1	0	0	0	0	0
Grand Pré	(3)	1	1	1	1	0	0	0	0	0
Harmonie	(8)	1	1	1	0	0	0	0	0	1
Saint-Valentin	(9)	0	0	0	0	0	0	0	1	0

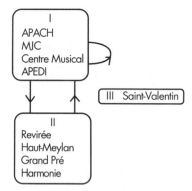

Figure 4.3   Links between classes in Meylan example

regularity criteria this tightly. The links induced by the initial relation between classes are shown in Figure 4.3. The resulting reduced matrix is:

	I	II	III
I	1	1	0
II	1	0	0
III	0	0	0

Alexis Ferrand (1982) points out in his study that Meylan municipal government has a hand in all four organizations in class I and directly operates some of them. Class II consists entirely of neighbourhood organizations, except Harmonie which is a folk music orchestra. These neighbourhood outfits have no common directors, but class I officers sit on their boards, giving the municipality a hand in their affairs too. Saint-Valentin is isolated. The equivalence mapped out here reflects the power structure for this set of organizations.

Obviously, Meylan is a very simple example. The results seem trivial and teach little more than what we would already suspect offhand about local power structures. But with greater numbers of individuals, these algorithms prove very useful for tracking regular and structural equivalence.

Matrimonial Exchange in Traditional Ethnic Societies

Equivalence is a way of creating categories that conform to a certain structure. It is a tool of analysis, but the researcher's natural inclination is to learn the rules operating in a survey population and governing its behaviour. Some societies are patterned into clans which determine the basis for matrimonial exchange. Men in one clan will be required to marry women from another specific clan. So clans are the product of structural equivalence here. The rules of matrimonial exchange are determined at clan level and apply equally to all members of the society. One advantage of such a rule is to preclude incest. A taboo on a certain behaviour pattern amounts to a requirement for another behaviour pattern. We shall consider a clan society with the following three rules:

1   No man may marry his mother.
2   No man may marry his sister.
3   No man may marry his daughter.

This society needs at least three clans that we shall call A, B and C. We can assume, for example, that men from A must marry women from B, B men must marry C women, and C men must marry A women. Children born to an A woman are B, those born to a B woman are C, and those born to a C woman are A. This system translates into two relations. The first, which we shall call m, is common to all three clans and defines which clan shall furnish a wife as a function of the male's clan origin. This relation can also be presented from the woman's standpoint and called w.

m		Will marry woman from			w		Will marry man from		
		A	B	C			A	B	C
Man	A	0	1	0	Woman	A	0	0	1
from	B	0	0	1	from	B	1	0	0
	C	1	0	0		C	0	1	0

We can express filial ties by deriving children's clan membership from their mothers'. It looks like m. Sons and daughters go into the same clan, so the relation is identical.

    Families commonly combine relations, taking into account grand-parents, in-laws etc. This would mean setting up relations for 'my father's (mother's) father', 'my father's (mother's) brother' for uncles, and 'my brother's (sister's) daughter (son)' for cousins, etc. But since we are work-ing with a single relation governing potential marriage partners and the clan membership of offspring, we only need raise the relation to successive powers.

$$
\begin{array}{cccc}
m & m^2 & m^3 & m^4 \\
010 & 001 & 100 & 010 \\
001 & 100 & 010 & 001 \\
100 & 010 & 001 & 100
\end{array}
$$

It appears that $m^3 = I$ (where I designates an identity matrix whose values arc all 0 except for the main diagonal where the values are 1) and $m^4 = m$. Matrix m^2 gives clan membership for children, and m^3 gives that for grandchildren as a function of father's clan. Therefore, a man may marry his great granddaughter or grandmother. The mother's clan is given in m^2. Thus m is the clan of the father, paternal uncle etc. A multiplication table for the relation is readily derived:

$$
\begin{array}{c|ccc}
 & I & m & m^2 \\
\hline
I & I & m & m^2 \\
m & m & m^2 & I \\
m^2 & m^2 & I & m
\end{array}
$$

This society of clans (i.e. equivalent classes) is designed for compliance with its rules of marriage and filiation and with the three incest taboos. We have structural equivalence because compliance is mandatory.

Structural equivalence as we have presented it was first developed by ethnologists (White, 1963; Lorrain and White, 1971) to describe kinship. Incest is the most common marriage taboo. From the standpoint of blocks, this taboo resembles a ban on reflexivity, i.e. the marriage relation is only compatible with empty diagonal blocks.

A ban on certain marriage combinations forces suitors to seek partners outside their native clan. And this is indeed what happens in an over-whelming number of societies which function as a finite number of groups, as analysed by Lévi-Strauss. A ban on endogamy imposes exogamy:

> Furthermore, in the technical case of marriage 'by exchange' so-called, or in any other marriage system whatsoever, the result of the incest prohibition is funda-mentally the same, viz., that as soon as I am forbidden a woman, she thereby becomes available to another man, and somewhere else a man renounces a woman who thereby becomes available to me. The content of the prohibition is not exhausted by the fact of the prohibition: the latter is instituted only in order to guarantee and establish, directly or indirectly, immediately or mediately, an exchange. (Lévi-Strauss, 1949)

The rules of this exchange principle in systems with a finite number of groups leads to the creation of rules that dictate bride sourcing. Lévi-Strauss distinguishes between restricted exchange among an even number of groups, where groups are paired off, and open-ended exchange among an odd number of groups, where bride swapping balances itself out among all groups.

In a system of restricted exchange, the taboo on marrying a sister imposes a filiation rule. This is nicely seen in Kariera society. Lévi-Strauss (1949) reports on the Kariera tribal system that prevails in both eastern and western Australia. Kariera are divided into four subgroups: Banaka, Karimera, Burung and Palyeri. He reports: 'Banaka necessarily marries Burung, and Karimera, Palyeri. The rule of descent is that the children of a Banaka man and a Burung woman are Palyeri, while the children of a Burung man and a Banaka woman are Karimera. Likewise, the children of a Karimera man and a Palyeri woman are Burung, and reversing the sexes with the classes remaining the same, they are Banaka.' The system is summarized in the following figure, where the = sign joins sections which intermarry and the arrows link the mother's section with her children's section.

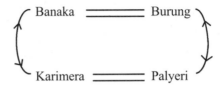

This reasoning is relevant to clustering individuals. If we examine marriage and filiation in terms of individuals, as we do for Western societies, we can reconfigure the four subgroups into a matrix of blocks. The simplified marriage matrix follows.

	Banaka	Burung	Karimera	Palyeri
Banaka	0	1	0	0
Burung	1	0	0	0
Karimera	0	0	0	1
Palyeri	0	0	1	0

Zeros stand for an incest taboo covering the society's subgroups. The filiation matrix is somewhat different, however. The entry in each cell expresses the type of couple (or husband's clan, which is one and the same). We use it to derive the type of couple for the children, which obviously varies with their sex. We have entered 'B' for boys and 'G' for girls to fit the data into one table (Table 4.8).

The normative character of the marriage rules gives the graph a very regular, simple appearance. Western societies offer more leeway in the choice of marriage partners but, as Chapter 2 shows, our leeway is less than total. Whether it is possible to identify marriage rules for modern

Table 4.8

	Type 1 Banaka man Burung woman	Type 2 Burung man Banaka woman	Type 3 Karimera man Palyeri woman	Type 4 Palyeri man Karimera woman
Type 1	O	O	G	B
Type 2	O	O	B	G
Type 3	G	B	O	O
Type 4	B	G	O	O

open societies is still a topical research issue. Lévi-Strauss and other ethnologists have opted for a statistical approach to this issue. Others (White and Jorion, 1992) have been trying to develop ways of detecting substructures in vast social systems. They use dual kinship graphs as introduced by Guilbaud (1970). A circle represents a couple, a line stands for a man and a dotted line stands for a woman. The following graph shows John, Mary and their three children, Peter, Lucy and Jack.

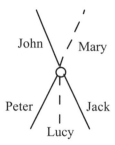

Kinship studies involve at least two distinct relations. One determines the choice of a partner and the other determines filiation. The system only works if the equivalence rule defining the clans respects both. Generally, researchers must also respect both in the field: if a society is defined by multiple relations, any classification system of individuals will only be significant if it respects all relations simultaneously.

Multiplexity

Sociometric studies often need to cover several relations simultaneously. A study of relations among scientists in neighbouring disciplines might investigate the following:

1 Who cooperates with whom?
2 Who quotes whom?
3 Who may have been whose student?

This would lead to three distinct matrices for this population, one for each type of link. If we are to take all the data into account for a classification of the individuals, the most rigorous method consists of considering, for every dyad (a, b), the full set of relations between them. We shall call this set the (a, b) bundle and express it as F_{ab}. We can now seek out an equivalence that respects the bundles, i.e. an equivalence f such that, if a and b belong to different clusters and are connected by F_{ab}, and if c and d are such that $f(a) = f(c)$ and $f(b) = f(d)$, then either $F_{ab} = F_{cd}$, or F_{ab} is empty, or F_{cd} is empty. This rule ensures what Reitz and White call juncture homomorphism. It is regular for every relation under study in a system. It is illustrated by the following, in which each type of line represents a type of relation:

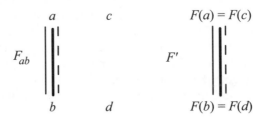

Notwithstanding, strict equivalence is far rarer in modern industrial societies than in ethnographic data because of less rigid rules. The complexity and diversity of relations make it necessary to settle for statistical approximations of equivalence.

Statistical Approximations of Equivalence

Software users are faced with choosing between tools that try to respect the spirit of structural equivalence and those faithful to that of regular equivalence. The notion of 'spirit' is important because, given the complexity of relations in most cases, any attempt at respecting the 'letter' of equivalence will only yield unreadable garbage.

Structural Equivalence Methods

Structural equivalence assumes all individuals in a cluster enjoy exactly the same relations to others. In the network matrix, rows and columns for two equivalent individuals must show identical values. This condition can be softened by classifying together people most like each other. To do this, you start by reckoning a similarity index for individuals before actual classification.

As an example, we shall use data collected by Samuel F. Sampson (1969). He studied 18 novices who had entered a monastery at different times. Six had entered the monastery before a series of liberalizing reforms. Two of the 12 who arrived after the reforms came to the fore as leaders and attracted five supporters. Sampson calls them the 'young Turks'. In the study, these seven are numbered 1 (John), 2 (Gregory), 7 (Mark), 12 (Winfrid), 14 (Hugh), 15 (Boniface) and 16 (Albert). Another five constitute a 'loyal opposition'. They are 4 (Peter), 5 (Bonaventure), 6 (Berthold), 9 (Ambrose) and 11 (Louis). Three others are perceived as immature 'outcasts'. They are 3 (Basil), 17 (Elias) and 18 (Simplicius). The final three are perceived as 'waverers'. They are 8 (Victor), 10 (Romuald) and 13 (Amand).

Sampson recorded enormous amounts of data on them and used four sociometric questionnaires. Relations were rated in terms of esteem/no esteem, like/dislike, positive/negative influence and praise/criticism in that order. Each rating was presented on a scale with a positive value at one end and a negative one at the other. At each of five interviews, novices were asked to rate three of their number at each extreme value on each of the scales.

The data in Table 4.9 are the positive ratings from the third series of interviews. The values in the matrix show how many times novice i gave novice j a top rating in response to one of the four questions. The data are therefore partial (Reitz, 1988).

Table 4.9   Interview data for monastery novices

	10	5	9	6	4	11	8	12	1	2	14	15	7	16	13	3	17	18
10	0	1	1	0	1	0	0	0	0	0	0	0	1	0	1	0	0	0
5	0	0	2	0	3	3	0	0	0	1	0	0	0	0	0	0	0	0
9	0	1	0	0	2	0	2	1	2	1	0	0	0	0	0	0	0	0
6	0	1	3	0	4	2	0	0	0	1	0	0	0	0	0	0	0	0
4	3	1	0	4	0	4	0	0	0	0	0	0	0	0	0	0	0	0
11	0	3	2	0	2	0	2	0	0	0	1	0	0	1	0	0	0	0
8	0	1	2	3	4	2	0	0	1	0	0	0	0	0	0	0	0	0
12	0	0	0	0	0	0	0	0	3	3	1	0	2	0	0	0	0	0
1	0	1	0	0	0	0	1	4	0	1	2	0	1	0	0	1	1	0
2	0	1	0	0	0	0	1	3	4	0	0	0	3	0	0	0	0	0
14	0	0	0	0	0	0	0	3	4	3	0	4	0	1	0	0	0	0
15	0	0	0	0	0	0	0	1	2	4	3	0	2	0	0	0	0	0
7	0	0	0	0	0	0	0	3	0	4	0	2	0	4	0	0	0	0
16	0	0	0	0	0	0	0	1	0	4	0	4	4	0	0	0	0	0
13	0	4	0	0	0	3	0	0	0	0	0	0	3	0	0	0	0	1
3	0	0	0	0	0	0	0	0	4	0	0	0	0	0	4	0	4	2
17	0	0	0	0	0	0	0	0	0	3	0	0	0	0	1	3	0	3
18	0	0	0	0	0	0	0	0	1	4	0	0	0	0	0	3	4	0

To obtain a similarity index between individuals i and j, we shall apply the method from Chapter 3 to calculate the Euclidean distance between values in the rows and columns for the novices. We have subtracted the values from the maximum distance given in the matrix because we want to work on an indicator of similarity, not distance. The similarity matrix can

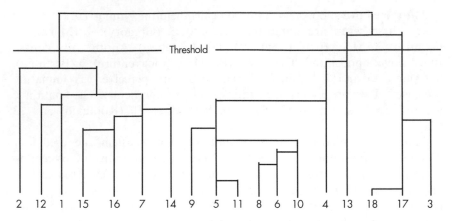

Figure 4.4   Clustering of monastery novices

then be routinely processed with a hierarchical clustering algorithm. In this case, we shall apply a single linkage clustering algorithm (see Appendix for details).

Figure 4.4 shows the following three clusters for the threshold point under consideration: (2, 12, 1, 15, 16, 7, 14), (9, 5, 11, 8, 6, 10, 4, 13) and (18, 17, 3). The first group overlaps perfectly with Sampson's young Turks. The second group includes the waverers and the loyal opposition. The last contains the outcasts.

Another widely used algorithm based on the same starting principle is CONCOR (Breiger et al., 1975). It judges similarity between two individuals as a function of their links to others. But it bases measurement on the Pearson correlation coefficient instead of Euclidean distance. This produces an initial correlation matrix C. Matrix C is derived from a matrix of observations O by finding the element c_{ij} which correlates row/row, column/column or both rows and columns (but row/row in the present case) as follows:

$$c_{ij} = \frac{\sum_{k=1}^{n}(x_{ik} - m_i)(x_{jk} - m_j)}{\left[\sum_{k=1}^{n}(x_{ik} - m_i)^2 \sum_{k=1}^{n}(x_{jk} - m_j)^2\right]^{1/2}}$$

where

$$m_i = \frac{1}{n}\sum_{k=1}^{n} x_{ik}$$

This correlation matrix serves to calculate $C(2)$, the correlation matrix for rows in C; and $C(3)$, the correlation matrix between the rows for $C(2)$; and

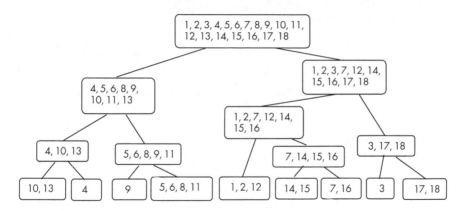

Figure 4.5 Dendrogram for monastery novices

so on until we converge on a matrix of values that are either +1 or −1. This resulting matrix can be reconfigured to show all the +1 values in two blocks on one diagonal and all the −1 values on the other diagonal.

+1	−1
−1	+1

This procedure defines two clusters of nodes. It can be reiterated for each cluster to yield four clusters and repeated as many times as needed until the desired level of partitioning is achieved. CONCOR ends up yielding a tree or dendrogram of embedded clusters. The tree for Sampson's data is given in Figure 4.5. Such partitioning creates a hierarchy that serves to reshuffle the initial matrix into blocks of greater or lesser density, as in Table 4.10.

CONCOR is a very flexible tool but some researchers are uncomfortable with such a 'black box' because nobody knows what significance to give to correlations of correlations. The substance of the results can only be judged *a posteriori*. CONCOR clearly does locate all equivalences in a network of strictly equivalent individuals who form an even number of groups, but strict equivalences are foreign to most real-life networks. In such cases, CONCOR appears to build groups of strong relational density, or at least groups whose internal density is far higher than their density of external relations. So it amounts to describing cohesion. It is rather like making a bet that, in the absence of strict equivalence, you stand a good chance of identifying more or less equivalent people by forming groups of relatively high cohesion. This attitude is not totally baseless because, although equivalent individuals will not always share links, as we have seen, all members of a clique are necessarily structurally equivalent. It is therefore not unreasonable to look for approximately equivalent individuals by trying to 'maximize' the density of the diagonal blocks in the permutation matrix.

Table 4.10   Reshuffled novices data

	10	13	4	9	5	11	6	8	12	2	1	15	14	16	7	3	17	18
10		1	1	1	1										1			
13				4	3										3			1
4	3			1	4	4												
9			2		1			2	1	1	2							
5			3	2		3				1								
11			2	2	3			2					1	1				
6			4	3	1	2		3		1								
8			4	2	1	2	3				1							
12										3	3		1		2			
2				1				1	3		4				3			
1				1				1	4	1			2		1	1	1	
15									1	4	2		3		2			
14									3	3	4	4		1				
16									1	4		4			4			
7									3	4		2		4				
3			4								4						4	2
17			1								3					3		3
18									4		1				3	4		

All of these models are useful tools for building effective clustering models, i.e. they produce equivalences that help researchers make discretionary decisions (Doreian, 1988).

Regular Equivalence Methods

Algorithms that base partitioning on exact regular equivalence only work in very simple cases. So here again, we are using algorithms that provide approximations. The definition of regular equivalence, given earlier, can be illustrated in the following way:

$$a \equiv b$$
$$\downarrow \quad \downarrow$$
$$c \equiv d$$

If a and b are equivalent (i.e. in the same cluster), and if a has a link to c, then b must also have a link to some element in c's cluster, assuming that a, b and c are not necessarily distinct, to keep the definition general. The principle behind approximating algorithms stems directly from this definition.

If we consider elements a and b, we can assess equivalence by reviewing all other element pairs that might be placed in another equivalence cluster. So we calculate a similarity index for each distinct dyad of elements. The value for this index rises with the number of other dyads that match for regularity, given that these other dyads can be considered as equivalent. REGE (Reitz and White, 1989) is one of several such algorithms that operate by iteration.

Table 4.11   Economic sector data

		(1)	(2)	(3)	(4)	(5)	(6)	(7)	(8)	(9)	(10)	(11)
Agri.	(1)	0	0	0	0	0	0	0	1	0	0	0
Oil	(2)	1	0	1	0	0	0	0	0	0	0	1
Chem.	(3)	1	1	0	0	0	0	1	0	1	0	0
Steel	(4)	0	0	0	0	1	1	0	1	0	0	0
Mach.	(5)	1	0	0	1	0	1	1	1	0	0	0
Cars	(6)	0	0	0	0	0	0	0	0	0	0	1
Tex.	(7)	0	0	0	0	0	1	0	1	0	0	0
Wood	(8)	0	0	0	0	0	0	0	0	0	0	0
Paper	(9)	0	0	0	0	0	0	0	0	0	1	0
Publ.	(10)	0	0	0	0	0	0	0	0	0	0	0
Trans.	(11)	0	0	1	0	0	0	0	0	0	1	0

We shall illustrate its use with an example drawn from the French economy. The French national statistical institute (INSEE) regularly issues tables giving a breakdown of sales and receipts showing how many francs went from sector i of the economy to sector j and how much i earned from j. This matrix can be processed to show how dependent one sector of the economy is on another as a supplier or a market.

Our example uses a simplified version of a 1992 table with 11 sectors (agriculture, oil, chemicals, steel and metalworking, machinery, cars, textiles, wood, paper, publishing, and transport). On the basis of totals in intersecting cells, the data were first adjusted to offset distortion due to the differing sizes of each sector. We then retained all values above a certain threshold to obtain Table 4.11.

The various algorithms in our software gave very comparable results.[2] The algorithms all agree on clusters (1, 7, 9 and 11), (4 and 5) and (8 and 10). The positions for 2 and 6 vary. Here is one example:

cluster I   1, 7, 9, 11
cluster II   8, 10
cluster III   2, 3, 6
cluster IV   4, 5

The operation turns up certain regular blocks and empty blocks (Table 4.12), but the regularity is only approximate. The diagram of intercluster relations in Figure 4.6 therefore valid from a simple homomorphic – but not regular – standpoint. The position of the wood industry is explained by the fact that INSEE classifies tree farming under agriculture but includes industries such as furniture-making in the wood sector.

Vulnerability-Based Equivalence

Several approaches have been developed to avoid approximations. RESO is one algorithm that will yield exact breakdowns of directed and undirected graphs (Dalud-Vincent et al., 1994).

Table 4.12   Economic sector clustering

		(1)	(7)	(9)	(11)	(8)	(10)	(2)	(3)	(6)	(5)	(4)
Agri.	(1)					1						
Tex.	(2)					1				1		
Paper	(9)						1					
Trans.	(11)						1	1				
Wood	(8)											
Publ.	(10)											
Oil	(2)	1			1							
Chem.	(3)	1	1	1								
Cars	(6)				1							
Mach.	(5)	1	1			1				1		1
Steel	(4)					1				1	1	

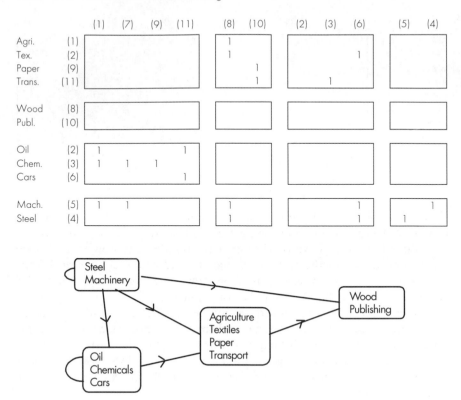

Figure 4.6   Economic sector intercluster relations

This approach is based on a vulnerable node (weak point) that is dependent on a cutpoint (see Chapter 3) because it would become isolated if the cutpoint were removed. Cutpoints that engender vulnerable points are called 1-cutpoints. The algorithm starts by breaking down the graph into its various components (weak connectivity in an undirected graph, strong connectivity in a directed one). It then discards any isolated nodes it identifies. The algorithm then performs the following on each component:

1 Identify cutpoints.
2 Identify 1-cutpoints among all cut nodes and deduce vulnerable nodes.
3 Classify vulnerable nodes in cluster I and eliminate from the graph.
4 Classify any new vulnerable nodes generated by the preceding elimination into cluster II and eliminate from the graph.
5 Iterate classification and elimination until no vulnerable nodes remain.
6 Place any cutpoints found in any of these sieving operations into the next cluster.
7 Return to the first step until sieving comes to a standstill.

In summary, the algorithm situates all the components on a graph and proceeds to identify succeeding levels of vulnerable nodes as it works its way to the core of a component. Each set of vulnerable nodes is put into a special equivalence cluster which means these nodes have the same articulation role in the network. We shall not give a formal definition of this equivalence here. It suffices to know that a relation of equivalence must exist in so far as the algorithm has generated a unique partition. No distinction is needed between relational equivalence and equivalence in terms of the algorithm.

The underlying methodological approach of this algorithm differs from that of others described so far. The definitions of structural or regular equivalence do not guarantee unique equivalence (unless it is maximal). The definitions only say *a posteriori* whether or not the equivalence of a given partition is structural or regular. This approach works the other way. Here we are *constructing an equivalence* – a single equivalence for a given graph. No approximation is made and the specificity of discrete data is preserved because there is no conversion into continuous data. Notably, no metric system, necessarily arbitrary with discrete data, is used.

Individuals in a component are clustered as a function of comparable vulnerability. They are exposed to the same risk of becoming isolated if one or more individuals drop out of the relation under study. The core(s) is (are) less vulnerable because no core member risks isolation if someone drops out. Individuals in each circle around the core are increasingly vulnerable as their distance from the core rises. Figure 4.7 illustrates this form of partitioning a graph component.

Applied to the Nolay sociability survey presented in Chapter 1, this algorithm shows that core individuals were those that had lived there

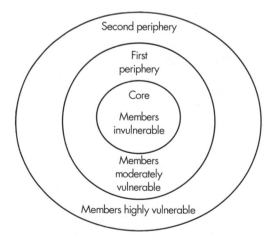

Figure 4.7   Core-periphery partitioning

longest (20+ years). This is the only variable that always correlates significantly to identify cores among the graph components. Age is only weakly
relevant. A senior citizen who had recently moved in stood a low chance of
belonging to the core while a teenager who had lived nowhere else stood a
very high chance. This fact is all the more remarkable because it works for
every social group in the town (i.e. every graph component picked up by
the algorithm). In other words, all groups or social circles showed the same
local integration mechanism. It is as if a new arrival starts by making a few
contacts, establishes more links as he stays on and continues making
progress towards the core which he reaches after living in Nolay long
enough.

As a second example, we processed the Sampson matrix used earlier to
illustrate CONCOR (Figure 4.8). For simplicity's sake, we have rounded
down to 1 all values >1 because RESO disregards edge values. The algorithm detects two singletons (intermediaries 10 and 13) and three strongly
connected components. The first component clusters all young Turks, where
7 is a cutpoint and 16 is a weak point. After elimination, RESO identifies 15,
14, 1 and 2 as further weak points and leaves 12 as the core. Loyal oppo-
sitionists are all clustered in the second strongly connected component.
Here, 5 is a weak point and 11 is a cutpoint. After their removal, 4 and 8
appear to be weak points and this leaves 6 and 9 as the core. The last
component clusters the excluded 3, 17, 18 and resists further breakdown.
These RESO results are entirely compatible with Sampson's own interpretation of the data.

Dual Roles and Attributes

This presentation of the various accepted definitions of equivalence exposes
major differences. Each reflects a particular standpoint and it is up to the
researcher to select which best suits the problem at hand. Each algorithm is
based on hypotheses of its own. Researchers should always bear these
differences in mind before attempting to compare results.

Moreover, individual roles or positions often carry attributes. A physician
or professor is a role backed by appropriate schooling. Some positions are
visibly labelled, e.g. servicemen wear uniforms and rank insignia. Other
attributes are more subtle or equivocal but still allow the observer to form an
opinion about position on a social ladder. So it is reasonable to question
the value of extensive social investigations into relations among individuals when simple observation of attributes might well achieve the same
results. Obviously, if attributes gave exact readings of role or position,
simple observation ought to yield as much as a full-blown study. If we are
researching structural equivalence that corresponds to one or more highly
codified rules, we will probably be able to reconstitute clusters quite easily.
But the problem becomes far dicier when looking for regular equivalence
that corresponds to interchangeable attributes. Experience shows slippage is

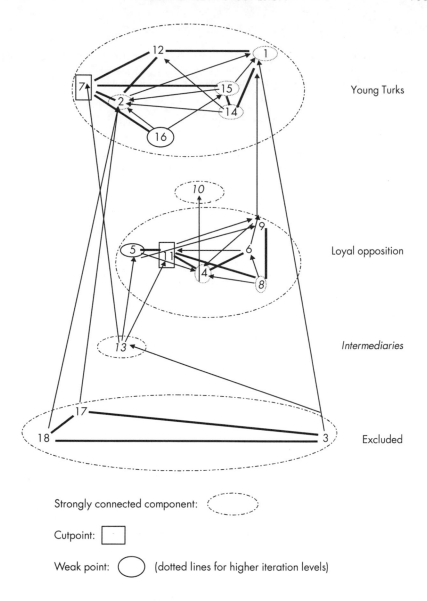

Figure 4.8   Connection and vulnerability among Sampson's novices using the RESO algorithm

very easy, and the urge to simplify research procedures often leads to unthinking adoption of a few basic indicators such as age, sex and profession without wondering about their relevance to the problem. Effective role reconstitution and the search for relevant concepts is a reaction against such slippage. For this reason, the sometimes highly technical work being done on the concept of equivalence remains very important.

Notes

1   Standard practice for a relational matrix where the diagonal is 1 is to compare a given row i and its marginal n_i with row j and marginal n_j.
2   See Patrick Doreian (1988) for a comparison of various algorithms on several examples.

5 SOCIAL CAPITAL

We have just seen how to distinguish groups and clusters in a complete network and how to study their relations. Chapters 5 and 6 will focus on the actors to understand the effects of the positions they occupy. The job market is one way of tackling the concept of social capital. This concept eloquently implies that an individual's relations are both asset and liability.

Job Market

Human Capital and Networks

The job market is a recent subject of social research. Only in the mid nineteenth century did the idea prevail that a person had a right to a job as a means of ensuring an independent living and therefore governments were late to conceive of full employment as a desirable goal (Salais et al., 1986). But once we start thinking about full employment and its corollary, unemployment, we need to theorize about how jobs are found, kept and lost. The first sociologists to apply social network analysis to the job market came up against other models developed by economists. As Salais (1990) points out, 'the economic theory of employment and unemployment is far from coherent. It is a hodgepodge of theoretical strata, young and old, but still going strong.'

The theory of human capital has made a key contribution here. It says work is just another tradable market commodity. From the employer's standpoint, employees have different amounts of human capital, i.e. different levels of investment in education and training that promise higher or lower productivity. Employers pay for marginal productivity and individuals travel the job market to maximize return on self-investment. This model explains the development of pay scales. The theory has been sophisticated by including the cost of mobility to the employee, but the basic principles subsist unchanged.

But an essential hypothesis is proper information flow. The job market only works properly if employers know what labour is available and job-seekers know about vacancies and salaries. It is therefore interesting to see how employers and job-seekers set about acquiring information.

Some researchers consider that the cost of information gathering to a company should be included in the model. Obtaining reliable information on which skills are available should be a prime concern in a company that is hiring. This explains why basic data such as age, education and grades are good indicators of human capital, all easy for employers to obtain. It may also explain why some employers attach so much importance to education that they will pay handsome salaries to executives who are overqualified and hold skills which do not necessarily square well with the job.

There is a wealth of studies on how job-seekers gather information. The studies suggest that the job market is more complex than the model allows, especially at the level of interpersonal relations which play a key role. As with human capital, social capital should not be underestimated. The study with the strongest impact on theoretical thinking to date was by Granovetter (1973). It was carried out in the Boston suburb of Newton (population 98,000). He focused on people who had changed jobs between two censuses. He sent out 266 questionnaires and held interviews with the most interesting respondents. He wanted to know how they had found their jobs. He considered three possibilities: personal contacts, formal application and direct approach.

Granovetter's definitions are worth a closer look because the nature of a relation can be hard to pin down. He defines personal relations restrictively. A personal contact is someone the subject knows and meets for reasons other than job-hunting and who acts a middleman either by informing her of a vacancy or by personally recommending her to the employer. Formal job application is mostly through classified advertisements and public or private employment agencies. Direct approach covers spontaneous mailings or door-to-door footwork by the job-seeker himself *a priori* and with no middlemen.

Some 56% of subjects found jobs through personal contacts. The other two techniques each succeeded for 19% of respondents. For those using personal contacts, 31% reported they found their job through family members and 69% through professional contacts. Granovetter notes that those most successful found their job through a professional contact, not friends or family, i.e. weak ties and short relational chains work better than strong ties.

Interviews showed that family contacts furnish tips on vacancies similar to the jobs they hold themselves far more often than introductions to persons empowered to hire. Granovetter suggests that when a job-seeker mobilizes a strong tie, that person feels obliged to come up with something, even if it is less than optimal for the job-seeker. It also explains why the best job openings are not filled in this way. However, friends and family are more likely to lead to more radical job changes than professional contacts. As a rule, most families have little contact with respondents' job worlds. Strong tie users are also younger than their weak tie counterparts. Granovetter then assessed the efficiency of contact frequency and reported that the ties that generated the most contacts and tended to be the strongest were also the least efficacious (Table 5.1).[1]

This leads to the problem of relational chain lengths. Granovetter finds short chains work best. A direct or indirect referral opens the door to

Table 5.1   Contact frequency in Granovetter's survey

Contact frequency	%
Often (at least twice a week)	16.7
Occasionally (more than once a year)	55.6
Rarely (once a year at most)	27.7

contact someone directly. There is a temptation to equate weak ties with long chains. For any chain of length L, in which each person can mobilize N contacts, you can theoretically hope to contact

$$1 + N + N^2 + \ldots + N^{(L+1)} = (N^{(L+2)}-1)/(N-1)$$

And contact numbers rise rapidly. For example, if $N = 5$, we obtain 31 contacts where $L = 1$; 156 where $L = 2$; and 781 where $L = 3$.

Long chains are not the most widely used in job-hunting. Most often, only one or two intermediaries are involved. However, the longer the chain, the closer we come to formal application and this spills over into the field of job market theory.

Strong and Weak Ties

Granovetter's results (1974) suggest differing levels of efficacy between strong and weak ties. Weak ties help find jobs that respondents find more satisfying than jobs through strong ties. He was the first to really formulate a theory along these lines. In his pioneering article 'The strength of weak ties' (1973; 1982), he classifies strength as a function of the following four criteria:

1   duration (includes time spent together as well as time elapsed since first encounter)
2   emotional intensity
3   intimacy
4   exchange of services (backscratching).

We might add multiplexity as the fifth criterion to understand the plurality of link interactions.

We can now apply this definition to consider three persons, A, B and C. We shall assume A has strong discrete links to B and C. If this is so, there is a good chance B and C have met, because both B and C spend a lot of time with A. This raises the probability of chance trilateral encounters in the company of A. And once in the company of a common friend, they will tend to establish a link. Moreover, any two people sharing a strong link tend to resemble each other and share a number of common tastes and interests. So if B and C resemble A, they will tend to resemble each other too and share certain traits, which in turn will promote the establishment of strong links between them. Psychological arguments also apply. If B has a strong link to A and no strong link to C but C has a strong link to A, this generates a dissonance that will lead B and C to make the system coherent by establishing closer relations. This all leads to the idea that strong links tend to be transitive.[2] Inversely, if A has a strong link to B but a weak one to C, B and C stand a poor chance of meeting. If they do meet, they stand a poor chance of discovering common traits and will have no special reason to establish closer relations. The link between B and C has a strong chance of being weak or non-existent.[3]

Transition to the global level is effected through the notion of a bridge. An edge is a bridge between two parts in a graph when it is the only link that spans the two parts, i.e. every node in one part can only reach a node in another part via that link. Edge 9–7 is a bridge in the following graph:

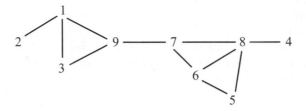

In a graph of real-life relations between people, bridges are rare. However, some links amount to bridges for all practical purposes in that a chain becomes much longer, and more likely to fail, if we do not go through a particular person for, say, an address or piece of information. Beyond a certain length, chains may even become ineffective for establishing contact. An efficiency principle is at work that turns a 'local bridge' into a *de facto* bridge. An edge can be considered as a local bridge if it is the shortest path between two parts of a graph, i.e. where all other chain lengths are >2. In the next graph, 9–7 is a local bridge between (1, 3) and (5, 6).

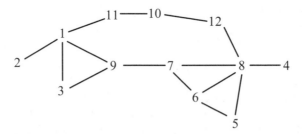

But Granovetter says a strong tie is never a local bridge. If we imagine that edge A–B is a strong link and we apply the transitivity principle strictly, any individual C with a strong link to A must have a strong link to B, so A–B is not a bridge because path A–C–B is available. For the strong link A–B to become a bridge, neither A nor B should have any other strong links in the relations, which is most unlikely.

Because strong links tend to be transitive, they tend to create closed self-sealing groups. Information that circulates through strong links will rapidly reach all members of a closed group. Weak links, i.e. bridges, serve to connect groups and move information among them. This is why weak links play a major role in circulating information from one self-sealing group with strong links to another.

The result is that weak ties must outperform strong ties to find a job, flat or personal introduction because they open windows to the outside world and access to people and information at large.

On this point, Nan Lin (1982) took up the Milgram approach (see Chapter 1) to test the weak tie hypotheses. He recruited a random sample of households in the Albany–Schenectady–Troy metropolitan area of New York state for his study. He notes that high-status households were over-represented in the sample ($n = 300$) and ethnic minorities were underrepresented. Each respondent was given two parcels to deliver to an addressee. Addressees were of four types: black female, black male, white female and white male. All lived in Schenectady itself. Addressees were balanced for variables such as age, length of local residence, marital status, church attendance and membership in civic organizations. Addressees were strangers and respondents needed intermediaries to accomplish delivery. About 30% of the parcels finally got through. The race barrier proved difficult to overcome. Whites did not know how to approach blacks for the task at hand. Delivery percentage was higher for parcels entrusted to males and addressed to females. Social status also comes into play: parcels from high-status senders to lower-status addressees tended to get through. But above all, Nan Lin's special attention to intermediaries enabled him to report that weak ties proved far more efficacious and significant than strong. His experiment confirms Granovetter's hypotheses.

Other job-hunting studies exist. All give converging results. They have added valuable detail to the role of intermediaries. Remarkably, we articulate theoretical propositions about types of relations and confirm them with equal ease whether the goal is to find a job or deliver a parcel. The hypotheses can be summed up as follows:

1 Your chances of obtaining a positive result increase with your ability to contact high-status persons.
2 Between two people of comparable social status seeking a positive result, the one who exploits weak ties stands a better chance of success than the one using strong ties.
3 The type of link a high-status person uses has no impact on the result, i.e. strong and weak ties can work equally well. However, low-status persons will probably obtain better results through weak ties.

That said, the first hypothesis has influenced numerous studies, but itself raises a theoretical and empirical problem that drove Granovetter to question it at one point. We shall begin by reviewing the empirical issues.

Job-Hunting

Granovetter had tested his model on white-collar workers near Boston at a time of low unemployment. Confirmation of the superior global efficacy of weak links came from studies under similar job market conditions. Two studies in the wake of Granovetter's confirmed this efficacy when it came to job information access and to jobs themselves, but they stress status differences in the relations that individuals can mobilize and their impact on the job-seeking process.

Simon Langlois (1977) shows the importance of age. Of the 1,589 persons in his sample who were already working when they joined the Quebec civil service, 35% of those aged 16–20 found their job through personal relations, a figure that climbs to 54% in the 36+ age group.[4] The network of professional contacts that develops over the years becomes increasingly mobilized as individuals become older. However, differences in job levels must be taken into account too. Executives and office workers show job-seeking behaviour patterns that tally fairly well with Granovetter's theory: 35.5% find jobs through weak ties, 15.8% through strong ties and 48.7% through so-called intermediary ties. However, the figures lean the other way for engineers, lawyers, physicians and psychologists in government employment: 30.8% use weak ties and 51% use strong. This leads one to wonder why strong links are more popular in certain occupational categories.

The results from a study on engineers by FASFID, the French engineering industry association, argue similarly (Degenne et al., 1991).[5] The proportion of engineers who reported their current employers sought them out rises with age. The figure is 15% for engineers under age 29 and 28% at age 50+. Young or old, this highly qualified population is immune to unemployment. The efficacy of their weak links increases with age. Their elite diplomas confer considerable job mobility if they so choose. They actively cultivate wide personal networks where they can advertise their availability and enjoy high profiles in their current positions.

Family plays a far bigger role in low-skill populations, especially when jobs are scarce. Here, 21% of first-time job-seekers find work through family, and 72% of the 21% report that the person they know who provided their first job is none other than their mother or father. An earlier French study (Marry, 1983) reports three forms of nepotism as follows:

1 direct entry to the family-owned firm
2 employment in a firm which employs a family member on the strength of the latter's recommendation
3 employment in a firm as a result of a family member's personal influence on the hirer.

Of first-time job-seekers who found work through nepotism, 74% report their father is working; only 1% list him as unemployed. Inversely, about half of first-time job-seekers who turn to the state employment bureau list fathers as unemployed. Therefore, strong links are particularly important to unskilled job-seekers and the loss of such links means the loss of virtually all chances of finding work through personal contacts.

Universities deliver more than diplomas, which are increasingly more important and less sufficient. They deliver personal networks that weaken over the years but remain relevant and easy to activate. Some alumni associations are very mindful about keeping up these networks. Any dropouts obviously forfeit most of these network benefits, whose value rises with the diploma's level and prestige, especially if they left owing to poor academic performance.

Although Langlois surveyed a privileged white-collar population, he too concludes that 'Efficacious circulation of job tips through weak ties in personal networks seems mostly typical of senior executives and civil servants, while strong ties continue to play a bigger role in other job categories.' Moreover, Granovetter (1982) notes that weak ties only assume tangible value if they furnish tips that job-seekers can actually exploit. From this standpoint, underqualified job-seekers are in no position to exploit the resources of any weak links they may well have.

Another factor not to be ignored is culturally specific organizational context. Rosenbaum et al. (1990) noted that the transition from the schoolroom to the workplace is set up very differently in Germany, Japan and the USA. In Japan, there are regular get-togethers with potential employers. Germany splits vocational training between the classroom and the shopfloor, giving the employers' network a first-hand knowledge of apprentices and vocational training levels.

So the strong-tie/weak-tie formula does not apply indiscriminately to any population. Actors base job-seeking strategy on who and what they can mobilize. Some will use weak ties but others will find strong ties the only real option (Forsé, 1997).

Market Segmentation

The results just outlined suggest the job market is a social reality that differentiates how it treats individuals. It also replicates inequalities, because privileged people will defend their privileges. So the job market is segmented and this is incompatible with Granovetter's theory at first glance.

The first segment, or primary market, consists of secure jobs. Job security is precious to an employer because the most efficacious skills are acquired on the job. It is also precious to the employee, not only because it earns recognition in the form of pay hikes but also because the system engenders a real lifestyle: 'Beyond the relation to the company, it's a relation to society and an economy, especially through consumer patterns that encourage planned purchases of durable goods . . . and more generally, into a lifestyle of stability' (Silvestre, 1990; Piore, 1975).

The secondary job market is everyone not in the primary market. It is the world of precarious employment. Companies play on both to cope with fluctuating demand. They lock in rare skills that ensure institutional continuity, and offload excess skills onto the secondary market until needed at some later date. To get the most out of key employees, companies trim non-core activities to a minimum. So very different forms of employment are becoming institutionalized, e.g. office temporaries and subcontracting.

In recent years, some researchers have noticed a split in the primary market between an upper crust of highly skilled executives with full control over their careers and mobility, and the rest whose security lies in a personal commitment to the company. Mobility is managed differently in each of these three markets:

> Mobility is a trajectory from one position to the next in the primary market as well as a social bond and a learning experience, i.e. the construction of total belonging. In other markets, mobility and the learning experience are inseparable but, if we count education received outside the company as mobility, it still amounts to dominated construction of belonging in the secondary market and of autonomous belonging in the upper primary market. (Silvestre, 1990)

The upper primary, lower primary and secondary job markets also have different internal mechanisms when it comes to choosing between weak ties and strong. Office workers and young engineers in the primary market exploit weak ties better. Manual labourers have no skills and few contacts while skilled labourers enjoy status in a peer group, so both will exploit strong ties better. Peer status also explains why physicians, lawyers and elite graduates work through relatively exclusive professional associations that cultivate strong ties. Lastly, personal reputation plays a key role in the upper primary market.

But Granovetter's model assumes an unstructured and *unsegmented* professional environment. Furthermore it only looks at the employee's behaviour, not the employer's.

Economic Action and Social Networks

The concept of segmentation and the empirical results urge us to recommend reading Granovetter back to front so that his concept about the strength of weak ties is read in the light of his later article on economic action and social structure (Granovetter, 1985). This article criticizes both neoliberal market theory for underrating social relations and market segmentation theory for overrating social relations. Granovetter says the fundamental issue then becomes how to reinsert economic actors in their social environment such that the principles of rational economic behaviour assume a relevant form.

Landing a job is a matter of negotiation between employer and candidate. The employer wants minimum uncertainty about the candidate's behaviour to maximize productivity. The candidate wants the best possible salary and working conditions as well as opportunities to increase her human capital.

Everyone can use relations to job-hunt. Given that weak ties constitute bridges between closed circles, let us take the example of an unskilled first-time job-seeker. He stands a poor chance of contacting someone outside his immediate circle with enough status to land him a job. Should he nonetheless chance upon such a contact, that person would have no special reason to lobby vigorously on his behalf. So the person would not minimize uncertainty in the potential employer. Information through such weak ties is not exploitable. However, if a company and a school have an apprenticeship agreement that has been working for several years, a degree of confidence may well arise. Uncertainty is lower. Any apprentice with a school recommendation stands a good chance of being hired.

Now let us imagine we are running a study and interviewing a youth who found work through family. We need more than just data on this strong tie. We need to elicit and record the social circumstances of the interaction, and we need a history of the relation between the employer and the referrer. This is social capital because it is the product of an accumulation of negotiations based on mutual confidence that simplify, or obviate the need for, further negotiations. Likewise, France has a body of elite engineers, of whom some are heirs to a long line of engineers and corporate presidents while others are genealogical newcomers to engineering. The family of the latter cannot play as strong a job-hunting role.

In the end, the indication of status carried in a link counts for more than whether it is strong or weak. If a job is truly a vocation that requires experience and adaptability, an employer has every interest in hiring a candidate recommended by current employees. Indeed they have no interest in recommending an underperformer who would tarnish their own positions and reputations. Likewise, the new employee will feel bound to live up to the confidence of people she knows. She will avoid disappointing them. However, if the job function requires abstract criteria such a college degree and the candidate is easily replaceable, the employer stands to gain by hiring on the abstract criteria. It saves investing in a personal relation. The candidate responds mostly by stressing the value of his credentials. In this case, weak tie logic works best. Nonetheless, weak and strong ties are both capital. They generally fall under the heading of social capital. Given the efficacy of capital theory at explaining job-hunting in cases such as the above, we can now examine how different researchers define it.

Social Capital

The idea goes back to Hobbes (1651) who says in *Leviathan*, 'to have friends is power'. Here he establishes a distinction between an individual's social and political resources and implies that a person's living standard depends on the resources at her disposal. Weber uses this last idea in his analysis of social inequalities. He asserts individuals can improve living standards with three types of resources: economic, political and symbolic. Economic resources govern her chances of access to wealth and assets. Materially, this obviously refers to income and an estate, which are unequally distributed in society. Symbolic resources govern access to social distinctions, i.e. prestige. A job carries a salary but it also carries some degree of social prestige. Political resources govern access to power. Income, prestige and power determine social status, i.e. position on a social ladder. There are scales to rate all three resources but congruence is not automatic. The most powerful people may not be the wealthiest and some low-prestige jobs generate enviable incomes. That said, patchy congruence does not mean the three variables are independent.

In neo-Weberist terms, each of these resources represents some form of capital. And capital is no metaphor here. These are resources people can *invest* and *spend*. Individuals can also barter economic, political and symbolic resources, even if only economic resources have strict cash equivalence. Individuals can also invest in one resource to increase their assets in the other two. Although Weber did not say so, social capital obeys the same rule.

Ever distinct from other forms, social capital consists of an individual's personal network and her chances of accessing whatever is circulating there, e.g. information. It may also increase the yield of other forms of capital. For example, we have already seen that one form of human capital, a college degree, is a prerequisite to some jobs but no guarantee in itself. Landing the job also requires relations who provide job tips and even personal recommendations. As Pierre Bourdieu (1980) suggests, social capital can substantially enhance human and educational capital in this case. In other words, the best jobs sooner go to those who best exploit their social capital, assuming all candidates are equally qualified. Of course a personal network is a distinct type of resource. The social capital of a personal network, which depends on its content and structure, differs from human capital, which is a strictly personal resource consisting of assets such as education and qualifications.

In usage, the concept of social capital also assumes the social action is directed at a goal that requires cooperation or competition from other actors. From this standpoint, social capital involves expectations and reciprocal obligations between individuals. If A does B a favour in a relation of mutual trust, A can reasonably consider B owes him a favour in return. B will eventually have to pay it back. A's social capital is the sum of all favours that every B in his network owes him. This argument assumes that individuals act not only on the basis of past relations or the efficacy of the present action, but also as if future returns on capital were already operating in the present situation. However, this is not to say that all individuals are actually capable of detailed calculations of the return on investment of their sociability. It is rather only a model that can be summarized in the following way: if we assume that a relation of communication or barter is an investment, the set of all such relations is a capital base and not just a 'treasure chest'. The next question is how to appraise it.

An individual's social capital is more than just the number of people he knows. Returning to Hobbes, personal power is plainly more a matter of having powerful friends than numerous friends. Nor can social capital be restricted to direct relations only. In job-hunting, the value of a friend is not only the information she holds, but the information she can access through her network too. If weak ties are indeed as precious as we claim, it is because they are far more efficacious than strong ties at tapping into new networks. Numerous studies (including De Graaf and Flap, 1988) into the relationship between personal networks and actual hirings agree that there is no correlation between network size and the chances of finding a job. This result has general validity for other domains.

Therefore, the concept of social capital does not boil down to the volume of contacts because not all contacts have the same *value*. This value depends on the structural characteristics of the relations. To illustrate the point, James Coleman (1990) cites the difference between open and closed structures but the concept is nicely summed up in Burt's structural hole theory. This theory offers a tool to measure the efficacy of an individual's social capital.

Structural Holes

The theory of structural holes ties together known results scattered in the literature. Let us take the example of an actor who needs certain information to achieve a goal and finds that some members of his network have it. Time is the least he will have to invest in his relations. The information may not be free but, at equal cost, the network can produce significantly different results. We shall consider two networks, one of low density and the other very high.

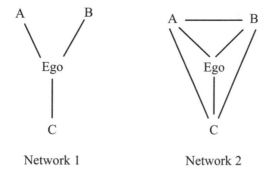

Network 1   Network 2

In the first network, A, B and C have no relations. In the second, all ego contacts are linked. Here, however, the ego's relations to B and C are redundant because her link to A enables linkup via path ego–A–B or ego–A–C. Thus this network has only one non-redundant contact. But the first network shows no redundant ego relations because the ego cannot use her relation to one partner to contact the others. The ego's position is clearly stronger in the first network. She alone determines the content and timing of information to everyone else, a power she forfeits in the second network as soon as she informs a single contact. The second network relays a diversified mix of information less efficaciously. Increasing the number of *redundant* contacts does not improve efficacy; increasing non-redundant contacts will. In short, the ego's social capital is inversely proportional to the redundancy in her network.

Burt (1992a) formalizes this important property when he explains structural holes: 'I use the term structural hole for the separation between non-redundant contacts. Non-redundant contacts are therefore connected by structural holes.' In other words, 'A structural hole is a relationship of non-redundancy between two contacts.' The first network shown above has three holes and the second has none. Structural holes carry other advantages for those who enjoy them.

Unlike what we might expect from the simple examples just cited, structural holes are not just a problem of density. Empirically, two criteria govern the creation of a structural hole: cohesion and equivalence. Cohesion says redundancy arises when two of the ego's relations share a direct link. The greater the cohesion (or density), the fewer structural holes. For example, cliques have zero structural holes. Nothing prevents information flow and only speed will vary as a function of the frequency of contacts.

The equivalence criterion takes into account indirect relations between the ego and the people in her network. As a reminder, two individuals are structurally equivalent if they share the same relations to the same people. They may not be in mutual contact but their relations are still identical because they can access the same information sources. Thus they are redundant from the ego's standpoint. In the following example of a network, A, B and C are structurally equivalent. They have no links to each other, but two of them are redundant contacts for the ego. Given the ego–A link, the ego does not need his links to B or C to reach α, β or γ. The ego can still reach B and C without direct links to them if she doesn't mind indirect links.

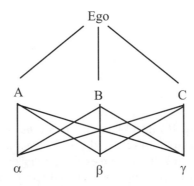

An absence of links does not guarantee zero redundancy or the existence of a structural hole. In short, there is a structural hole between two of the ego's contacts either because they do not share a direct or indirect link or because they are not structurally equivalent. Schematically, redundant links are not basic arcs according to the definition in Chapter 3.

Burt goes too far when he asserts, without saying why, that the efficacy of a network (e.g. the yield of any information sought) shows linear dependence on the number of structural holes, because this assertion contradicts what has been demonstrated in the basics of the mathematical theory of communication. Communication channels have static and therefore entropy unavoidably accumulates with transmission, eroding information quality. The best way of preventing this is to introduce redundant message transmissions, reckoning that static will distort message elements in a random pattern. Multiple dispatching of the same message should enable receivers to reconstitute the original message. Spoken language applies this principle. Weaver finds 50% redundancy in the English language. In French, three phonetic markers distinguish the plural *les animaux* from the singular *l'animal*: the 'e'-sound in the article, the 'z'-sound at the start of the noun and the final 'o' sound. Two are redundant. Redundancy is not futile; it guarantees efficacious communication. It also operates in communications networks where it confers the same guarantee. It is necessary up to a point. Only beyond that point, which unfortunately cannot be measured *a priori*, does it become superfluous. We hold that efficacy is about striking the right balance between redundant and non-redundant relations, not maximizing structural holes.

As stated, the value of structural hole theory is that it provides a global framework and coherent vocabulary that ties in various approaches scattered in the literature. For example, structural hole theory accounts for both the *tertius gaudens* and the strength of weak ties. We shall give the standard account of the *tertius gaudens* link in triads before reassessing it in terms of structural holes.

Coalitions and Triads

A triad is a social system of durable links among three elements, persons or groups. Georg Simmel was the first to spot its importance. Studying socialization, he perceived social structures as a balance between positive and negative forces, and more particularly between conflict and cooperation. He also says conflict is a mechanism of integration. A common enemy bonds individuals and helps define a group. Conflict is thus an especially important form of interaction. Conflict generates frontiers between groups and each frontier is a potential flashpoint. Analysing conflict mechanisms, Simmel (1950) discovered the fundamental, somewhat archetypal, role of trilateral interplay: 'The dyad, therefore, does not attain that super-personal life which the individual feels to be independent of himself. As soon, however, as there is sociation of three, a group continues to exist even when one of the members drops out.' In conclusion, Simmel is saying sociology really begins with the study of triads.

A relation between two actors has no existence other than binary, but if a third joins in we can speak of a network whose systemic traits are more than the sum of each actor's individual attributes. Simmel had the vision to realize that the difference between dyad and triad is much sharper and more fundamental than that between triad and tetrad or n-ad, and that any set of n actors can always be reduced to a network of k triads (even if he does not raise the issue of shared and unshared nodes). Thus, the triad is the basic unit of social interaction.

Simmel says most triads subdivide into a pair and a third party. To show this, he introduces a distinction between direct and indirect links in a network:

> When three elements, A, B and C, constitute a community, there is added to the immediate relationship which exists, for example, between A and B, the immediate relationship which they gain by their common relation to C. This is unquestionably a sociological enrichment, apart from the bond by the straight and shortest line; each pair of elements is now joined by a broken link. Points upon which the pair could find no immediate contact were put in reciprocal relationship by the third element, which offers to each another side, and joins these, nevertheless, in the unity of its personality. Separations which the parties could not of themselves reconcile are accommodated by the third, or by their being included in a comprehensive whole. On the other hand, the direct union is not merely strengthened by the indirect, but may also be destroyed. There is no relationship so complete between three that each individual may not, under certain circumstances, be regarded by the other two as an intruder. (Simmel, 1950, quoted in Caplow, 1968)

Triad dynamics sum up nicely in the role of the third party:

> From the conversation among three persons that lasts only an hour, to the permanent family of three, there is no triad in which dissent between any two elements does not occur from time to time – a dissent of a more harmless or more pointed, more momentary or more lasting, more theoretical or more practical nature – and in which the third member does not play a mediating role . . . This function makes the round among the three elements, since the ebb and flow of social life realizes the form of conflict in every possible combination for two members. (Simmel, 1950, quoted in Caplow, 1968)

The above observation leads Simmel to list the third element's three functions or strategies:

1 *Mediation*   The third element mediates conflicts and facilitates negotiations. This assumes both members perceive him as sufficiently impartial.
2 *Tertius gaudens*   Here the third element exploits the conflictual relation between two comparable power bases. If each base attempts to enlist her into alliance against the other, she can play both sides, raise the stakes and win out against both when they run out of ammunition.

3 *Despotism* This is the function of 'divide and conquer'. The third
   element instigates conflict between the other two so as to preclude any
   alliance against herself. The resulting split underpins her power base,
   but precariously so, because it vanishes as soon as the split heals.

Here Simmel addresses the key issue of coalitions and their genesis. Numerous social psychological studies have attempted to explain empirically
observed results. Theodore Caplow (1968) describes the coalitions that
developed around a pachisi table, a board game where players roll dice to
advance tokens. The first to reach the final square wins, but each player
starts off with a certain capital he can negotiate with opponents, and a rule
added by Vinacke and Arkoft makes negotiations indispensable. This rule
requires everybody to move with every roll of the dice instead of individual
rolls for each player. After numerous experiments, Gamson (1961) developed a theory of coalitions. He distinguishes between a minimal winning
coalition, which starts losing when one member drops out, and the cheapest
winning coalition, which is that winning coalition whose combined resources
are closest to critical mass for victory. He lays down the principle of 'equit-
able expectation' whereby 'Any participant will expect others to demand
from a coalition a share of the payoff proportional to the amount of
resources which they contribute to a coalition.' Gamson then reasons out the
strategic consequences for rational actors:

> When a player must choose among alternative coalition strategies where the total
> payoff to a winning coalition is constant, he will maximize his payoff by maxi-
> mizing his share. The theory states that he will do this by maximizing the ratio of
> his resources to the total resources of the coalition. Since his resources will be the
> same regardless of which coalition he joins, the lower the total resources, the
> greater will be his share. Thus, where the total payoff is held constant, he will
> favour the cheapest winning coalition.

This allows the prediction of minimum winning coalitions for a wide range
of triads. Caplow distinguishes eight that are illustrated in Figure 5.1, and
Gamson says six stand 'good' chances (Table 5.2).
   Caplow (1968) concludes:

> As we have seen in the pachisi experiments, the need to choose among alternative
> partners and to agree on the division of prizes often leads players to formulate
> rules about the choice of partners and the division of prizes from whatever
> materials come readiest to hand. The relative distribution of resources is always a
> convenient framework for the assignment of new tasks and the division of new
> prizes. Thus a status order, once established, tends to reinforce itself by
> reproducing previous inequalities in new transactions between the individual and
> the collectivity.

Pachisi reveals an essential feature of triads: the strength of weakness and
the weakness of strength. This underpins the strategy of *tertius gaudens*.
The weakest player exploits his weakness and wins by turning it to his own
advantage. When the trilateral balance tips one player into a weak position, it is often streetwiser to team up with the weaker partner than with
the stronger who may eventually crush you.

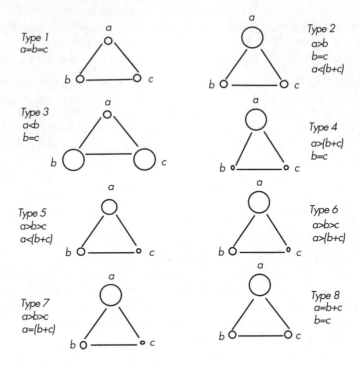

Figure 5.1   Winning coalitions in triads

Table 5.2   Gamson's predictable coalition tables for triads[1]

Type	Minimum winning coalitions
1	Nil effect
2	b - c
3	a - b or a - c
4	None
5	b - c
6	None

[1] Types 7 and 8 are not evaluable here because they fall outside the scope of Gamson's hypotheses.

Thus, triads often catalyse. The mere presence of a third element, how-ever passive, tends to modify the original dyadic relation. This is why a triad can never be reduced to the sum of three dyads. Structural analysis integrates this fundamental lesson when it states the principle that a dyad cannot be studied (except psychologically) without consideration for its position in an environment. A network structure is always more than a mere 'sum total' of dyadic relations. Networks sooner pertain to mech-anisms that combine interpersonal relations and intercircle relations.

According to Burt, *tertius gaudens* (TG) is third party to two or more actors in competition, in conflict or having no relations among themselves:

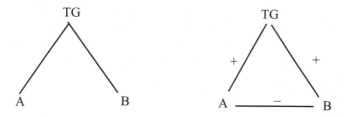

In either case, *tertius gaudens* derives a benefit from the tension between A- and B-type actors. He exploits his structural position to set himself up as some sort of middleman. However, this privileged position is founded on non-redundant relations (e.g. cohesion in the example above). If A and B establish a positive relation, the structural hole disappears and *tertius gaudens* loses control over the network and its commodities.

Weak Ties and Cutpoints

This argument is useful to reinterpret and better understand Granovetter's analysis of weak ties. Both empirically and statistically, the strength of a link boils down to the frequency of contacts it engenders: above-average frequency characterizes strong links and below-average frequency characterizes weak ones. If we accept that all links in a clique (i.e. dense network) are strong, it instantly follows that links between cliques, which are fewer by definition, will most probably be weak. The following examples depict an ego in one clique and her relations to two other cliques via cutpoints A and B.

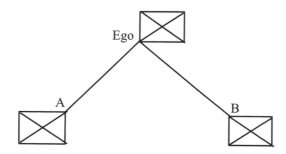

Relations within each clique are strong because we assume that maximum density implies close relations. So ego–A and ego–B links are weak. If intraclique contacts are of above-average frequency, it follows that other contacts fall below the average. Or so goes the 'statistical' argument, but Burt shows this situation is based on a structural hole. Here, ego–A and ego–B relations are non-redundant. With no structural holes, we would be faced with one big clique and find ourselves totally unable to determine link strengths, *a priori* or theoretically. Zero or weak redundancy is indeed the hallmark of clique relations. The upshot is that weak links are the most likely to indicate the presence of structural holes.

If weak links and structural holes do describe the same phenomenon, then why complicate Granovetter's relatively sound and well-established argument? As Burt writes, 'Tie weakness is a correlate, not a cause.' When studying information flow, the basic difference to the end result is whether or not the links are redundant. Weak ties draw their strength from structural holes that arise when one cutpoint becomes a bridge between two groups. The beneficiaries can then develop a strategy (ego, A and B in the above example). The *tertius gaudens* strategy becomes a real option when a pattern of structural holes promises some gain to be gleaned from competition between two disorganized contacts (*i*, *j* in the next graph).

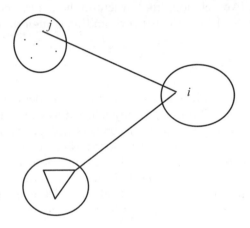

Measurements

The preceding graphs show simple examples and any application to real-life networks requires tools of measurement. We shall summarily review Burt's (1992a) measures.

Raw data come in the following three forms:

(a)   sociometric choices between individuals
(b)   common involvement in circles
(c)   intensity of relations between actors.

We shall now present the simple configuration of a binary square (but not necessarily symmetrical) sociometric choice matrix. To find the structural position for each actor as a function of both direct and indirect links to all members of a network, the O matrix is transformed into a Z matrix with the statistical approach to structural equivalence given in Chapter 3. At this point, Burt lists eight indicators to assess the structural position of all actors in a network.

Contacts

If i stands for the ego and N_i is the size of his network, we begin by adding up the ego's direct and indirect relations R_i (where $0 \leq R_i \leq N_i$).

Non-redundant contacts

Non-redundant contacts NR_i are characterized by their autonomy within the ego's network. Where $NR_i = 1$, all members enjoy strong links to each other. Where $NR_i = N_i$, network members share no links to one another. The number of links is given by

$$NR_i = \sum_j \left(1 - \sum_q p_{iq} m_{iq} \right), \quad q \neq i, j$$

Here, p_{iq} is the proportional investment in relations with q (interaction with q divided by the sum of i's relations),

$$p_{iq} = (z_{iq} + z_{qi}) / \sum_j z_{ij} + z_{ji}, \quad i \neq j$$

m_{iq} is the marginal strength of the relation to q (interaction with q divided by j's strongest relation),

$$m_{iq} = (z_{iq} + z_{qi}) / \max(z_{jk} + z_{kj}), \quad j \neq k$$

and z_{ij} is an element of matrix Z and $0 \leq m_{iq} \leq 1$.

Contact efficiency

Contact efficiency CE_i is the fraction of non-redundant contacts in the ego's total relations:

$$CE_i = NR_i / N_i.$$

Average marginal strength of relations between contacts

The simplest way of measuring the density of the ego's network is to add up all values z_{jq} for all dyads (j, q) in i's network ($\sum_j \sum_q z_{jq}$) and to divide the sum by the maximum number of possible contacts $N_i(N_i - 1)$. Alternatively, Burt proposes the following formula to measure the average marginal strength of contacts ND_i among members of the ego's network:

$$ND_i = \left(\sum_j \sum_q z_{jq} / \max(z_{jq}) \right) \Big/ (N_i(N_i - 1)), \quad j \neq q$$

If $ND_i = 0$, there are no contacts among members of the ego's network, but they are maximal where $ND_i = 1$.

Proportional density

If we only want weak connectivity, the following formula for proportional density PD_i applies:

$$PD_i = \left(\sum_j \sum_q \delta_{jq}\right) \Big/ (N_i(N_i - 1)), \quad j \neq q$$

where $\delta = 1$ if $z_{jq} \neq 0$ and 0 otherwise.

If $PD_i = 0$ there are no relations among ego contacts, but if $PD_i = 1$ all dyads interconnect. In a network where all dyads have weak connections, ND_i has a low value while PD_i is much higher.

Constraints of type 1 structural holes

The above calculations for constraint on each actor will also yield reciprocal values for autonomy. Autonomy depends on the distribution of structural holes around the ego in terms of (1) holes between contacts and (2) holes within groups of contacts. We shall differentiate them by speaking of type 1 and type 2 holes.

We shall consider that contact j constrains the opportunities of actor i when i is investing a major share of her contacts in the relation to j but i has few structural holes she can use to negotiate a favourable yield on her investment. 'Investment' is intended here in the sense of the proportion of contacts in i's network that connect to j. If this proportion is substantial, and despite the fact that i may no longer sustain her relation to j, some of her other links still connect her to j. Here we are putting i under heavy constraint. We obtain the opposite result if j is isolated from all her other contacts. If j is i's only contact, constraint is maximal. In summary, j constrains i if j has exclusive relations to individuals in i's network and there is no substitute for j. The value for the constraint (c_{ij}) is given by

$$c_{ij} = \left(p_{ij} + \sum_q p_{iq} p_{qj}\right)^2, \quad q \neq i, j$$

Any actor j connected to all of i's other contacts exerts heavy constraint on i because i has no structural holes. Any request from j will prove difficult to avoid or negotiate. Inversely, any j isolated from i's contacts only exerts mild constraint on i. Redundancy is all the greater in the i–j relation as the number of j's contacts in i's network increases.

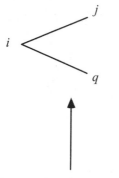

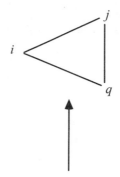

j constrains i but does not vector constraint from q

Even without a direct i–q link, i may still suffer constraint from q through path q–j–i

The sum of c_{ij} constraints for j yields total constraint C_i on i as follows:

$$C_i = \sum_j c_{ij}$$

If $C_i = 0$ the ego has numerous disconnected, readily replaceable relations, but if $C_i = 1$ the ego has only one contact. The average constraint on i is (C_i/N_i) and therefore the relationship $(c_{ij}/(C_i/N_i))$ measures the proportion of j's constraint on i with respect to average constraint on i. This relative constraint is 1 when j's constraint equals average constraint on i.

Constraints of type 2 structural holes (oligopoly)

If at the outset we have a grouping of actors that classifies each in a group according to a predetermined criterion, we can find an oligopolistic value O_j for each group that varies inversely with the number of structural holes inside the group. This positions us to examine a second type of structural hole.

In this type, the greater the number of structural holes in j's group, the lesser the constraint j exerts on i. In terms of cohesion criteria, $O_j = 1$ in any clique and becomes minimal for any individual with no relations ($O_j = 1/nj$). In this last case, constraint from any actor can be avoided by playing off actors against one another. We have taken account of type 1 structural holes in ego relations and defined c_{ij}. We now need only multiply that value by O_j to obtain a more global value of j's constraint on i: $C_{Gij} = c_{ij} O_j$. The fewer the structural holes between groups, the heavier c_{ij} becomes; and the fewer the holes within groups, the higher O_j rises. Consequently, C_{Gij} increases because of the absence of structural holes both within and between groups. In the following example, $C_{Gij} < C_{Giq}$:

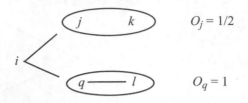

If we have no such data, O_j is arbitrarily assigned a value of 1 and we return to a type 1 structural hole analysis of constraint.

By finding the difference between p_{ij} and c_{ij}, we can measure the desirability of a relation between the ego i and any actor j, where p_{ij} is i's relational investment in j and c_{ij} is j's constraint on i. The difference boils down to i's net structural profit in the i–j relation.

Hierarchy

We shall close discussion of indices with an index to assess hierarchy in a network. Burt uses Theil's entropy index which he calls the 'hierarchy' H_i to measure the concentrations of constraint in dominant relations:

$$H_i = \frac{\sum_j \left(\dfrac{c_{ij}}{C_i/N_i}\right) \ln \left(\dfrac{c_{ij}}{C_i/N_i}\right)}{N_i \ln N_i}$$

If $H_i = 0$, i is under equal constraint from all his relations; and if $H_i = 1$, all constraint comes from one actor.

Autonomy and Articulation

An individual's autonomy $(1 - C_{Gi})$ is obviously inversely proportional to the sum of constraints C_{Gi} upon him. It rises with the quantity of structural holes around him, both within his groups of direct contacts O_j and with direct contacts among themselves c_{ij}. In other words, constraint rises with redundancy while autonomy improves with the exclusivity of relations.

An actor's social capital is a function of her autonomy. Autonomy is potential strategic capacity and access to resources resulting from an actor's position in a network. We have seen the two available strategies, articulation and *tertius gaudens*. They return us to the fundamental concept of social network analysis, that the structure of relations constrains individual behaviour while simultaneously offering opportunities that vary with individual network position. An actor's access to any strategic opportunity depends on her social capital. Contact frequency, contact numbers and other purely dyadic attributes are of secondary importance.

In communication networks with restricted information access, any actor who can position herself to become a mandatory intermediary can exploit

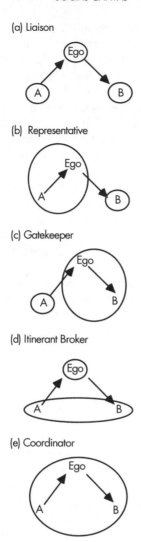

(a) Liaison

(b) Representative

(c) Gatekeeper

(d) Itinerant Broker

(e) Coordinator

Figure 5.2   Articulator roles

the position to her own ends. Such individuals can be identified in several ways, but is there only one strategy and one role type for the articulator? Gould and Fernandez (1989) have drawn up a typology suggesting the role type is not unique but depends on the position of others with respect to existing circles. Here the term 'circle' applies in the broadest sense, i.e. a group of actors who are equivalent in the network according to a given criterion. Figure 5.2 shows how Gould and Fernandez distinguish five articulator roles, where A and B are two individuals that connect through an ego.

(a) *Liaisons* connect individuals from different circles while belonging to a circle of their own. In this case we assume the ego has no vested interest in the communication or negotiation that she fosters. She is simply a go-between. Her strategy is that of any articulator: she can break off relations.

(b) *Representatives* belong to the same circle as A while B is of a distinct circle. Link directions suggest A has delegated the ego to represent her in negotiations with B. This articulator represents her circle to the outside world. Her strategy must therefore be more complex than the liaison's.

(c) *Gatekeepers* are positioned like representatives within a circle. This articulator screens outside access to members of his circle.

(d) *Itinerant brokers* belong to a circle distinct from that of A and B. This articulator facilitates intragroup communication. She becomes essential whenever negotiations break down inside a group and need external jumpstarting.

(e) *Coordinators* operate much like itinerant brokers but belong to the same circle as A and B. They are 'in-house' third parties who coordinate action within their own group. Itinerant brokers and coordinators call to mind Merton's 'cosmopolitan' and 'local' influentials respectively.

Obviously, this typology sketches out idealized portraits. In effective networks, actors mix or switch roles more or less successfully. But this typology does have the advantage of ready applicability in the field. If you have raw network data on a company, political party or any other context, network analysis techniques will speedily identify the circles as a function of a given selection criterion and situate the actors within them. Actually, it might be interesting to vary the criteria to see how they affect roles.

In each case, the articulators are always the ones with a structural hole at their disposal, a point we have already learnt from Burt. But here it appears that the array of circles around the structural holes can exert significant impact on the articulator's role and her strategies. Simultaneous consideration of all three types of data (dyadic relations, relational directions and circle membership) will sharply enrich the results of your study.

Notes

1 Not all researchers distinguish between strong and weak ties in the same way. Nan Lin (1982), for example, defines strong ties as family, friends and neighbours and reserves weak ties for acquaintances.

2 Heider, Davis and Rapoport have extensively investigated transitive tendencies in strong links. See Granovetter's (1982) bibliography for numerous references.

3 Granovetter considers there is no link when two people do not know each other or merely exchange purely conventional greetings without real contact.

4 This gender-balanced study covered 2,553 ministerial employees in February 1977.

5 FASFID conducts an employment study of engineers every four years. The data are from
   the 1987 study, which drew responses from 941 women and 14,905 men.

6 POWER AND CENTRALITY

We now turn to centrality, the actor's second fundamental trait, without losing focus on the actor and the effects of her structural position. Centrally positioned individuals definitely enjoy a position of privilege over those relegated to the circumference. They are hubs, where we can reasonably expect power to concentrate. Numerous studies agree that centrality is bound up with power, both in organizations and in more informal networks, but they also report the link is neither straightforward nor unequivocal.

In 1948, Bavelas was already testing the hypothesis that central positions confer influence. With fellow social psychologists from MIT he ran a series of studies on small groups, concluding that centrality impacts a wide range of issues from leadership to personal satisfaction in group members. Shortly thereafter, sociologists applied the concept to more complex social systems. Cohn and Mariott (1958) found it helpful to explain integration policy in India. Beauchamp (1965) used it to understand organizational efficacy, and Czepiel (1974) to study diffusion of innovations.

While confirming that centrality is an essential structural attribute, these and other studies also underscored the difficulty of quantifying it. Although it seems intuitively obvious, centrality also seems to elude any generally acceptable definition. And definition will affect how we measure a given phenomenon, which in turn alters the conclusions drawn from the data, especially about something like power.

Centralities

Centrality in networks operates somewhat like inequality in social stratification. Several perspectives are possible, each relevant in its own way. In both domains, there are absolute and relative viewpoints that intersect with a local or a global one. In a classic article which we will be using, Linton Freeman (1979) deduces three forms of centrality.

Degree Centrality

Degree centrality is the simplest and most intuitive. It measures an individual's centrality according to the number of connections to others, i.e. degree in undirected graphs and indegree/outdegree in directed graphs. Central individuals have strong connections to other network members; peripheral individuals do not. A measurement scale can readily be designed to consider indirect links through a given number of intermediaries, but we shall restrict ourselves here to direct links. In other words, the centrality index C_{ADi} of any node i in a graph is equal to its total number of direct links. In the example shown, this index is 4 for node 1, 3 for nodes 2 to 5, and 1 for all others.

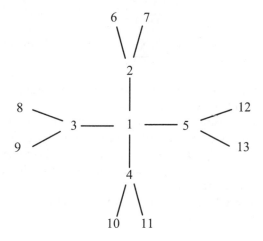

However, these indices reflect purely local centrality that disregards the structural features of the graph and of the individuals with links to a local centre. However, a local centre with links to peripheral nodes is less 'central' than a local centre with links to other centrally located nodes. And if several graphs are to be compared, the absolute number of links loses all baseline value. A person with links to four others in a group of 100 occupies a very different position than he would in a group of 12.

This difficulty is readily overcome with an index of relative or weighted centrality for each node, calculated by dividing her score for absolute centrality by the maximum possible centrality for the graph. The results obtained are comparable in so far as relations are of the same type for all graphs concerned. Just as link quantities between graphs with different node totals may not be compared (but densities may nonetheless), weighted centrality indices offer a basis for comparisons.

The maximal degree centrality of a node corresponds to the centre of a star, i.e. connection to the maximum number of links possible. If n is the total number of nodes, the centre of a star is given by $C_{ADmax} = n - 1$. The weighted degree centrality of node i is obtained by dividing the absolute degree centrality of node C_{ADi} by the maximal centrality: $C_{NDi} = C_{ADi}/(n - 1)$. The result is expressed as a percentage, and 0 denotes an isolated node while 1 designates the centre of the star network.

For comparison purposes, we also need to judge the global centre of the network because the centre of a decentralized network and that of a centralized one are two very different positions. To avoid confusion, we shall use centrality to describe the situation of any node in a graph and reserve centralization to speak of the network as a whole. As a rule, the weighted centrality index for a given network C is given by the sum of differences between the maximal centrality of one point and the centrality of every other point. This sum is then divided by its maximal value such that

$$C = \frac{\sum_{i=1}^{n}(C_{\max} - C_i)}{\max\left[\sum_{i=1}^{n}(C_{\max} - C_i)\right]}$$

This relationship can be calculated using either absolute or weighted centrality scores as input. C is always a value between 0 and 1 that indicates to what degree maximal centrality exceeds the centrality of all other points. If $C = 0$ all nodes enjoy equal centrality, but where $C = 1$ one node dominates centralization completely. This is the position of the most central point. Obviously, centralization will vary according to the definition adopted to measure individual centrality.

Based on the preceding formula, degree centralization C_{AD} using absolute centrality for each node is given by

$$C_{AD} = \frac{\sum_{i=1}^{n}(C_{AD\,\max} - C_{ADi})}{\max\left[\sum_{i=1}^{n}(C_{AD\,\max} - C_{ADi})\right]}$$

The greatest sum of differences in the denominator is $n^2 - 3n + 2$, such that the degree centralization for a given network is given by

$$C_{AD} = \frac{\sum_{i=1}^{n}(C_{AD\,\max} - C_{ADi})}{n^2 - 3n + 2}$$

The greatest sum of differences for the denominator becomes $n - 2$ when the calculations are based on weighted centrality values, and the equivalent formula is then

$$C_{ND} = \frac{\sum_{i=1}^{n}(C_{ND\,\max} - C_{NDi})}{n - 2}$$

Degree centrality stresses the local viewpoint and measures transaction activity or capacity for each member of a given network but disregards her capacity to control them. However, we can also perceive an individual as more central when her dependence on other members for transactions throughout the network decreases (i.e. as she needs fewer and fewer relays to complete a transaction). From this standpoint, her centrality and independence climb in tandem; independence and control are synonyms here. There are two ways to express this second aspect of centrality.

Closeness Centrality

The first way of evaluating the centrality of an individual according to this criterion is to make a judgement about her closeness to others. This is a more global measurement that brings into play the closeness to all network members, not just connections to immediate neighbours.

Returning to the previous example, we see that 6 depends on 2 to reach 7, and 2 depends on 1 to reach 5, while 1 depends on 5 to reach 12. Individual 1 is central because she is never remote from anyone. None of her path lengths to any other node exceeds 2. Individuals 2, 3, 4, and 5 are less central because their path lengths to peripheral individuals reach 3. And these last individuals need path lengths of up to 4 to interconnect.

Bavelas, Leavitt and Beauchamp developed this concept but Sabidussi (1966) quantified it by defining the centrality of a point as the sum of its geodesic distances to all points on the graph. What this actually yields is a measure of remoteness or inverse proximity which can be read as inverse centrality: the points furthest from other points are the least central and vice versa. We have already defined a geodesic in Chapter 3 as the shortest path length between two nodes of a graph. As we are only considering undirected graphs here, we shall call d_{ij} the number of nodes in the geodesic that connects i and j. Sabidussi proposes the following formula to measure the closeness of node i as the sum of geodesics to all other nodes:

$$C_{APi}^{-1} = \sum_{j=1}^{n} d_{ij}$$

The resulting value expresses absolute closeness which Freeman uses to calculate relative closeness with the same principle that applies to degree centrality, i.e. comparison with maximum centrality which once again becomes equal to $C_{max} = n - 1$. Thus

$$C_{NPi}^{-1} = \frac{C_{APi}^{-1}}{n-1} \quad \text{or even} \quad C_{NPi} = \frac{n-1}{C_{APi}^{-1}}$$

C_{NPi} is the index of weighted closeness expressed as a percentage between 0 and 1. It is easy to interpret and is useful for comparing networks. It has been used to show that, as an individual's closeness to others increases, so does her access to information (Leavitt, 1951), power (Coleman, 1973), prestige (Burt, 1982), influence (Bavelas, 1950; and Friedkin, 1991) and higher social status (Katz, 1953). It follows that those individuals furthest from the centre are also furthest from sources of information, power, prestige or influence.

As above, we can obtain an indicator of global network centralization. Closeness centrality is most readily derived from the weighted centrality index. The maximum for the sum of spreads in maximal relative centrality is $(n^2 - 3n + 2)/(2n - 3)$. Thus, the global centralization index is given by

$$C_P = \frac{\sum_{i=1}^{n}(C_{NP\,max} - C_{NPi})}{(n^2 - 3n + 2)/(2n - 3)}$$

Betweenness Centrality

Betweenness offers a more precise way of measuring an individual's centrality.[1] Linton Freeman suggests that some weakly connected individuals (i.e. persons of low degree centrality) may still be indispensable to certain transactions. The greater an individual's actual or potential intermediary value to all members of a network, the greater his control over communication flow and independence of others to communicate. Such an individual can easily influence the group by withholding and/or distorting information that passes through her hands. She is also in a better position to coordinate information for the entire group. From all of the above, she plainly occupies a central position. But again we need a tool of global measurement.

The betweenness of a given point to two other points is its capacity of standing on the paths or geodesics (i.e. minimal length paths) that connect them. Note that two points may have several geodesics. The closeness centrality index does not take this into account, and so we need a new index.

If nodes j and k can indeed use any of several geodesics, the probability they will use a specific one is $1/g_{jk}$, where g_{jk} is the number of geodesics between j and k. The capacity of a third point i to control communication between j and k is given by $b_{jk}(i)$, that is i's probability of standing along any geodesic that j and k have selected. It varies with the total number of geodesics between j and k that contain i, which is expressed as $g_{jk}(i)$ and equals $b_{jk}(i) = g_{jk}(i)/g_{jk}$.

To calculate absolute betweenness centrality for i, it only remains to add up its betweenness for all dyads on the graph:

$$C_{ABi} = \sum_{j}^{n}\sum_{k}^{n} b_{jk}(i), \quad j \neq k \neq i \quad \text{and} \quad j < k$$

As above, this result should be complemented by a weighted index. Here the maximum centrality of the point is given by $C_{max} = (n^2 - 3n + 2)/2$. Consequently, relative betweenness centrality is given by

$$C_{NBi} = \frac{2C_{ABi}}{n^2 - 3n + 2}$$

Values for this index again vary between 0 and 1 and are comparable between different networks. The betweenness criterion says global network centralization C_B is given by either of the following relationships:

$$C_B = \frac{\sum_{i=1}^{n}(C_{AB \, max} - C_{ABi})}{n^3 - 4n^2 + 5n - 2} = \frac{\sum_{i=1}^{n}(C_{NB \, max} - C_{NBi})}{n - 1}$$

Although these indices express the same concept as closeness, they are more demanding in a way. Any point in a connected graph is characterized by its closeness to other points and even the most outlying point has some closeness score. However, its betweenness index is only greater than zero if it is positioned to act as an intermediary. In the previous example, central point 1 has 100% closeness while the four outlying points score 57%. This paradoxical result is offset by calculating the relative betweenness index. Here, the central point again scores 100% for relative betweenness but the outlying points (which cannot ever intermediate) all score 0%.

We have now covered three definitions of centrality. Degree centrality is an individual's capacity to develop communication within a network. It is expressed by the number or proportion of links to a local environment. Closeness and betweenness centrality measure an individual's capacity to control communication in a network, which depends on his relations to all members of a network and not necessarily on the number of links to immediate neighbours. Closeness measures control less accurately than betweenness. From the standpoint of global network centralization, strongly connected centralization is the hallmark of lively communication while strong closeness or betweenness shows that a minority of actors control the communication.

These three methods do not necessarily yield congruent results, but it is worth noting that they all take the same approach to the problem of measuring the proximity of a set of indirectly connected individuals. Stars give best results, circles the worst. Star and circle are like one telephone system that routes all subscribers through a main switchboard and another based on direct interconnections. However, centrality does not take into account the volume of communication or exchanges between individuals and therefore only applies to unvalued graphs.

Flow Betweenness

Freeman et al. (1991) set out to learn how flow betweenness affects centrality. They advance a new yardstick for betweenness that applies to valued graphs based on the unvalued betweenness model. Their model considers node i an intermediary if two other nodes need i to ensure maximum flow of transaction traffic between them. If f_{jk} is maximum flow between j and k, and $f_{jk}(i)$ is flow through i, the degree of dependence on i for maximum flow between any two non-ordinal points is given by

$$C_{AFi} = \sum_{j}^{n} \sum_{k}^{n} f_{jk}(i), \quad i \neq j \neq k \quad \text{and} \quad j < k$$

This index leads to the consideration that flow between two points should be calculated at global network level. Flow depends not only on the flow capacity of the direct link between two individuals but also on the entire capacity of all (independent) direct and indirect paths that connect them.

This absolute index is completed by a weighted index when it is divided by the total flow for all nodes in the graph. It is given by

$$C_{NFi} = \frac{\sum_{j}^{n} \sum_{k}^{n} f_{jk}(i)}{\sum_{j}^{n} \sum_{k}^{n} f_{jk}}, \quad i \neq j \neq k \quad \text{and} \quad j < k$$

An algorithm is required to calculate the value of maximum flow between two points, and we refer readers to Ford and Fulkerson (1957) for full details. We shall only note that it does not apply to unvalued graphs, which are a special type of valued graphs where all flows between nodes are equal to 1.

This algorithm yields results that differ from those obtained with the simple betweenness index C_B except in graphs with no cycles. In graphs with cycles, the difference in results is due to the fact that C_B is based solely on the shortest paths that will carry flow between two nodes while C_F reckons into the equation all independent paths capable of carrying it. It is therefore more realistic to apply C_F unless there is reason to believe that people are restricting flow to shortest paths. This is also a good way to correct certain paradoxical results that other indices will turn up now and then. We shall return to the Meylan relational graph (Figure 4.1) for an example. The Meylan graph is valued but we can use an unvalued version that merely indicates the presence or absence of relations. Table 6.1 sums up centrality scores for each node.

The first three indices in the row for Harmonie show very high values despite its eccentric position on the graph. This is because it is a compulsory intermediary to reach Saint-Valentin, but the result feels wrong and needs adjustment by flow betweenness scores (on both valued and unvalued graphs). Both indices give Harmonie a far lower score. This example points up the wisdom of reviewing all results before passing final judgement on the greater or lesser centrality any point may incarnate.

Table 6.1   Centrality index table for Meylan civic organizations

No.	Name	Degree	Closeness	Betweenness	Unvalued flow betweenness	Valued flow betweenness
(1)	APACH	87.50	88.89	21.43	28.77	42.00
(2)	APEDI	62.50	66.67	2.38	14.67	12.15
(3)	Grand Pré	50.00	61.54	0.00	7.69	4.92
(4)	MJC	87.50	88.89	21.43	28.77	24.00
(5)	Haut Meylan	37.50	57.14	0.00	4.88	3.28
(6)	Revirée	25.00	53.33	0.00	1.14	0.72
(7)	Centre Musical	62.50	72.73	4.76	14.67	14.29
(8)	Harmonie	50.00	66.67	25.00	13.41	7.58
(9)	Saint-Valentin	12.50	42.11	0.00	0.00	0.00

Note that network centralization as measured by flow betweenness is given by the same formula that applies to simple betweenness, i.e.

$$C_F = \frac{\sum_{i=1}^{n}(C_{NF\,max} - C_{NFi})}{n - 1}$$

From Centrality to Power

All techniques presented thus far evaluate the centrality of the actor without regard for the individuals to whom he connects. But we need a distinction between an outlying local centre and a core centre, because being the centre of a group of relatively isolated individuals is very different from being the centre of a set of highly integrated individuals.

Formal calculation of an index to express this difference poses a number of problems. First we face a vicious circle where determining the centrality of node i assumes we know the centrality of all nodes j that connect to i, but their centrality depends on hers. This is given by $C_i = \sum_j r_{ij} C_j$ where r_{ij} is the value of the i–j relation that can be defined variously, e.g. socio-metric choices, geodesic distance or maximum flow.

In the wake of Elihu Katz (1953) and Claude Berge (1967), Phillip Bonacich (1972) proposed an algorithm to resolve this problem. Using matrix notation, he re-expressed the above formula as $\lambda c = Rc$, where c is the vector of centrality scores for each node, R is the sociomatrix between nodes and λ is a scale constant. In this equation λ is by definition an eigenvalue of R, and c is R's associated eigenvector. Thus we obtain centrality indices for each individual by selecting the weighted eigenvector that matches the greatest eigenvalue in matrix R. This solves the technical problem but not the sociological one.

Bonacich asserts the indices measure an actor's power. Indeed, a central actor connected to other central actors can certainly be considered powerful. After all, she holds a dominant position, as shown by the index just obtained, whenever an exchange or negotiation arises.

According to Knoke and Burt (1983), this index measures centrality or power satisfactorily in an undirected network but simply measures actor prestige or fame in a directed context because it only includes received choices (i.e. indegree) for each actor. Indeed, an actor's fame or prestige rises with the number of individuals who cite him and the amount of fame or prestige they enjoy themselves.

This raises another problem. If, as we have seen, a central actor is a mandatory intermediary, she is in a position to control communication. But how sure can she be that her powerful and prestigious relations will always defend and support her position or prestige?

Cook et al. (1983) have opposed the idea that power and centrality (in the sense of a mandatory middleman) were necessarily synonymous. Relations with relatively uninfluential actors can prove invaluable in certain negotiations. And relations with actors with too much power can sometimes prove a handicap because they have too many relational options. Likewise, Caplow's coalition theory (see Chapter 5) suggests that the power of other actors reduces rather than enhances the ego's power. If we hypothesize that every actor wants to dominate any coalitions he builds, we must allow he will only succeed to the extent that he avoids overly powerful partners. Thus power is more subtle than a mechanical sum of powers held by others. In at least some cases, it must be measured in the light of a centrality that can ward off other overly central actors. The same applies to prestige which quickly eclipses in an immediate environment of higher prestige. It is readily arguable that an actor's prestige falls in such an environment but rises as soon as she clearly stands apart from the crowd. A high-prestige circle outshines the prestige of individual members while a high-prestige person confers prestige on the circle she joins.

Bonacich (1987) developed a new way to measure centrality and test the hypotheses about each of these situations. He took up the preceding equation and added a new parameter. Centrality is now given by

$$C_i = \sum_j (\alpha + \beta C_j) r_{ij}$$

where α is an auxiliary parameter that does not affect relative centrality. It is merely chosen such that the square of the length of vector C (i.e. $\sum_i C_i^2$) equals the total number of nodes in the graph. However, the value of β changes centrality scores considerably for every individual as follows:

(a)   If $\beta = 0$, an actor's centrality increases with the number of his direct relations to others, give or take a proportionality constant. We again have the degree centrality mentioned earlier, where centrality increases with the number of an actor's direct relations to others, however eccentric they may be.

(b)   If $\beta - 0$, the ego's centrality increases with the centrality of the ego's relations, which are reflected in rising values for β. A positive value for β sets up a context where an actor's power depends on that of his relations. If $\beta = 1$, we are back to the preceding index but the incidence of the ego's network centrality grows as β climbs. Low β values impart preponderant weight to the ego's centrality in a local network structure (i.e. the ego's immediate neighbours). High β values credit the ego's centrality with connections to outlying individuals.

(c)   If $\beta < 0$, the same logic applies. The higher the absolute value for β, the greater the importance of outlying individuals to the ego's centrality. The lower the value of β, the more restricted she is to immediate neighbours until β reaches the absolute value of 1, in which case only her direct relations are considered. When β goes negative, however, centrality has an inverse effect on the ego's relations, which are weakened by links to other central actors. This expresses the concept that an individual loses power by entertaining links to overly powerful individuals.

Thus the new index measures all three types of centrality but it does not determine values for β. The sociologist has to assign values for β herself as a function of context and working hypotheses. The following remarks may help.

In absolute terms, the value of β should bear some link to transitivity. In an informal network where A's power over B does not give A any power over C, transitivity is weak even if B has power over C. However, transitivity rises as the context becomes increasingly hierarchical. An army general's authority extends beyond relations to staff officers down to the rifleman who actually executes the order. Transitivity runs top to bottom through the hierarchy of officers, NCOs and enlisted personnel. Such a context rates a high β value, whereas a value of 0 reflects power confined to a dyad. In summary, the greater the transitivity, the higher the value to assign to β, and high transitivity signals strong hierarchy when the subject is power.

From a theoretical standpoint, power cannot be defined merely in terms of a dyadic relation, except in certain cases. Weber defines power as the probability that an order will be executed. This definition has the merit of establishing the necessarily relational nature of power. Power is not an independent entity or individual attribute; it needs a relation to exist. As organizational sociologists note: 'There is no power, there are only powerful ties.' Notwithstanding, Weber's (1922) definition should be expanded to include relational transitivity. Attention should also be paid to whether an actor's powerful relations buttress her position or undermine it, without forgetting that any balance of power is dynamic and subject to change.

Roy and Bonacich (1985) faced this sort of situation when they studied interlocking directorates in US railway companies in the early twentieth century. The 'central' companies of this structure were relatively small railways in a 'balkanized' arrangement based on separate interests and weak overlap. The strongest railways were those at the centre of local interest groups but the network was globally decentralized and weakly integrated. Thus local centres were more powerful than the global centre. The situation changed with later buyouts and mergers that spurred greater integration and centralization.

In conclusion, the global centre has more power than local centres in a highly centralized network but the opposite may be true of a decentralized network. Another example is the highly centralized French government, whose power is reinforced by that of local government; while regional cities weaken central government in highly decentralized Germany. Just as there is no doubt that power and centrality go hand in hand, it is equally clear that the bond is most ambiguous.

North American sociology has attempted to refine the concept of power by distinguishing direct exercise or domination from influence or effort to recruit support for a given cause. Knoke (1990) conjugates power and influence to yield four different types of power behaviour.

		Influence	
		Absent	Present
Domination	Present	Coercion	Authority
	Absent	Power broking	Persuasion

Network analysts have obviously pondered how to construct and observe domination and influence. And because this evokes concepts inseparable from that of a relation, these concepts should stand at the heart of network analysis (see Chapter 7 for an analysis of influence).

Power and Exchange

Power is best understood in terms of what networks exchange. Richard Emerson and Karen Cook studied networks in this way by investigating exchange among actors with one or more resources of interest to others. They say there is connectivity if an exchange occurring through a link is affected by other exchanges through other links (we shall restrict our focus to networks with this property). For example, a fall in the volume and frequency of coffee sales lifts the volume and frequency of tea sales.

Connectivity is positive where an exchange increases the probability of other exchanges. It is negative where this probability falls. In retail distribution, a rise in sales from manufacturer to distributors raises the probability of cascading increases between wholesalers and retailers. In a competitive market environment, if B_1 and B_2 are competing to procure maximum quantities of a given finite product from A, her sales to B_1 will exert negative impact on B_2 (and vice versa). A ball circulating between team members in a football game is a series of positive exchanges, or 'passes', but exchanges between teams, or 'intercepts', are negative. In a positively connected network, coordinated action and group integration depend on cooperation among network members. In a negatively connected network, both depend on competition. Most real-life situations present a mix of positive and negative exchanges. An organization will require cooperation to achieve a set goal but competition will rise because participating actors will have individual goals which, although compatible with the common goal, remain partially incompatible between actors. Once this distinction is understood, we can move on to construct a global theory of exchange. Obviously, exchange situations are not static and it is important to pin down the parameters of change.

The global theory of exchange is based on the principles of collective action given by Coleman (1973). It assumes rational behaviour from actors and analyses action in terms of actors and events, both affected by an interactive mix of self-interest and control. Assuming directed action, an actor's interest is defined by the impact of the goal's achievement on her personal welfare. The actor's control over achievement is the share of the payoff she can award herself. Her control over achievement of an indivisible payoff is her probability of determining achievement. If no single actor can achieve the goal alone or award herself the total payoff, the system of actors is defined as a network of mutual dependencies. Each actor and her special interests are dependent on the other actors for achievement. Coleman shows that rational actors will, under such conditions, exchange some or all of their control with other actors and this produces what is called a collective action network.

In such a network, links between individuals are determined by the degree of uncertainty that affects the flow of the resources in circulation. This theory covers neither compulsory exchanges nor those of zero effect on all actors in the system. If we have a trilateral relation where A and B exchange gifts and B and C go on weekend excursions together, we do have a network but not an exchange network in the sense just defined. However, if our three friends visit each other regularly, we obtain an exchange system because the time A spends with B may affect the time he spends with C. It usually does not matter what is being exchanged. It may be goods, services, job tips or whatever.

Some exchange theory axioms are relevant to the relationship between exchange and power. David Willer (1992) lists the following two:

(a) Actor i seeks exchange with j if and only if i is more powerful than j or i's power relative to j equals or exceeds her power over any other of her relations.
(b) If i exchanges a resource with j, i receives more than j if and only if i is more powerful than j.

Once exchange relations are empirically sorted into positive or negative, we are equipped to understand power in terms of an actor's position in a network. For simplicity's sake, we shall reduce the graph for the set of relations to a homomorphic graph where all positions have equivalent exchange potential. The following graph shows only two structural positions, A and B.

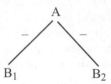

A's position is strongest because she controls resource flow to B_1 and B_2, who have no alternative supplier. Thus we conclude that A is more powerful than B. According to Emerson (1962; 1972), power is inversely proportional to dependence. A's power over B with respect to resource x she controls depends on the value of x to B and the availability of x from alternative suppliers. In other words, B's dependence on A varies with the benefit B actually derives from exchange with A and the relative value of the exchange in comparison with exchange with other sources.

We have already seen that if there is indeed a link between centrality and power, progression between them is not linear. The experiments of Cook et al. (1983) confirm this diagnosis for negatively connected networks, i.e. where actors are competing for a given resource. Marsden's (1982) simulations also confirm it. In a positively connected network, however, power seems to rise with centrality because local centres behave towards the global centre more like simple intermediaries (which is not the case when all relations are competitive). Is there any reticular reason for this ambivalent situation?

Cook and Emerson (1978) suggest that the concept of vulnerability may be especially relevant here. In a connected graph, a node becomes vulnerable when the removal of another node on the graph isolates it from all other remaining nodes. For example, no node is vulnerable in

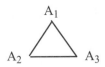

but B_1 and B_2 are vulnerable in

because A's removal would isolate them. Nonetheless, the vulnerability for each node as expressed in a numerical index raises a number of problems. Therefore, Dalud-Vincent et al. (1994) propose a totally discrete method of classifying nodes as a function of vulnerability. As outlined in Chapter 4, this method serves to show the relationship of vulnerability to distance from the centre of a graph: vulnerability decreases with the proximity of a node to the core(s).

The vulnerability of any connected point is tested by withdrawing a point from the graph, which simulates a situation where the latter refuses an exchange and the consequences will vary depending on whether the network is positive or negative. This is shown in the following example:

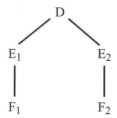

If we take out D, then E to F exchanges survive; but the removal of E isolates all remaining nodes. E is therefore less vulnerable than D or F. But in a cooperative network, D's withdrawal immediately interrupts all exchange within the network, which would not necessarily be the case in a competitive network where D's withdrawal would not impede E's competitive exchanges with the occupants of F positions because F is now entirely dependent on E.

It is reasonable to affirm inverse correlation between power and the vulnerability of a position. However, the centre of a cooperative network has at least as much power as intermediary positions do because the centre is less vulnerable (i.e. we have a case of 'classic' centrality), but intermediary positions are more powerful than the centre of a competitive network because the centre is more vulnerable than they are.

Given that power is unequally distributed, there is cause to wonder about the existence of a centre of gravity where one can logically expect balance. Such a point does exist if we hypothesize that exchange levels tend to gravitate towards a state where every partner becomes equally dependent on every other partner. Karen Cook and Tokio Yamagishi (1992) speak of the principle of 'equidependence'. Let's imagine A and B have $24,000 to share. There is balance or equidependence when each has $12,000. But if A has a relation to C that entitles A to a $10,000 cut on the exchange, only $14,000 is left for A and B to divide into $7,000 shares. So A ends up with $17,000 and B is left with $7,000. This yields an equidependence exchange ratio of 17:7 which measures equidependence and reflects the structural power of the actors involved.

Note that this balance reflects unequal distribution of power. Can the actors find a more egalitarian distribution of power? Four mechanisms are indeed conceivable. The first two are trivial: (1) weaker actors can back out or (2) stronger actors can increase their cut. The second two are less so

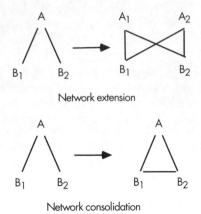

Figure 6.1   Achieving egalitarian distribution of power

(Figure 6.1): (3) weaker actors can diversify partners (network extension) and (4) weaker actors can unite to restrict the more powerful actor's options (network consolidation).

To achieve a more egalitarian distribution of power, any actor whose power base is a structural hole in a negative exchange system must either extend her network or consolidate it. Numerous laboratory studies on the dynamics of exchange systems agree.

Yardsticks for Power and Prestige

Power and prestige are measured by determining how actors with special goals and interests exchange resources for a variety of purposes in such a way as to influence the course of events to their own advantage. The equidependence principle is one useful tool here but we also need a distinction between the competitive market situations dear to economists, and networks of local elites or organizational actors. In an ideal free market environment, any two actors can theoretically exchange resources. In a network, more parameters are involved. In particular, actors must share mutual trust and links may be direct or indirect. In addition, each position has a specific 'value', e.g. cutpoints have options of control and exchange not available to other nodes. All these factors must be taken into account to determine the power, prestige and influence of each actor.

Several models can perform this determination. Burt's model has the advantage of being available in the software package Structure® (Burt, 1992b) described in the Appendix. Predictably, we permute the matrix for observed data O (e.g. sociometric choices) into a Z matrix with the element z_{ij} that expresses the strength of a relation between i and j (see Chapter 3).

Choice status

Choice status CS_i is the number of actors who reach the ego i divided by the total number of actors who could potentially reach him in a network of n actors:

$$CS_i = \sum_j \delta_{ji}/(N-1), \quad j \neq i$$

where $\delta_{ji} = 1$, if j can attain i ($z_{ij} > 0$) and 0 otherwise. CS_i varies from 0 to 1. It is 0 if no actor can reach i and 1 if anyone can reach him. Note that this calculation, and the others that follow, only cover the ego's 'received links', i.e. arrows directed at the ego in directed graphs. Prestige is an altogether different matter.

Extended relations

Relations are weighted for strength, which amounts to calculating the average marginal strength of received relations ER_i as follows:

$$ER_i = \sum_j \left[z_{ji}/\max(z_{jk})\right]/(N-1), \quad j \neq i$$

ER_i varies from 0 for no citations to 1 for maximal relational strength, when i enjoys strong links to every actor.

Exclusive relations

This index RE_i expresses the degree to which an actor has become the exclusive relation of all others in a network. It is given by the average proportional strength of received links as follows:

$$RE_i = \sum_j \left[z_{ji}/\sum_k z_{jk}\right]/(N-1), \quad j \neq i, k$$

RE_i varies from 0 to 1. The expression in brackets [ ] expresses j's investment in his relation to i.

Power

Power more readily grows out of exclusive relations to key actors than to marginal ones. We reckon this into the equation with a weighting for the degree to which j's relations to i are exclusive because of j's power. The power p_i of i is thus given by

$$p_i = \sum_j \left[z_{ji}/\sum_k z_{jk}\right]p_j \quad (z_{jj} = \max(z_{jk}) \text{ if } z_{jj} \text{ is arbitrary})$$

Because the power of i depends on that of j and vice versa, we call in an algorithm. We faced the same problem when evaluating power as a function of centrality, and the solution is the same: look for specific values and vectors. According to the above formula, i's power increases with demand for her network. As Coleman (1973) and others point out, this amounts to considering that power (or prestige) acts as a price mechanism in an economic model of global market equilibrium.

Reflected power

Mark Mizruchi et al. (1986) suggest breaking down power into the components of relations directed to i and those symmetrical with i. Reciprocal relations between i and others reflect relations of reciprocal power of the one upon the other, which Burt terms 'reflected power'. It is expressed as a percentage by

$$RP_i = 100 \times \sum_j z_{ji}\, z_{ij}, \quad j \neq i$$

In a way, it expresses i's impact on the network and the feedback it engenders. Structure® includes the statistic $p_i/\max(p_i)$ which varies between 0 and 1; 0 designates a powerless individual and 1 an all-dominating individual.

Local Elites

The application of these yardsticks to local elites or actors in an organization is rare owing to an unfortunate shortage of data. Nonetheless, Marsden and Laumann (1977) applied a similar model to five local events in a small US town. They estimated power by considering 10 different resources controlled by actors in the study population. They found 90% correlation with a direct measure of subjective influence (number of times an individual is cited as a 'local leader' regardless of any relations to respondents). Actor scores for power also correlated well with centrality scores. Power and prestige ratings for each actor enabled the team to predict which local events would actually occur with 60% accuracy because they knew which actors had a decisive impact on making things happen.

Historically, the study of local elites based on structural analysis dates back to political sociology in the 1950s and 1960s. Although Chicago sociology and other paradigms have upstaged political sociology, it has been making a comeback since Floyd Hunter's (1953) monograph on Atlanta and Robert Dahl's (1957; 1958; 1961) work on New Haven. However they offer scant detail about the political network of actors or how collective decision-making processes actually operate. It was only in the 1970s and 1980s that studies of local power systems really applied network analysis to interorganizational communication structures and exchange networks in a bid to grasp the differing degrees of actor involvement in the collective decision-making processes.

In particular, Edward Laumann and Franz Pappi (1976) ran four studies in the Federal German Republic and USA that demonstrated the value of network analysis to understanding local power structures. The two monographs on the town of Altneustadt, Germany (population 20,000) are the most widely known, but the other two on Towertown and River City, Illinois also enabled interesting comparisons. The Altneustadt studies focused on local elites and organizations while the Illinois studies addressed more formal organizations.

Laumann and Pappi's study design was based on Talcott Parsons's famous AGIL functional analysis tool. Applied to local organizations, AGIL stands for the four categories of adaptation (e.g. banks and companies), goal attainment (municipal government and court system), integration (labour unions, political parties and civic organizations) and latent maintenance models (e.g. schools, churches and health care services). These different functional models of local organizations exchange a certain number of resources, i.e. (A) money, (G) power, (I) influence and (L) non-monetary tradables.

This almost outrageously Parsonian typology did yield a list of key organizations worthy of study. The researchers then interviewed the heads of each body about their personal networks (according to the classification system given above) and their ties to elites in other organizations. The small survey population (51 persons in Altneustadt) enabled Laumann and Pappi to set up sociometric choice matrices that broke down elite relations into three categories: business, local politics and socializing. Matrix analysis revealed that the actors with the greatest centrality were also generally considered the most influential in local affairs. Centrality gave them access to resources they could use to steer local decision-making processes.

Clique analysis revealed the contours of local elites. Three cliques orbited the conservative CDU and social democratic SPD parties; another clique gravitated around local small business; and the remaining actors were isolated. But these isolated actors were bridges between the CDU and SPD cliques who only shared one direct link.

The elites of the CDU clique were all cited by other elites but only cited each other. Multidimensional scaling analysis on path lengths revealed the following two structural principles for the Altneustadt elites:

1 Only central actors coordinate and integrate action in a given local structure (marginal actors do not).
2 Actor closeness reflects three functional subsystems (Figure 6.2): religious leaders and educators; businessmen; and scientists (Altneustadt has a research institute). All actors in every subsystem are potential local partners of any coalition that may arise to solve a local problem.

These three domains share a common core consisting of town council members and key corporate executives. Small businessmen, church leaders, teachers and scientists all stand outside the inner circle. Prominent local leaders stand closer to the centre than county government officials. These

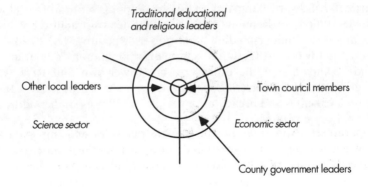

Figure 6.2   Local elite structure in Altneustadt, Germany

observations hold true for all three networks of the study: business relations, local politics and socializing. Joseph Galaskiewicz (1979a; 1979b)
reports similar results from Towertown, where townsmen of strictly local
prominence monopolize the network core.

   In all cases, centrality correlates with prestige (most cited actors) and the
capability to influence local decision-making towards vested interests of
the central actors (Knoke, 1983). There are three reasons. First, central
actors enjoy better access to information and other resources than marginal
actors. Next, they are more actively involved in local issues. And last, they
play a decisive role in building coalitions during early negotiations upstream
of actual decision-making.

   Coalitions always form along the frontiers of various structural positions
identified through network analysis. The frontiers may vary according to
the issues and vested interests at stake. In Altneustadt, the organization of
a rock festival pitted the 'religious' subcategory of 'traditionalists' in the
Catholic Church against the 'scientists' among the 'modernists', but a land
survey issue about municipal borders coalesced all local elites against the
county officials.

   Laumann and Pappi showed that the coalition whose sum total of
reputations carries the most prestige will always win out. Thus there is a
link between prestige and influence. However this link requires careful
assessment because effective influence is the product of a complex process
that is sensitive to the structural position of actors belonging to multiple
networks, each of whom has specific resources that can sway decision-
making toward her own vested interests.

Organizations

Organizations are definitely one area where network analysis makes strong
original contributions. Unfortunately, few studies have so far applied it to

research the link between centrality and power. Still, it is natural for sociology to wonder about the relation between different relational systems and the ability of certain actor groupings to achieve their ends. Such indeed was what Vincent Lemieux (1982) sought in proposing to begin by distinguishing networks from 'apparatuses' (organizations). He offered six principal criteria.

1   *High role specialization*   Role specialization is lower in networks than in apparatuses. Apparatuses explicitly restrict roles and implicit roles arise when networks are superposed onto an apparatus. In networks, any specialization opens the door to a greater plurality of roles.

2   *Low multiplexing*   Relations are sharply defined in an apparatus but more multiplexed in networks.

3   *Low link redundancy*   Relations show high redundancy in sociability networks because of the plurality of roles and the essentially informal links they engender. An apparatus necessarily consists of formal links whose express purpose is to minimize redundancy. Such streamlined links yield organization tables whose structure is far simpler than that of an equivalent social network.

4   *Established frontiers*   Network frontiers are less precise than apparatus frontiers and, above all, they are not policed. Any border policing needs that may arise are not done on a contract basis. Because an apparatus protects its frontier by force of law, it is easy to decide if a given individual belongs or not. Who belongs to a given network is less obvious. For example, some people will ignore the very existence of certain distant cousins, but they are definitely her relatives. Do they belong to her network nonetheless? This raises the tricky issue of potential relations.

5   *Formal action coordination*   An apparatus coordinates action through explicit custom-tailored operating procedures, at least in part. Constitutional rules or company bylaws come on top of these procedures to coordinate coordination. Lemieux notes networks have no such meta-coordination. No one is assigned to oversee coordination although there are borderline cases, such as neighbourhood gangs, where the leader is vested with a degree of authority that leads her to coordinate action. In this case, we have a quasi-apparatus with officious meta-coordination, i.e. coordination not sanctioned by law or contract. In sociability networks, most coordination occurs from neighbour to neighbour without contracts.

6   *Strong hierarchy*   Networks map out as strongly or semi-strongly connected graphs and therefore contain little hierarchy. An apparatus has a hierarchy and appears as a quasi-strongly connected graph.

Catherine Flament (1991) applied this approach to a set of civic organizations on the French Riviera. She investigated both their local internal organization and their relations to respective national head offices.

(a) She used link redundancy to oppose bodies as a function of internal organization. Either they were set up much like formal bodies with a board of officers who carried out most duties with little input from members, or they operated with committees where members organized events together and reinforced mutual links.
(b) Multiplexing served to compare the roles of employees and activists in each organization. She notes that individuals play more roles when a project aims for a broad goal rather than a specific target.
(c) Frontiers transpired through a body's relations to other bodies. Relations were either competitive if an organization defended its activist niche and government grants, or cooperative if it sought outside partners.

Flament supplements Lemieux with an additional criterion. Her study includes links between the local office of a civic organization and its national head office. She takes account of hierarchy (connectivity) and link strength or weakness. She notes that older national bodies with a tradition of being tightly organized tend to have strong hierarchies and strict membership rules. In another category of bodies, however, local autonomy is the rule and hierarchy is absent. Flament classifies formal institutionalized links as strong and others as weak. This set of criteria segments the population of civic organizations into three classes that operate in distinct and coherent ways:

(a) *grouped institutions*, which have an apparatus-type structure with 'strong formal links'
(b *groups*, which are exclusive introspective bodies and where organizational analysis criteria do not apply
(c) *networked groups*, which are apparatuses that have developed what Lemieux would call network features (e.g. individual autonomy and multiplexing of cross-cutting links).

This classification is relevant to explain the historical development of civic organizations and their efficacy. Flament concludes

> The apparatus type of organization was the backbone of (French) adult education in a market environment of low competition where the size of government grants depended on negotiating skills and at a time when social and cultural services needed to expand on a large scale. Today government is shedding such commitments and competition is rising from the private sector, local governments and others. Furthermore, quality not quantity is now the issue, as well as the capability to respond to complex problems. In the context of such an uncertain environment where innovation is the key to higher productivity, networked organizations appear to show superior performance . . . Civic bodies whose income is growing are networked organizations that have diversified their sources of revenue. Other bodies are showing stagnant income levels while others face sharp cutbacks if there is a change of party in local government or national government pulls out . . . Networked organizations are also those who are offering new and innovative services for youths (e.g. job services and housing) or who are active in environmental protection.

Intra-Organizational Relations

We shall consider an organization such as a company or government agency. We need to identify a certain number of relations if we are to analyse how it functions. First there are the formal links. Some persons have authority, give orders and rate performance which affects promotions and salary. The set of all these formal links of authority maps out into an organizational table. It is usually an explicit document because it establishes ongoing obligations among persons even if it is not exempt from self-contradiction. This type of relation is usually well identified and injects neatly into a matrix for formal analysis.

Other formal relations include those governing information flow. Information flow needs scheduling so that everyone with a need to know receives data on time. But information exchanges do not introduce the same sort of hierarchy as above. In some departments or agencies, everyone needs full information regardless of rank or grade, but not in others. Secretaries need every detail about their boss's plans and activities yet they are still subordinates. They will pass on some, but not all, information they hold to lower levels of the organization as necessary. Informal hierarchies arise because some people can elect to pass on or withhold information. They happen in the grey area where formal rules meet effective functioning. Organizational sociologists have long been familiar with the behaviour patterns of information withholders and the constitution of power bases that the organizational table had not foreseen.

The third and last type of link to investigate is friendship and back-scratching. Such relations generate bonds that are vital for the proper functioning of an organization. A perennial quip says the fastest way to gridlock an entire organization is to strictly apply all the rules and nothing but the rules. The informal links that help circulate information unquestionably amount to informal fillips that sustain effective functioning (Crozier and Friedberg, 1977).

Thus there are several levels to an organization, which a minimum of serious investigation will express into matrices for each relation. Organizations are like layer cakes where each layer represents a particular relation. Any diagnostic study should attempt such a systematic breakdown of relations.

We shall suppose we want an exact definition of a corporate executive. Of course executives are easily recognized in a company setting. But each company has its own style and features. Executives as a category are actually an abstract list of common traits that we go on to illustrate with tangible examples. We need to make many such abstractions based on observation of relations. Knowledge of individual traits alone is not enough. An individual with no executive duties may be earning an executive's salary and enjoy formal classification as one. Inversely, a non-executive may fill an executive role. Even after discarding all executives with no executive duties, we still face a functional discrepancy between employee status and effective role because actors are constantly tinkering with their actual positions.

Law Office Case Study

Emmanuel Lazega (1992) applied these principles to a recent study. The study is remarkable for selecting a collegial and fairly unbureaucratic organization, which is somewhat rare for sociologists to do. This organizational definition is Weber's but he settled for simply classing collegial bodies beneath bureaucracies. Only recently did sociologists recognize the value of collegial organizations or try to study them very rigorously. Lazega quotes Waters (1989), who says: 'Collegial structures are those in which there is a dominant orientation to a consensus achieved between the members of a body of experts who are theoretically equal in their level of expertise but who are specialized by area of expertise.' Collegial does not mean unbureaucratic, but the decision-making process involved is more complex. For example, the decision-making process of a university operates through a series of peer committees. The formal structure makes only a partial contribution towards systemic integration, and Lazega goes on to show, in his study of a New England law office, that the contribution of informal relations is at least of equal importance.

The law office in Lazega's study covered 71 business lawyers (36 partners and 35 salaried associates). They worked at three locations in Boston, Hartford and Providence. The firm specializes in litigation and corporate counselling. The study investigated integration among the firm's different locations, specializations and two types of remuneration. Through network analysis, Lazega came up with two mechanisms.

The first mechanism is cohesion-based. By asking lawyers (1) who they asked for advice, (2) who they worked with and (3) who their friends were, Lazega showed that each formal network consists of small cliques that act as bridges across frontiers drawn by location, specialization and lawyer status (partner or associate). Moreover, the informal networks have specialized functions. Cooperation networks bridge the gap between associates and partners. Advice networks connect people in different locations. And friendship networks cross back and forth between litigation and counselling. Lazega concludes that 'informal structures are not the sole basis for organizational integration. Each type of link makes a specific contribution to integration in the firm, especially when a risk of conflict appears between members.' The diagonal in Table 6.2 illustrates the integration mechanism (all links are strong since they connect clique members).

It thus becomes clear that informal links promote integration by off-setting formal internal links which undercut integration. Lazega focused structural equivalence analysis exclusively on links of cooperation to identify the second integration mechanism.

Table 6.2   Cross-cutting links in a New England law office

| | Cross-cut link | | |
	Remuneration status	Location	Specialization
Cooperation	x		
Advice		x	
Friendship			x

The second mechanism is not new in itself. It was noticed long ago that actors in different fields need to cooperate and this leads to inter-dependence which becomes an integration mechanism in an organization. The contribution of structural equivalence analysis here is to identify the forms interdependence will assume in a context of informal relations.

The law firm's policy is to avoid the feudalism of stable legal teams where one partner always works with the same associates. This rule is designed to prevent any party of lawyers from imagining they can split off with 'their' clients. But structural analysis discovered the emergence of several groups where one partner regularly worked with the same people. So there is a flagrant gap between the firm's explicit policy of atomization and the actual tendency toward stable teams. These teams also preserve the balance of power among partners. From this standpoint, business sense seems to win out over pure organizational thinking. And this has not disaggregated the office into several 'micro-firms' because these strategies are indeed rational: 'The structure of working relations tends to make it impossible to control both the client base and the legal staff; this prohibits the members of any single position from monopolizing both power bases.' In short, no team can achieve critical mass and split off into a separate firm. This type of power base sharing bestows collegial organizations with a second integration mechanism.

We have not presented the calculations for the above but they are all based on proven techniques of network analysis. The techniques offer a systematic approach to relations between structures and to actor behaviour patterns in an organizational environment. Systematic analysis of informal relations was what enabled Lazega to identify the effective structures at work among individual actors or positions within a network at the law firm and to understand their contribution to integration. At this firm, they establish bridges that crisscross formal frontiers and preserve the existing balance of power, thus pre-empting cleavage which poses a bigger threat to collegial organizations than to pure bureaucracies.

Interlocking Directorates

Lazega's (1994) study clearly illustrates the value of network analysis to understanding intra-organizational relations, but relations between organizations are also worthy of attention. And a wealth of such studies are available.

Industry, services, banking and corporate bodies all entertain various kinds of relations. Some are directly business-related as in the case of an auto manufacturer who buys in brake systems from a subcontractor. The finished product is then sold through distributors. There are many ways of identifying exchanges but it often proves difficult enough to know where to draw frontiers between them. The existence of branch offices and differing links to subcontractors, subsidiaries and affiliates can make the frontiers of a company difficult to pin down.

Berkowitz (1988) experienced this difficulty with units and exchanges in his study of Canadian enterprise. He sees companies competing in markets for their products and tries to analyse competition by reconstructing relevant aggregates. He attaches special importance to discovering who actually controls a company. This is easy when one shareholder holds a controlling stake, but a company with numerous minority shareholders complicates matters. Yet each wields real power. His solution is to make a graph of minority interests that takes accounts of transitive influence. This enabled him to break down the field of investigation into discrete units.

Berkowitz then used this breakdown to identify which sectors were equivalent. The difficulty that arose here was that companies had different types of production with different profiles. He abandoned his attempt to regroup them and focused on the dual problem of regrouping comparable types of production in the same companies or corporate groups. This approach established positional equivalence from the standpoint of production. However, classification must also take account of market access for each company if it is to make economic sense. Lastly, two production activities were only grouped together if they appeared inside the same company and if they were competing in the same market. This approach means processing vast amounts of data to cluster economic activities that will serve as a testbed for hypotheses about actor behaviour.

In addition to cross-shareholdings, companies operate other links when managers sit on several boards of directors. Such data are easy to look up for, say, the nation's top 50 corporations or the world's biggest 100. From a formal standpoint, this amounts to a network that graphs just like the civic organizations of Meylan (see Chapter 4). We start with a rectangular table with rows for the companies and columns for board members. We then derive a matrix that lists how many members sit on both boards of any pair of companies.

However, John Scott (1987) adds a distinction. First he notes the case of a key executive who holds a mere seat on another board. In this case, he simply represents company A on the board of company B. The existence of this affiliation suggests other links (e.g. cross-shareholdings, business relations). Then he notes the case of a member who owes his board seat to business relations or cross-holdings. For example, Smith is on the board of financial services company A. He obtains a seat on the boards of companies C and D. The C–D link appears on the graph, as it should, but it only reflects A's discrete affiliations to C and D. Instead of performing a routine symmetric matrix for the interlocks, Scott prefers to distinguish between type A–B board seats (which should be directed *a priori*) and type C–D seats (which have no grounds to be directed). To this end, we start with a table that plots board members against companies and round it out with data about the specific position of each board member in her own company and corporate group.

Beth Mintz and Michael Schwartz (1981b) worked from board director lists published in *Fortune* and other business magazines. They insist that companies should be analysed at the right level of aggregation:

> A great number of director exchanges implies major intercorporate influence, significant intercorporate dependency, or an intermeshed social network of corporate leaders. Any combination of these underlying realities implies a high potential for common action. A specific firm will be heavily interlocked if it has a great many structural ties to other firms, if it is the centre of a group of economic interdependencies, or if its leadership are personally connected to a great many other leaders. In any of these situations, highly interlocked companies may be central to coordinated action.

They used corporate data from 1962 and 1966 but met serious obstacles in monitoring structural evolution as some of these companies folded, merged or faced new startups. Of the 1,131 companies surveyed in 1962, 1,111 were left in 1966. In 1962, 13,574 individuals yielded 5,699 links between 1,003 companies.

In another article, Mintz and Schwartz (1981a) distinguish between hubs and peaks. Hubs are companies with spokes to many other companies and therefore show high centrality. Peaks are companies whose only links extend to companies less central than themselves. Some hubs are also peaks; peaks are not necessarily hubs. With these criteria, they found that financial groups were clearly the most central of all. Even local banks turned out to be peaks. At the very core were four big banks and three insurance groups. The practical conclusion is that seven institutions can operate the links they entertain to regulate budding conflict between any two corporations.

Joel Levine (1972; 1985; 1987) published an atlas in 1985 of links among major financial and industrial multinational groups. It contains country maps that show which companies occupy central positions, chains and cycles as well as distance and closeness generated by interlocking directorates.

The 1980s saw a wave of studies on interlocking directorates in North America but Europe has seen a few as well (Stokman and Wasseur, 1985; Scott, 1987). All specialists of this particular field now stress the need to understand the subtle mechanisms that generate elites and links between major corporations (Palmer et al., 1986; Berkowitz, 1988).

Notes

1 For recent developments on betweenness centrality, see White and Borgatti (1994) and Hage and Harary (1995).

7 DYNAMICS

Enormous research remains to be done in the dynamics of social networks, the subject of this chapter. Although we have no synthetic theory, there have been several attempts to gain a perspective on social change (Doreian and Stokman, 1997). We shall be examining in detail the most significant without seeking any artificial form of overall coherence.

Innovation Diffusion

The study of how any innovation (e.g. new technology, fashion wear) diffuses throughout an industrial society requires the researcher to place himself in the position of the user, her tastes and preferences, before trying to determine if the aggregate of choices obeys some sort of pattern. The key issue is to learn whether the sum of personal decisions to adopt or reject an innovation does not snowball into a collective movement whose logic is grounded in interpersonal relations.

Historically, Gabriel Tarde (1895) was the first to research this area. He believed the human tendency to imitate fellow beings was the fundamental law of all social phenomena. At that time, he noticed that innovations spread out through society along an S-shaped curve that, in his opinion, reflected three fundamental empirical states: 'Slow progress at the outset, fast progress of regular acceleration in the middle, before final gradual deceleration down to the end.' However, this paradigm did not pick up any real sociological momentum until 1943 when Bryce Ryan and Neal Gross investigated the diffusion of hybrid corn in an Iowa farming community.

Their groundbreaking studies showed it took nine years for all of these very modern agricultural producers living in a progressive society to switch to a hybrid corn seed that was being actively promoted. The seed had all the features of a 'good' innovation. It doubled crop yields and the doubling was conspicuous. It needed no new or special skills. Farmers could test seed samples on a small plot. Detailed information was available from qualified sources and they could inspect the results their neighbours obtained. Henri Mendras (1967) found the same resistance after a similar study in Béarn, France in the 1950s. This confirmed there was nothing unusual in the conditions of the Ryan and Gross (1943) study. Hybrid corn diffusion did follow an S-curve, and the first to raise the new corn were relatively cosmopolitan farmers with higher socioeconomic status than those who did not. Ryan and Gross paid scant attention to opinion leadership, but they did lay the foundations for a new approach to the study of communication and behavioural change which was adopted by growing numbers of sociologists. In 1975, Rogers and Thomas enumerated over 2,700 studies on innovation diffusion. Given the near exponential growth of studies in this field, today's total is substantially higher.

Regardless of the innovation under investigation, all studies seek out the diffusion channels and diffusion time, i.e. the time it takes an innovation to reach everyone in a social system. Studies confirm that diffusion follows an S-curve identical to the one for pathological contagion. In other words, new ideas, appliances and other innovations spread like epidemics. In the vast majority of cases, Verhulst's logistical function model still gives the best fit for innovation diffusion. Such a graph plots diffusion delay along the abscissa and the cumulative proportion of people adopting the innovation along the ordinate. It always yields an S-curve. Statistically, this relationship corresponds to the distribution function of the logistical law and, in its simplest form, is given by $F(t) = 1/(1 + e^{-t})$. The derived formula for the proportion of individuals who have adopted an innovation at any time (t) is: $F'(t) = F(t) [1 - F(t)]$. This formula says that, once diffusion has a minimum of momentum, the number of individuals who adopt an innovation at any given time is proportional to the number who have already adopted it and those who have not (the formula yields a bell curve). Thus, we are clearly facing a collective phenomenon. The aggregate of individual decisions picks up a momentum that is not independent of time of occurrence and progression over time is not linear.

It is now worth segmenting the bell or S-curve into rising and falling components to examine the personal traits of individuals during various diffusion phases. Tarde distinguished three phases but we can obtain greater accuracy by dividing the curve into five components (Figure 7.1). At t_0, the innovation affects no one. At t_1, diffusion reaches a handful of pioneers. They have opted for the innovation and the risks that go with it. For example, they may buy into a new computer norm without knowing if it will become an industry standard. In t_1-t_2, diffusion picks up speed and reaches the trendsetters. Trendsetters make snap decisions, but only after the pioneers have tinkered with the innovation for a while. In t_2-t_3, momentum continues building until the innovation reaches half the population. Diffusion now flips over into decline. We can speak of a majority, but we distinguish a leading-edge majority in t_2-t_3 from the trailing-edge majority in t_3-t_4. The latter finally adopts the innovation because 'everybody's got one' and they are starting to feel abnormal, a behaviour pattern we see in fashion clothes. At t_4, only a handful of diehards remain who will eventually adopt it against their better judgement, if only because no alternative is commercially available.

There is absolutely nothing hypothetical about this typology. Too many studies report it. It keeps turning up in studies although the actual proportions of individuals will obviously vary between innovations and survey populations. Thus, it is a valid way to accumulate comparable data, and is very useful to anyone with a new product to launch. Setting aside

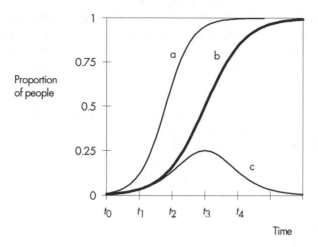

Figure 7.1   Diffusion of innovation: (a) proportion who know of a given innovation at t; (b) cumulative proportion who have adopted it at t; (c) proportion who adopt it at t

the importance of the actual features of a new product, it is also essential to target the right initial population. Advertising campaigns must appeal to the profiles of pioneers and trendsetters, because under normal conditions others will follow suit once these two subpopulations have been won over. Without going into detail, pioneers and trendsetters share a good number of common traits. The main difference is that pioneers are willing to take bigger risks; they are closer to the socioeconomic mean and track down new information more actively. Trendsetters have higher socioeconomic status and serve to legitimize the innovation. They are also influential in changing other people's opinions.

This epidemiological breakdown only classifies individuals in terms of action phases. But an entire and sometimes complex persuasion process gradually develops between the moment a person learns of the existence of an innovation and the moment she adopts it. First people have to hear about an idea, product or lifestyle. In industrial society, most people receive this information through the media, specialized agencies, friends or relatives. But whatever the source, information travels faster than the innovation itself although it too will move along an S-curve. At each phase, there is a delay before the informed person decides to adopt the innovation. It is short for pioneers, slightly longer for trendsetters and continues lengthening until a majority is attained. The delay reflects the time it takes someone to convince himself of the innovation's positive potential. All studies confirm that personal contacts play a vital role during this thinking period. The key to final adoption lies in the recommendations of friends, neighbours and family to confirm and legitimize the information in their possession.

Not all members of a network are equally capable of influencing other people's decisions. Some are opinion leaders, others are not. Numerous studies report that the social distance between opinion leaders and others is a key variable of the influence mechanism. In traditional hierarchical societies, leaders must stand a cut above the crowd, but no more unless they are to risk social rejection. In industrial societies, leadership roles do not always fall to the same people and they vary widely between networks and the type of innovation in play.

In a small Midwestern town, Katz and Lazarsfeld (1955) studied women's tastes in four areas: clothing and hairstyles, food and household appliances, civic affairs and politics, and movies. They interviewed 800 women on how they arrived at decisions and on the personalities of the people who influenced their choices. Their observations offer three main lessons. First, there are specific influence mechanisms for each social stratum and each of the four areas. Second, influence from the same social stratum is more important than influence from a higher stratum. Third, influential people are more enthusiastic about innovations than others, but this subjective factor is less important than sociodemogaphic traits (with an arguable exception for movies). In summary, small town Midwestern women prefer advice from peers except in politics and civic affairs and will seek it from peers of slightly higher socioeconomic status whom they consider as 'experts' in the issue at stake.

The influence mechanism is based on a communication and information network that operates through the mass media and personal relations. Media coverage is uniform but individual exposure and understanding of the information both vary. To understand information properly, you have to be looking and ready for it; only influential people have this active receptivity. Thus, opinion leaders are the prime conduit for useful information. Only when they have the information can they exert influence efficaciously. A person of total ignorance is beyond influence and will only respond to social authority. Discussion between the influential and the influenced leads to a decision of general adherence sooner or later. So we have what Lazarfeld calls 'two-step flow of communication' where information moves from the media to the influential and from them to less motivated potential users.

That said, influential people do not share a homogeneous profile. Some are prominent citizens. They hold positions as intermediaries between the circle they belong to and higher echelons of power. Moreover, their position is confirmed by the confidence they enjoy because of the favours they obtain for their clientele and the existence of this clientele justifies their position in the higher echelons. Influential people are individuals who have saved up real social capital. We might even speak of 'social capitalists'. They accumulate wealth and increase it. In the patron/client relationship, trust is intimately attached to the person, her membership in the group and her respect for its customs and traditions. The relationship to the 'outsider' is altogether different.

The outsider is not the same sort of community member as someone born into it. She comes from somewhere else. This suits her for the role of pioneer, since 'difference' is a permanent feature of her local image. Simmel (1908b) notes: 'All economic history shows foreigners who appear as merchants and merchants who are foreigners.' The foreign merchant (or travelling salesman) introduces to a circle various products it did not previously know. Businesslike formality facilitates transactions with outsiders who are circle members nonetheless.

Crozier and Friedberg (1977, drawing on Jamous, 1968) identify a third type of actor. They evaluate power in an organization in terms of games between actors. Actors who belong to several social networks can exploit the autonomy this multiple membership obtains to promote change within the organization under certain circumstances. The researchers note that: 'Through their multiple memberships and relational capital in various segments of their environment, those groups and individuals who can exert at least partial control over this area of uncertainty and harness it for the benefit of their organization will very naturally acquire considerable power within that organization. It is the power of the so-called "secant marginal".'

The prominent citizen, the outsider and the secant marginal are all in a good position to promote the diffusion of innovation. All have contacts outside their own groups; all hold marginal positions. Mendras (1967) reports how the prominent citizens of Béarn were the first to switch into hybrid corn. Simmel finds outsiders make good pioneers because they tend to attach less importance to local tradition. Jamous (1968) shows how secant marginals became the backbone of the 1959 French hospital reform movement, one of the biggest overhauls in French health care history.

All three types of person are intermediaries, but leaders are of two types. In Merton's (1949) study of 'Rovere', he distinguishes between local and cosmopolitan leaders:

> The localite largely confines his interests to the community. Rovere is essentially his world. Devoting little thought or energy to the Great Society, he is preoccupied with local problems, to the virtual exclusion of the national and international scene. He is, strictly speaking, parochial. Contrariwise with the cosmopolitan type. He has some interest in Rovere and must of course maintain a minimum of relations within the community since he too, exerts influence there. But he is also oriented significantly to the world outside Rovere, and regards himself as an integral part of that world. He resides in Rovere but lives in the Great Society.

Merton sees the following differences:

1 *Roots* Local leaders are grounded in their home town and would not think of emigrating, while cosmopolitans are always ready to pull up stakes if the opportunity is sweet enough.
2 *Relational* Networks Local leaders want lots of contact with other townfolk. Multiple contacts build networks upon which they can exercise influence, while cosmopolitan leaders are very discriminating in their relations. The latter select contacts with expertise, while locals

choose pleasant company who have a feeling for human relations and local history, not skills and knowledge.

3 *Civic spirit* Most influential people show above-average involvement in local organizations but cosmopolitans are into more organizations than local leaders. Localites at more at home in local bodies with personal contacts while cosmopolitans prefer organizations with bigger goals.

4 *Reading habits* Cosmopolitans read more than localites. Cosmopolitans have a bias for national periodicals while locals are more interested in local and regional events.

5 *Sociodemographics* Cosmopolitans tend to be young and upwardly mobile people whose social status is based on professional qualifications while localites are older individuals of firmly established status

Cosmopolitans stand out as conduits that pass on information from the mass media to people in their immediate environment. They have every chance of being a pioneer, while localites stand better chances of being trendsetters. Localites inspire confidence in their immediate environment and help people reach a decision.

Moreover, Merton also distinguishes 'top influentials' (cited by 15%+ of respondents) from 'middle influentials' (cited by 5% to 14%) and 'rank-and-file influentials' (cited by under 5%). As in other studies, respondents tend to cite people from their own stratum, but the highly influential tend to rank themselves above those who cite them. Moderately and slightly influential people cite respective peers.

Influential people of all levels organize themselves into networks that criss-cross existing networks in their community. Networks will vary widely in their features and formal openness to diffusing innovation. That is because networks do not operate in a social vacuum: they are features of a social structure. In traditional rural communities, communication obviously flows through a tight network of family, neighbours and local institutions or hierarchies. Moreover, the prevailing mindset stresses continuity plus the wisdom and emotional security of tradition and set ways. So any innovation meets prejudice at the outset. In industrial society, however, networks are highly specialized and this prejudice is absent. For example, a network of small town physicians constitutes a relatively autonomous network. Their special training isolates them from the population at large in so far as medicine is concerned and they will entertain privileged relations among each other. In addition, scientific training has habituated them to medical innovations. Therefore they readily subscribe to the value system of industrial society which extols innovation and change at the expense of the status quo and all that is familiar.

In either case, the form and existence of communication networks explain innovation diffusion. We still have very few data to correlate diffusion studies with network studies, but the next two examples will argue the issue and point up some differences.

Both examples involve a new methodological approach to diffusion studies. Early diffusion studies took scant account of interpersonal relations. Then they took them into account to understand the opinion-building process. It was not until Coleman et al. (1966) that studies attached real importance to the influence of effective social structures. And here, network analysis proved invaluable because it is specifically designed to ferret out the structure of communication within a system. Network analysis alone offers a systematic tool to reconstruct message flow and the structure that accommodates it. This is a key point because human interaction is the essence of innovation diffusion, the transmission of a new idea from one person to the next. As Everett Rogers (1979) writes: 'Any given individual in a system is likely to contact certain other individuals, and to ignore many others. As these interpersonal communication flows become patterned over time, a communication structure emerges and is predictive of behavior. Basically, communication network analysis describes these linkages in an interpersonal communication structure.' The example we shall borrow from Coleman et al. (1966) is more than illustrative and has spawned new lines of research. It concerns the diffusion of a new drug among physicians in four Midwestern cities.

The study surveyed how physicians decided whether or not to prescribe a new antibiotic. The Coleman team interviewed a survey population of 216 respondents and accessed all local pharmacy prescription records. This made it possible to check prescription information from physicians against the prescriptions themselves, a big advantage over most studies which usually work exclusively with respondents' responses. Interviews covered the career background, personal attitude to medicine, information sources and personal network of each respondent.

The drug diffused quickly in this homogeneous, highly specialized community. Within two months of commercial release, 15% of physicians had already prescribed it. The figure rose to 50% after six months and to 87% at the time of study, 17 months post-release. On a graph, diffusion makes a steep linear climb until the eighth month after release, when it arches over into a horizontal line. But the S-curve lacks the standard first segment, suggesting a population with no pioneers or trendsetters. This is superficially unsurprising: extensive testing precedes FDA approval. However, the first physicians to prescribe this antibiotic only prescribed it to limited numbers of patients and waited a certain time before expanding prescriptions to cover all medical indications. So there were trendsetters after all, who set up their own personal experiments on the drug. Extensive FDA testing does not completely obviate the need for 'a little personal experiment'. Such experiments proved conclusive for most physicians who would then go on to prescribe it on a routine basis. Trendsetters shared the following common traits:

1   regular contact with the local medical school
2   regular attendance at medical conventions

3   regular subscription to several medical journals
4   above-average contacts with pharmaceutical representatives
5   self-image as a scientist keeping abreast of his field rather than a doctor
    devoted to his patients
6   less than 25 years of medical practice.

These differences are not very pronounced and the decision-making process
is the same for trendsetters and followers in general (except for personal
experiments). Pharmaceutical representatives were cited as the information
source by 57% of physicians; periodicals and colleagues scored 33% and
10% respectively. Decisions were reached quickly in all cases and followed
consultation with colleagues. The most common information path is:
pharmaceutical representative; verification in the literature; confirmation
and moral support from colleagues. The entire sequence is the same for all
physicians.
   In such a homogeneous environment where the first prescribers rapidly
acquire a majority following, we can legitimately wonder if personal networks serve any real purpose, if in fact each physician isn't actually making
decisions all by himself purely as a function of her personal speed of
assimilating information and acting on it. The Coleman team answered this
by dividing the physicians into two groups: those who maintained links to
medical institutions and formal networks and those who did not. The curve
for the first group climbs fast and levels off after eight months, while the
curve for others is sinewy and almost flat until it starts ascension when the
first curve flattens out. So a strong network effect is at work in the first
group with a weaker effect for the second. Interpersonal relations play a
critical role here as elsewhere, even in the individualistic world of private
medical practice.
   The study asked respondents who they solicited for advice, medical shop
talk, and socializing. Trendsetters turned out to be those cited for all three
categories. Trendsetting physicians may well prove to be network hubs
precisely because of their popularity in their medical communities. But we
must consider the network as a whole to understand the diffusion process.
Here we see that diffusion of the new antibiotic occurred in four phases:

1   Dense professional links mediated influence to promote it.
2   Dense friendship links mediated this influence.
3   Isolated physicians responded to influence from their colleagues as a
    body.
4   Actual decision was made independent of links to colleagues.

The next example illustrates the same paradigm in an environment where
tradition carries far more weight. The study concerns family planning in
rural South Korea as researched by Rogers et al. (Park et al., 1974).
Interviews covered 1,000 women of childbearing age in 24 villages. We
shall restrict ourselves to 39 interviews in two villages he surveyed.

Village A was a family planning success story with 57% of couples practising, against only 26% in village B, although both villages had received comparable exposure to the nationwide campaign on birth control methods. The difference results from the following comparisons of the two village networks:

1   Informal clique structures overlap more extensively with the mothers' clubs in village A than in B.
2   Opinion leaders had closer links to the mothers' clubs in A and supported family planning.
3   The mother's club leader in A held a far more central position in the village communication network.

Rogers revisited these villages in 1975 and was unsurprised to learn that the mothers' club in B had folded. Incompetent leadership, financial problems and clique rivalries had won out.

Personal network data also confirmed the importance of each person's relational environment. Rogers notes that a respondent stands a high probability of adopting an innovation once half her personal network has done so.

However, we must distinguish between weak links and strong. Every ego network consists of both strong homophilic and weak heterophilic relations, all more or less interconnected. Homophily and attraction facilitate communication but simultaneously operate to resist new ideas. Paradoxically, strongly interconnected networks have low innovational potential (Rogers and Shoemaker, 1971). Networks need a minimum of heterophily and weak links if information is to flow easily from clique to clique. As explained in Chapter 8, we have an important concept here: it is weak links that integrate a network. Links between cliques in the two Korean villages proved weak (i.e. heterophilic) but strong (i.e. homophilic) within each. But in village A, the more numerous interclique links appear to have secured better integration than in village B, marked by high interclique rivalry.

Diffusion networks clearly vary with the type of innovation involved and how taboo-sensitive it is. When Rogers was testing this hypothesis, he compared three networks in each village: friendship, family planning discussion and abortion fixing. He selected them because they represented three levels of taboo sensitivity. Abortion must have been highly sensitive because it had been legalized only months before the study began. For both villages, contact numbers fall from friendship to family planning to abortion, i.e. the greater the taboo sensitivity, the lower the frequency of communications. Table 7.1 shows that taboo subjects are discussed in networks of moderate connectivity approached through weak links. This seems odd at first but is probably because individuals prefer to exploit structural holes for delicate subjects in order to avoid any boomerang effects that strong links might engender. Ferrand (1991) found similar results in a study of confidant networks in France (i.e. networks for

Table 7.1   Discussion of taboo subjects

Connectivity level	Village A			Village B		
	Friendship	Family planning	Abortion	Friendship	Family planning	Abortion
Village index	0.10	0.09	0.01	0.13	0.11	0.05
Average clique index	0.64	0.52	Nil	0.70	0.50	0.30
Average strength	2.90	2.90	1.00	3.30	3.20	1.60

Source: Rogers, 1979

sharing intimate secrets). He reports individuals select confidants among people who know each other very little or not at all.

We shall now proceed to methods that bring in additional criteria to test global network influence on diffusion.

Network Impact on Diffusion

The preceding studies show that innovation diffusion operates through mechanisms of interpersonal influence. Thus the formal features of a network shoulder the main responsibility for the dynamics involved (Valente, 1995). We shall show how to measure dynamics with an example that contains a sociometric choice matrix. It enables us to test various reticular effects, which would be impossible with dyadic closeness indices only. The example assumes that we know the time it takes each person to adopt the innovation from the time of introduction at t_0. We shall also assume that the form of the network explains the diffusion process and use that to discover how contagious one person's words and deeds are upon others. We shall consider the hypothesis valid if a person's position in a network correlates with the time needed by all other members to adopt an innovation, especially if we can demonstrate that their mimicking time is inversely proportional to individual distance from that person.

For notation purposes, t_i is the time it takes ego i to adopt an innovation and t_j is the mimicking time for network comember j. Contagion is deemed network-dependent when the relationship between t_i and t_j is a function of the weighting w_{ij} that the network attributes to the i–j relation.

Thus we must begin by assigning a value to w_{ij}. For convenience, we shall establish a scale from 0 to 1 with the following constraints:

(a)   The sum of weightings for a given i is 100% ($\sum_j w_{ij} = 1$).
(b) $w_{ii} = 0$ (individuals exert no self-influence).

The closer w_{ij} is to 1, the faster i mimics j's adoption of an innovation. To be consistent with our hypothesis, we shall weight the i–j relation as a strict function of the closeness in the network. However, we have already seen several ways of judging closeness. We can choose among cohesion and regular, structural or autonomous equivalence. We have no special reason *a priori* to prefer any of them to establish w_{ij} and must wait until we see which best fits the empirical data.

Cohesion rates the distance between two individuals as a function of how many clique (or pseudo-clique) affiliations they share. If the cohesion model is valid, influence is due to contact closeness. The higher the density of a dyadic relation, the faster and more efficacious the influence should be. This assumption is based on a simple idea we can illustrate with a network containing individuals A, B and C. If A adopts an innovation, C's chances of mimicking him rise as her path length to A falls. If A, B and C are a chain in that order, C has no chance of mimicry until B is won over. In a clique with a direct A to C link, however, B and C can adopt the innovation simultaneously. From the standpoint of persuasion, the clique configuration minimizes mimicking time. If C resists B's influence for any reason, it will still take her less time to adopt the innovation in a clique than in a chain because she may trust A more and will therefore be more receptive to her influence.

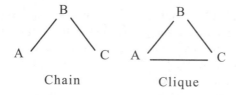

Chain   Clique

In short, the shorter the influence path between two people and the denser the network, the greater the chances one actor will replace another to persuade the ego to adopt an innovation.

Chapter 4 outlined the various ways of measuring dyadic cohesion. Burt derives a Z closeness matrix and z_{ij} from an O sociometric choice matrix (see Chapter 3). We also need to select which type of connectivity will best measure cohesion. To obtain a matrix of symmetrical closeness indices, we must select minimum and maximum values for (z_{ij}, z_{ji}) that will define strong and weak connectivity respectively. We shall assume $z_{ii} = 1$ if the ego has zero links. Burt (1992b) goes on to define π_{ij} as the weighting that will indicate to what degree t_j can replace t_i as follows:

$$\pi_{ij} = \frac{(z_{ij})^v}{\sum_q (z_{iq})^v}, \quad 0 \leq \pi_{ij} \leq 1, \quad \sum_j \pi_{ij} = 1$$

The final weighting for w_{ij} in the i–j relation is given by

$$w_{ij} = \pi_{ij}/(1 - \pi_{ii}) \quad \text{such that } w_{ii} = 0 \text{ and } \sum_j w_{ij} = 1$$

In the equation for π_{ij}, the exponent v serves to vary the range of influence on the ego. This value is a real number not equal to zero, with relational weightings proportional to the structural conditions involved. If $v=1$, the relational weighting is proportional to the structural conditions observed. An individual who cites four persons will see his relation to each weighted at 0.25. The more v exceeds 1, the greater the influence of those persons closest to him. The value for v cannot be determined *a priori* and requires testing, using criteria we shall examine, over a range of values until we find the best model of contagion.

Alternatively, we can use equivalence to measure dyadic closeness. With this yardstick, two people are assumed to adopt an innovation simultaneously because they are equivalent in a network, without necessarily sharing a direct link. Using structural equivalence, we apply Burt's technique of deriving the closeness index from a matrix using Euclidean distances between individuals (as used to obtain 'statistical' structural distance in Chapter 4). If d_{ij} is the distance between i and j, closeness is given by $d_{i\max} - d_{ij}$ (where $d_{i\max}$ is the greatest distance to i). We then calculate π_{ij} and w_{ij} as above (by replacing z_{ij} with the closeness index in the formula for π_{ij}).

The network effect on contagion (i.e. dyadic cohesion or equivalence) can be determined either as a global value for the network or for any member dyad. Finding a global network value is a matter of simple regression analysis using $t_i = (a\bar{t}_i + b) + e_i$ or equivalently $\hat{t}_i = a\bar{t}_i + b$, where e_i is the time interval between observed time t_i and the time interval t_i, estimated by the simple linear model; a is the slope and b is the intercept for the least squares regression line; $\bar{t}_i$ is the weighted average (for w_{ij} relations) of mimicking delays for all other individuals, thus $\bar{t}_i = \sum_j w_{ij} t_j$. If relations are correctly weighted and found to affect contagion, the model gives significant estimates for t_i. This is done by routinely obtaining the linear correlation coefficient and testing for significance.

Another way of assessing the effect of relations on contagion is to examine each dyad and compare mimicking times to see if they occur as a decreasing function of weightings for dyadic relations. This relation is shown in Figure 7.2, which plots weightings w_{ij} along the abscissa and absolute values for mimicking time differentials $|t_i - t_j|$ along the ordinate. The structure is deemed to affect contagion (low w_{ij} values imply high $|t_i - t_j|$ and vice versa) if points are found to cluster along a broadly downward curve (which may be worth trying to model). This sort of graph shows that

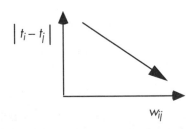

Figure 7.2   Contagion as an effect of weightings for dyadic relations

the stronger the link, or the equivalence between two actors (depending on how you calculate w_{ij}), the more they will tend to need the same amount of time to adopt an innovation.

Up to this point, we have been focusing on the time needed to adopt a material innovation, but this approach obviously applies to new opinions, lifestyle patterns or any other variable whose values we want to examine in terms of network effect.

There is yet another way of measuring network effect on diffusion. Forsé (1991) distinguishes four basic types of stars in directed graphs. Any social network can be pictured as a web with two types of individual relays. When a sociability study finds that A cites B who doesn't cite A (A → B), it means A is the conducting element and B only appears because A cites him. We thus speak of active citations where A cites B and passive citations where A is cited by B; in graph theory jargon, the terms translate as 'outdegree' and 'indegree' (see Chapter 3). A's set of active citations is obtained by merely adding up all the components in her row vector on the adjacency matrix, and the total for her column vector gives her passive citations. For both criteria, it may prove worthwhile to compare direct with indirect link scores by convergence, as we shall see later.[1]

We can also classify according to both weak or strong, and conductivity or dependence. Then we cross-match them to obtain four basic categories of the connectivity of an individual to those he cites or is cited by (Figure 7.3). This conveniently equips us to apply the raw data and to graph individuals by plotting passive citations along the abscissa against active citations along the ordinate. This four-part breakdown tells us which configuration applies to each person.

A glance at the diagonals on Figure 7.3 points up a state of tension between balance and imbalance. There are as many active citations in the upper left square as passive citations in the lower right square. We have a simple relay in the lower left square and a multiple relay in the upper right

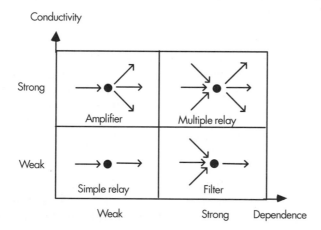

Figure 7.3   Categories of connectivity of an individual

Table 7.2   Connectivity in Nolay

Criterion	Multiple relays	Amplifiers	Filters	Simple relays
Length of residence (years)	10+	10+	10+	<10
Migration tendencies	None to low	None	Low	Higher
Age range (years)	18 to 29	30 to 44	45 to 64	65+
Job	Office/factory workers	Self-employed manual/office workers	Liberal professions, corporate executives, prominent citizens	Pensioners

Source: Forsé, 1991

one. The first diagonal is non-linear and presents a dynamic that differs radically from that of the second. But once again, we are dealing with two antithetical conditions: weak dependence and strong conductivity which yield amplification, versus strong dependence and weak conductivity which yield filtration.

Applying this grid to the Nolay survey (see Chapter 1), we see that these four types of stars coincide nicely with distinct social categories (Table 7.2).[2] We are not surprised to find conductivity correlating with long residence. Other results are less obvious but still explicable. For example, prominent citizens appear as filters, but this is because their fame attracts far more citations than they can produce themselves.

This last result suggests that each diffusion phase has a reticular form that may be the primary cause of the statistically observed accelerations and decelerations on the logistical diffusion curve. For example, the curve may take off at a shallow angle because opinion leaders operate as filters. The amplifiers and multiple relays in their wake may account for the accelerated ascent in the second curve segment, while simple relays may tilt the curve back down. But more data are needed for confirmation.

Structural Balance

The evolution of structural relations suffers from a lack of research, probably because of the difficulty of performing sequential observations over longer timespans. It is both difficult and cumbersome to monitor changes of opinion and behaviour by running a panel survey with periodic interviews of the same respondents in standard population samples. Panel surveys with relational data are worse still. Nonetheless, some studies on affinitive structure are available and instructive in terms of both results and methodology.

Social psychologists wondered early on if affinitive networks tended towards some form(s) of balance. Heider (1946) was the first to lay down the principles of what was to become the theory of structural balance. Of course, balance is a fundamental concept that permeates the entire sociometric tradition. It comes into play in any simultaneous study of two relations such as selection/rejection, cooperation/antagonism, approved/

taboo marriage, and is based on the following familiar maxims with a special twist at the end:

1 A friend of a friend is a friend.
2 An enemy of a friend is an enemy.
3 A friend of an enemy is an enemy.
4 An enemy of an enemy *might* be a friend.

We must now learn how well the behaviour of a professional society or other social group conforms to these rules. A philosophical issue is also at stake: do human groups have a natural tendency to evolve towards a state of balance? The idea dates back as least as far as Spinoza's *Ethics* (1677). The work is written as a logical treatise with propositions and demonstrations. The following propositions are from *Book III: On the Origins and Nature of Affections*. Heider (1979) quotes it as a source of inspiration and Spinoza's vision is both broader and deeper than what the theory of balance has borrowed, as we shall see:

> *Proposition XXII* If we conceive that anything pleasurably affects some object of our love, we shall be affected with love toward that thing. Contrariwise, if we conceive that it affects an object of our love painfully, we shall be affected with hatred toward it.

> *Proposition XXIII* He who conceives that an object of his hatred is painfully affected, he will feel pleasure. Contrariwise, if he think that the said object is pleasurably affected, he will feel pain. Each of these emotions will be greater or less, according as its contrary is greater or less in the object of hatred.

> *Proposition XXIV* If we conceive that anyone pleasurably affects an object of our hate, we shall feel hatred toward him also. If we conceive that he painfully affects the said object, we shall feel love toward him.

> *Proposition XXXIII* When we love a thing similar to ourselves, we endeavour, as far as we can, to bring it about that it should love us in return.

> *Proposition XLV* If a man conceives that anyone similar to himself hates anything also similar to himself, which he loves, he will hate that person.

We can express the problem formally by imagining a population with two antagonistic relations that we shall symbolize with plus and minus signs. We shall assume a complete graph, i.e. with all dyadic relations labelled as positive or negative. The theory of balance is based on the interpretation of triads according to the following categories.

In Figure 7.4, triads 1 and 2 are balanced. In triad 1, *b* and *c* both agree about *a*; they disagree about *a* in triad 2. Triads 3 and 4 are unbalanced. In triad 3, *b* and *c* agree; and they disagree in triad 4. A triad has balance if the sum of minus signs is 0 or 2. Triads showing odd sums are unbalanced.

The next step is to add up positive and negative balance for each triad in the network. These sums readily convert into the balance index that expresses the ratio of balanced to unbalanced triads. Frank Harary (1959) derives three hypotheses about relational dynamics from the index:

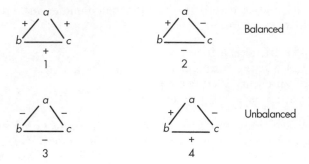

Figure 7.4   Structural balance

1   Unbalanced graphs tend toward balance.
2   Relational graphs tend toward completion.
3   Relational graphs tend toward balance.

Unfortunately, the hypotheses are formulated far too generally for empirical testing. Flament (1963) has shown that, for a complete and symmetrical graph to be balanced, it is necessary and sufficient to be able to classify all nodes in two classes such that relations within each class are all positive and relations between them negative. Nonetheless, the condition for balance remains extremely severe under a strict definition.

Most graphs reflect less than strict balance. Some are balanced, others are not. Some researchers even assert no empirical graph shows balance. Flament (1963) researched methods that would balance any graph with minimal change to plus and minus relation signs. But why assume that all graphs are complete? And why should all dyadic relations be either positive or negative? In effect, his research shifts the issue of balance toward classification possibilities for nodes.

It is more worthwhile to classify the peaks of a graph such that all positive links fall into the same block, with the negative links dispersed in the other blocks. The next graph, for example, is unbalanced but complies with this criterion.

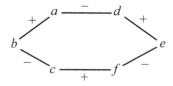

Flament (1979) also reports on an experiment where some subjects were put under stress and others left in their normal states. In the latter case, subjects preferred clustered structures (as defined above). Under stress they still prefer such structures but more weakly clustered, and they develop a distinct taste for dual-component structures.

Some of Pierre Parlebas's work on sports systems is relevant to such analysis. In 1986, he researched conductivity in athletes. Obviously, not all physical activity requires social interaction. Mountain climbing is one activity allowing single-handed interaction with nature. But most competitive sports mobilize people into teams with greater or lesser conductivity that promptly allow classification of interaction in terms of cooperation and antagonism, i.e. strict cooperation between players on the same team and strict antagonism between players on opposing teams.

This distinction becomes the criterion for node clustering on an interaction graph. Most games involve two teams playing by rules of ritualized duelling. Both teams have the same strictly antagonistic goal: a point scored by one team leaves the other down one. Such a graph is complete and all triads are present and balanced. Football and a host of other sports operate in this way. However, some sports involve three or more teams, each pitted against all others. Bicycle and relay races are but two examples where 'my enemy's enemy is my enemy too'. Multiple contestant races are type 3 triads that do not necessarily split into two blocs. While building his classification system, Parlebas encountered a great variety of sports he qualifies as competitive and institutionalized but encountered numerous non-competitive sports as well. However, he observes that the share of ritualized duelling sports continues to rise in widely televised institutional athletics (e.g. the Olympics).

Friendship and Accord

We are addressing a macrosocial tendency, but Spinoza's postulates on equilibrium are relevant on a smaller scale of analysis. They concern the evolution of affinitive relations according to agreement and disagreement among members on certain issues or on criteria for judging others. The goal is to test whether agreement encourages friendship and disagreement inhibits or severs it.

Lazarsfeld and Merton (1982) laid the foundations of this approach with a study of tolerance among 1,500 families in two very race-sensitive US cities. Agreement or disagreement on racial issues was one of two variables they used to classify dyads. The second was the existence of a friendship link. Dyads were put into one of the following categories:

FA   two friends of the same racial views
F'A   two non-friends of the same racial views
FA'   two friends of differing racial views
F'A'   two non-friends of differing racial views.

The next step was to predict how relations would evolve. *FA* and *F'A'* dyads were assumed to be more stable than the others. Lazarfeld applied Merton's qualitative analysis approach and came up with the transition

Table 7.3

Timepoint 1	Timepoint 2				Total
	FA	FA'	F'A	F'A'	
FA	50	20	10	20	100
FA'	30	20	0	50	100
F'A	50	0	40	10	100
F'A'	20	10	0	70	100
Total	150	50	50	150	400

matrix in Table 7.3 in which he starts out with 100 dyads for each category at timepoint 1 and ends up with the redistribution of dyads shown at the bottom of the table.

The number of harmonious dyads (*FA* and *F'A'*) tends to rise and the others to fall. But what happens by timepoint 3 if we hypothesize that the propensity of dyads to change categories remains stable over time (the Markov chain)? The same transition matrix now obtains the following distribution:

FA	*FA'*	*F'A*	*F'A'*
145	55	35	165

If we go on to imagine how this community evolves over a very long period, it is easy to demonstrate that the distribution ultimately stabilizes as follows:

FA	*FA'*	*F'A*	*F'A'*
133	57	24	186

Lazarfeld's interpretation of Merton's approach thus leads to a preponderance of what he calls harmonious dyads, but other dyads subsist. He points out that the stability of the transition matrix cannot be taken for granted because the overall distribution of dyads in the community as a whole may alter the probability of a dyad's migration to another category. But this leads into treacherous waters where continual observation over an extended timeframe is needed if we are to hypothesize soundly.

Lazarsfeld and Merton equated friendship with personal values. Another process, also inspired by Spinoza, concerns the evolution of affinitive relations according to whether two people share the same opinions about a third party. Johnsen (1986) studies this from a formal standpoint by considering that affinitive links are not necessarily symmetrical. A may hold a positive view of B, who may be negative or indifferent about A. This divides dyads into the following categories:

M   two positive arcs
N   two neutral or negative arcs
A   asymmetrical dyad with negative and positive arcs.

Four outcomes and their opposites are possible:

P1   People holding the same opinions of others are likely to become mutual friends (M type).

C1   People who are not mutual friends tend to hold differing opinions of others (N or A types).

P2   People who have the same opinion of others tend to have affinitive links (A or M).

C2   People who have no affinitive link tend not to have the same opinion of others (N).

P3   People who have affinitive links tend to have the same opinion of others (A or M).

C3   People who do not have the same opinion of others tend not to have affinitive links (N).

P4   People who are friends tend to have the same opinion of others (M).

C4   People who do not have the same opinion of others tend not be mutual friends (A or N).

Johnsen considers all 16 possible triads to see which propositions actually describe behaviour in a social structure (Figure 7.5).

Some triads are obviously compatible with Johnsen's propositions, others are not. For example, triad 2 confounds P1 because triad members 2 and 3 are not *mutual* friends but have the same opinion of member 1. However, triad 1 conforms to all eight propositions. If we hypothesize that only one of the propositions is true at the moment the process has become stable, then only triads compatible with that proposition should remain. Table 7.4 enumerates triad compatibility with each proposition.

The third triad alone confounds all propositions. The first proposition is a more restrictive variant of the second, which includes all triads compatible with the first. Likewise, the third proposition is a restrictive variant of the fourth. The propositions are not mutually incompatible and we could base a model on the first and third. It would be defined by the triads they share, 1 and 9. Further models can be founded on all other logical combinations of propositions and triads.

We can now examine real and theoretical macrostructures and see which propositions make good or perfect fits. This is done by enumerating the compatible and incompatible triads inferred from the relevant propositions. For example, the diagram for a duel (Figure 7.6) conforms to all propositions.

But the next model is more complex. It consists of five blocks of individuals who are mutual friends (Figure 7.7). Blocks at the same level are indifferent or inimical to each other. Links between blocks of differing levels are asymmetrical but directed the same way. The result is hierarchy. This makes the structure incompatible with the first proposition. Individuals in blocks 4 and 5 agree in their opinion of individuals in blocks 2 and 3, which should incite them to greater closeness when in fact their relations are mutually inimical or indifferent.

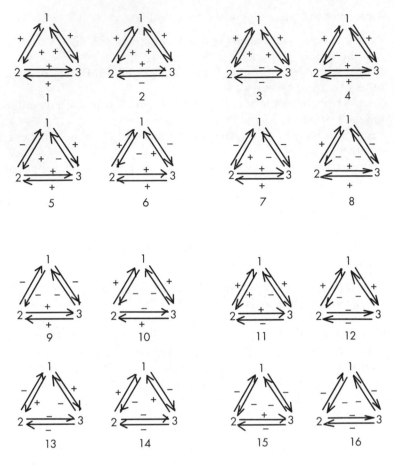

Figure 7.5   Types of signed triads

Table 7.4

Proposition	Triads
P1	1, 6, 8, 9, 10
P2	1, 2, 4, 5, 6, 8, 9, 10, 11, 12
P3	1, 5, 9, 14, 15, 16
P4	1, 5, 6, 7, 9, 10, 11, 12, 13, 14, 15, 16

Johnsen applied this approach to several examples of sociometric structures he culled from the literature. He found that the third and fourth propositions gave better fits than the other two. So, friendship sooner implies agreement than vice versa. Notwithstanding, the process is not yet well understood and needs longitudinal surveys plus detailed investigation in the context of how affinitive relations evolve over time (see Maisonneuve and Lamy, 1993).

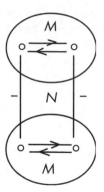

Figure 7.6   Duel between clusters

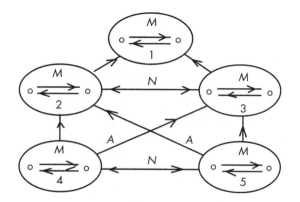

Figure 7.7   Emerging hierarchy from not necessarily symmetrical links

Collective Decision Models

With a yardstick for direct influence of actors on one another, we can determine each actor's pre-eminence, or personal power relative to the power in circulation from other network members. The next step is to weave these structural data into a model of the opinion-building and decision-making processes.

Coleman (1990) and Frans Stokman and Van den Bos (1992) have designed collective decision models of particular interest. Although sophisticated and tailored to specific contexts, both share a number of common principles which we shall broadly review using the notation of Stokman and Van den Bos.

The models assume a set of N actors concerned about a collective decision whose payoff is K. We also add in the following:

1   The power of any actor i over any collective decision k is expressed by v_{ik}, where V is the matrix of v_{ik}. It has N rows and K columns.
2   s_{ki} is the importance of collective decision k to actor i, where S is the matrix of s_{ki}. It has K rows and N columns.
3   c_{ij} is the estimated value of i's ability to influence fellow actor j, where C is the matrix of c_{ij}. It has N rows and N columns.
4   r_i is the resources i can bring to bear on fellow actors to affect the decision.

Given the above, c_{ij} is i's capacity to influence j as obtained from the matrix for element a_{ij} in the network: $a_{ij} = 1$ if i can contact j, and $a_{ij} = 0$ if he cannot. Thus we obtain

$$c_{ij} = \frac{(r_i a_{ij})}{r_j + \sum_{k=1}^{N} r_k a_{kj}}, \quad k \neq j$$

This model simply says that one actor's power to influence another is the sum of her resources plus the fact that she can contact him. The hypotheses are easier to fathom if we review the definition of an actor's power given in Chapter 6. But here power depends on an entire set of decisions.

If we disregard the network for the moment and focus on each actor's personal power over various decisions (expressed in matrix V) and the importance of the decisions to each actor (matrix S), then an actor's power (matrix P) is obtained with the formula $P = VSP$. In this case, an actor's power includes his capacity to influence decisions of importance to others. Such is the logic of a collective decision model.

If we take the network into account, we have an influence model that defines an actor's power as her ability to influence others about important decisions. Power is now given by $P = CVSP$.

If we elect to consider influence and decision-making as two distinct phases, we can merge the models in $P = CVSP + VSP = (CV + V)\,SP$.

Stokman finds the above models static and suggests a two-step model. The first step consists of interactive influence, a process where actor i's position on decision k at time $t + 1$ depends on time t, the capacity of others to influence the decision and the importance of the decisions to all actors. The formula is

$$x_{ik}^{(t+1)} = \frac{\sum_j s_{jk} x_{jk}^{(t)} c_{ji}}{\sum_j s_{jk} c_{ji}}$$

Decisions are taken once the influence process is over. For decision k at a given t, the probable outcome depends on the position of each actor, which in turn depends on the influence process and each actor's power over the decision. Outcome is given by

$$o_k^{(t)} = \frac{\sum_i x_{ik}^{(t)} p_{ik}}{\sum_i p_{ik}}$$

The models are conceptually elegant, but need huge input to test real-life decision-making processes. In particular, we need estimates for p_{ik} which express every actor's personal power over every decision. In a political context, we might look at each legislator's ability to put across her position in subcommittees, lobbies and other meetings upstream of the vote. But it is probably easier to work from an actor matrix although secret contacts may also weigh into the final decision.

The model is also difficult to apply in the field because it assumes a closed system with no external influences: once the actors have been locked into position, the system develops a dynamic of its own making. This was a major reason behind the disappointing results that Stokman and Van den Bos obtained from Laumann and Knoke's data on a series of US energy policy decisions. However, a simulation of the influence phase did show that the initial positions of the actors evolved as a function of other actors' positions and contacts in the network. The application of such models to real-life situations and careful autopsy of failures will continue to improve our understanding of collective decision processes in institutional settings.

Microeconomic View of Network Equilibrium

We have already seen that power is not necessarily distributed evenly throughout a network. Indeed, such is the case for most exchange relations. This steers us back to the question of inferring balance from observation of ongoing relations. Assuming that networks tend toward balance, we should be able to formulate hypotheses that will help predict outcome.

Burt (1992b) approaches this issue by distinguishing situations where actors are substitutable from those where they are not. The configuration with non-substitutable actors is simplest. It assumes independent actors. We now apply an equilibrium model similar to that developed by Coleman in the late 1960s (Coleman, 1966; 1973). Assuming rational behaviour, we can proceed to study interactions from a microeconomic standpoint.

We shall assume all actors can buy or sell relations on a competitive market. Actor i steps into the market with, of course, his own interests in mind, but also with a set of relations which other actors broadly value at price w_i. She can now use her own relational capital to bargain for other relations. On the marketplace, i's interest in j or in the potential usefulness of the $i-j$ relation can be expressed as an indicator of the strength of the $i-j$

relation. We shall call this indicator z_{ij}, and Burt's formula (see Chapter 3) is one way of obtaining it. We shall apply the following two constraints:

$$\sum_j z_{ij} = 1 \quad \text{and} \quad 0 \le z_{ij} \le 1$$

Thus $w_i z_{ij}$ is the proportion of resources i will commit to interacting with j.

That said, j's network also has a price tag or global utility value p_j. Therefore we have to strike a balance between i's supply and j's demand, and that equilibrium, if indeed it exists, must obviously occur simultaneously for all (i, j) pairs in the network. We shall suppose e_{ji} represents what i stands to receive when the network is in a state of equilibrium, subject to the two constraints just imposed:

$$\sum_j e_{ji} = 1 \quad \text{and} \quad 0 \le e_{ji} \le 1$$

The price of the relation with j at equilibrium becomes $p_j e_{ji}$. But equilibrium supposes that this price matches the resources i is prepared to commit to a relation with j. Thus the equation for equilibrium is

$$w_i z_{ij} = p_j e_{ji}$$

The problem is to find e_{ji}. We start by assuming unfettered competition, so that the value of $i(w_i)$ equals the purchase price of her network p_i. This allows us to reformulate the above equation as

$$p_i z_{ij} = p_j e_{ji}$$

or

$$e_{ji} = z_{ij} \left(\frac{p_i}{p_j} \right), \quad p_j \ne 0$$

Because the relation is symmetrical at i and j, we have equivalently

$$e_{ij} = z_{ji} \left(\frac{p_j}{p_i} \right), \quad p_i \ne 0$$

The value for z_{ij} is known here, but what about p_i and p_j? According to the equilibrium equation, we have $\sum_i p_i z_{ij} = p_j \sum_i e_{ji}$ and since $\sum_i e_{ji} = 1$, it follows that $p_j = \sum_i p_i z_{ij}$. We instantly see the analogy with the equations in Chapter 6 for actor power. What we are calling the 'price tag' here, or the utility value of i's network, can also be understood as i's power. Quite logically, i's market value climbs as she accumulates power. Now that we have an algorithmic solution to every actor's power in the network, we can easily move on to calculate the value of equilibrium between any pair of actors.

For every i, we have an observed relation to j, namely z_{ij}, and a value for equilibrium e_{ij}. The margin for outcome is given by the difference between these two values, assuming there is a general tendency toward equilibrium. Burt suggests linear regression to evaluate the global dynamic potential of the network. Assuming $\hat{e} = az + b$ (where a and b are estimated by least squares), we obtain a linear correlation coefficient for effective relations and equilibrium. Strong values for this coefficient indicate practically no gap between the two actors. Low values indicate strong non-equilibrium in effective relations and therefore a wide margin for outcome.

All of the above assumes non-substitutable actors. However, many market and other situations involve substitutable actors and this requires a more sophisticated model.

We shall imagine i is prepared to interact with k, and s_{jk} expresses how easily i can replace k with someone else (with the usual pair of constraints $\sum_i s_{jk} = 1$ and $0 \leq s_{jk} \leq 1$). Burt recommends establishing substitutability by evaluating the structural equivalence of j and k. Other criteria are possible, but we can reasonably suppose that the more two actors are structurally equivalent, the easier the one will replace the other. We can therefore copy Burt and write

$$s_{jk} = \frac{(d_{\max k} - d_{jk})^p}{\sum_l (d_{\max k} - d_{lk})^p}$$

where d_{jk} is the Euclidean distance between j and k (see Chapter 3). In this fraction, p is a positive integer whose value is determined a priori to vary the degree to which i can replace j and k according to their equivalence. The minimum value for p is 0 and reflects total substitutability. The value approaches independence as it rises in the manner already shown. Finally, we select the value that best suits the available data for the network and the hypothesis we want to test.

Now j's perceived value to i in the i–j relation always remains z_{ij}, but the second model uses u_{ij} to express the actual market value of interacting with j which varies with the perceived value of k (where j is a potential replacement). We thus have $u_{ij} = \sum_k z_{ik} s_{jk}$. This formula implies that j is not substitutable if $u_{ij} = z_{ij}$. Where $u_{ij} > z_{ij}$, j can replace k but k is the more valuable alternative. Where $u_{ij} < z_{ij}$, j can replace k and j is more valuable. In short, the greater the importance of the i–k relation to i and the better j can replace k, the more valuable the i–j relation is to i.

Returning to our equilibrium analysis, we need only substitute u_{ij} for z_{ij} in the equilibrium equation for independent actors. If replacements are possible, we have

$$e_{ji} = u_{ij} \left(\frac{p_i}{p_j} \right), \quad p_j \neq 0, \quad p_j = \sum_i p_i u_{ij}$$

As above, p_i and p_j are values for the power of i and j. However, they must be recalculated because they should be based on u_{ij} and not z_{ij} as before. Here, power depends not only on strong links to other powerful actors but also on substitutability by other actors in the network. That distinction having been made, we perform the same calculations as before with the second model and interpret the results in the same way. In particular, the gap between the value of a relation in a state of equilibrium and the actual market value of the relation (after substitutability has been reckoned in) reflects once again the network's margin for outcome.

Notes

1 Chapter 3 explains that these scores are obtained by raising adjacency matrices through succeeding powers. It is worth testing to find at what point raising by powers stops modifying the rankings of individuals as a function of the number of indirect active or passive citations they obtain. According to the Perron–Frobenius theorem, rankings of individuals always reach a stable configuration (see Berge, 1967: 128–131). We call it the convergence state.
2 The same holds true with data on indirect links at the convergence state.

8   MULTIPLE AFFILIATIONS

The literature on social networks frequently refers to dyadic relations between individuals and to those between groups. Examples of groups include alumni associations or Masonic lodges. The term 'network' most often has a colloquial rather than a sociological meaning. It is a shotgun term for the links people must be sharing if they belong to some sort of entity with relational coherence. Likewise, the literature treats networks both as a set of relations among all members and as an aggregate of dyadic relations. We build models of relational groups based on cliques or sets of structurally equivalent actors while others try to shift the focus off groups and into dyadic relations, as occurs when we try to infer a network from who frequents a particular place.

But are these two approaches describing two different realities? The origins of these two opposing approaches lie partly in the history of sociology. Social psychologists have concentrated on sociometric data that express, say, who selects whom to perform a certain task in a group. Ethnologists tend to find it more natural to frame interaction around real-life social groups. When analysing the elementary links of kinship, clans are more readily identifiable than the relations that create them.

From a purely formal standpoint, there is no special reason to select dyads as the building blocks of structure. Or as the unique units of a network. Nothing stops us from perceiving a network as a set of units of varying sizes, provided they are relevant. Mathematics encourages such generalization through its own practice of generalizing graphs into hypergraphs (see Appendix). A hypergraph is a family of subsets, just as a graph is a set of dyads. As noted in Chapter 2, some sociologists have chosen sets of individuals as the basic units of social structure. They call these units 'social circles' (Kadushin, 1966; 1968; Seidman, 1981; Foster and Seidman, 1982).

But every society presents a wide range of social circles and any individual belongs to several. In each case, membership takes a different form that structures relations in a specific way. This is the focus of the present chapter. But first we need a good definition for 'social circle'.

Social Circles

The colloquial meaning of a circle is a group of people who know each other and share affinitive links, but structural analysis needs a more precise definition. The matrices in Chapter 3 help establish more formal distinctions we can use to explore structure more extensively.

Circle Types and Principles of Definition

We shall imagine a given population and formulate a very general idea of relations. We construct a binary matrix for a particular interpersonal link. It may be based on real or symbolic personal attributes, or perhaps the circumstances in which the relation is established or maintained. It may be governed by social norms. We measure the relevance of each complementary factor by adding an extra matrix to the relational matrix. For example, one matrix column might stand for a PhD. If individual i has one, we put a 1 in the cell where row i intersects that column. This correlates the fact that i has a PhD with the specific relation that it sets up to less educated j.

Likewise, we use columns to indicate events that population members do or do not attend. This matches up an interpersonal link such as friendship with an activity such as frequenting the same restaurants or social events.

We can also add columns for rules that accompany certain roles. Complementary data will vary enormously but this does not mean we are adding apples and oranges. In fact, each element preserves its specific features and all that changes is the way they are represented for input to the graph.

The matrix we shall use for our analysis is the following. Here, X is a population with x_i elements such that every X we insert corresponds to a set of rows and columns for all x_i elements; and $Y1$, $Y2$, $Y3$ stand for sets of attributes expressed as $y1_i$, $y2_i$, $y3_i$ . . . .

	X	$Y1$ $Y2$ $Y3$
X	XX	XY
$Y1$ $Y2$ $Y3$		Y_iY_j

The $X \times X$ submatrix shows links between individuals for whatever relation is being studied, and we fill in interactions according to our predefined criteria. The $X \times Y$ areas match up attributes with the individuals who have them. The $Y_i \times Y_j$ areas match up attributes among themselves where needed. This matrix is very schematic and is rarely applied to real field data, but it has the virtue of pinning down the parameters being analysed in a network. The $X \times X$ submatrix accommodates several types of blocks, i.e. rectangles depicting a relation between certain rows and columns (Table 8.1).

Table 8.1

	X1	X2	X3	X4	Y1	Y2
X1			1111 11**S**1 1111		1011 0101 0010	
X2		1111 11**C**1 1111 1111 111				0111 0101 0111 0010
X3						
X4				1010 O**R**10 1011 0101		1111 1111 1111 1111

C blocks

A C block consists of the blocks along a diagonal. Any block filled with 1 shows that the individuals in it share links. If there is a 1 in every block along the diagonal, the corresponding individuals amount to a clique where everybody knows everybody. Whence the name: C for clique. C blocks depict affinitive groups.

S blocks

The S stands for structural equivalence and the blocks are rectangular because they express relations between A and B, two distinct groupings in a given population. They consist entirely of 1s and mean that every member of A interacts with every member of B, which is automorphic or structural equivalence by definition. In real life, this may mean compulsory relations or even warfare and banishment.

R blocks

R is for regular. As above, these are rectangles that match up two distinct submatrices. However we do not assume they all have a 1. The minimum requirement for an R block is that everyone in A has a relation to at least one member of B. Here we recognize the familiar criterion that defines regular equivalence and differentiates roles.

P blocks

P is as in partition. We shall define P blocks by examining the submatrices that match up our population with various attributes or complementary elements. All possible blocks of this type are rectangular and we may consider them as containing 1s or as at least being R blocks. A block full of 1s bundles people who share the same attributes or find themselves in the same place at the same time. An R block means an individual needs at least one group attribute to belong to the group. These conditions may alternate or even cumulate. We can also resort to all manner of blocks with densities intermediate to a straightforward R block and a block of 1s. At this point the concept of similarity comes into play, which says that the more attributes two individuals have in common, the more similar they will be, and that groups will coalesce according to similarities among people.

All of these blocks serve to identify three principles that define groups. The first is *cohesion*. We see cohesion in C blocks. The group is defined by the links of its members. Relations here are usually affinitive.

The second is *identity*. Identity is a relation of distinctness or opposition. We see it in S blocks which are non-diagonal and carry 1s. In reality, S blocks define strict opposition between two groups. Every member of one group is different from every member of the second. In real life, it can cover a wide range of situations. It may mean a distinctive fraction of the population which gives itself a special identity, e.g. through exclusive rites and rituals such as Christian baptism; or emblems like scout uniforms. Extreme opposition is another example. War pits all citizens of one nation against all those of another. Another variant is when a group elects to reject certain members, as happens to criminals, heretics and scapegoats. Groups establish their identity by whom they reject. The identity principle engenders special attributes that identify who is in or who is out. ID cards, membership cards and criminal records all operate according to the identity principle.

The third is *complementary roles*. It appears in R blocks and shows exchange. Two subsets distinguish themselves by establishing and pursuing correlating roles. Complementary roles show up in university degrees and military rank insignia, for example. In most populations, all three principles operate simultaneously and lead to the identification of three types of groups (Figure 8.1).

What then is a social circle? Well, the first thing to look at is the personal involvement of people in their relations. If 'social circle' is to have a truly operational definition and we follow Bouglé's assertion that membership in a circle influences the behaviour of all members, then we logically infer that the identity principle is operative. Thus, a group of people is not a social circle simply because everyone knows everyone or helps each other. We can speak of a circle if members knowingly admit to membership and membership affects member behaviour in some way.

It is not enough for an individual to belong to a clique in a relational graph or for her to shoulder a role with which she does not identify. We must take account of all groups that the individual knowingly belongs to, so that we can study her behaviour as a function of what each group suggests or requires.

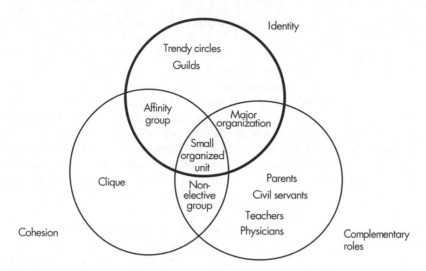

Figure 8.1   Principles defining circles

Strictly speaking, 'social circle' thus designates groups founded on the basis of mutual recognition. Some circles operate exclusively on the identity principle but organizations use both identity and complementary roles while affinity groups rely on identity and cohesion. Other circles operate all three principles. Strict circles are shown in bold on Figure 8.1, with normal lines for circles in the looser sense of the term.

The next question is how personal attributes contribute to circle building. Don't spots somehow make a leopard? In practice, this question only arises with complementary roles, because the emblems of mutual recognition merge with actual membership if the identity principle is operating alone, while affinity groups need to coopt if they are to survive. Returning to complementary roles, this principle may furnish the primary drive to form a group at the outset before other traits develop that lend permanence to the social relation, e.g. the soldier whose leadership skills result in a battlefield commission that carries over into the peace that follows. In short, the relation engenders the attribute. Meritocracies, however, operate the other way around.

Civil services use competitive examinations and education to screen who they hire and to confer responsibilities. This illustrates how one social relation (authority) becomes institutionalized on the basis of an attribute acquired in a very different social relation (education). Generally, personal traits do affect role attribution but are most often only prerequisites or are insufficient in themselves.

Nonetheless, rules and norms are hallmarks of any social circle. The identity principle is sovereign and defines the basis for inclusion in the group and mutual recognition. We then bring in the other two principles so that we can qualify circles and understand how they tick. Role differentiation will be greater in some circles than others, and interaction levels will be more or less personal.

Marx basically defines a social class as a set of structurally equivalent individuals but this does not suffice to describe a social circle. We only have a circle once members become aware of their equivalence and start constructing a common identity. This is what he calls a 'class in its own right'. The trouble is that several alternative identities are simultaneously operative. A factory worker may identify with the working class but he also identifies with his employer and performs according to company expectations. This can spin off role tension and conflict because the behaviour his company expects of him may not square with the behaviour the working class expects of him, especially if he joins a labour union or radical party. Individuals juggle allegiances as best they can to further their own self-interest at any given moment: this is called personal freedom.

This chapter started by asking what difference it would make to our perspective if we defined social structure in terms of social circles and not interpersonal links. We should have a good feel for the answer by now. From an objective posture, the most natural approach is to graph binary interactions and disregard the effects of external allegiances on them. Graph analysis is indeed the best available way of studying informal links or just relative social positions (Degenne, 1986). But if the target is to understand an individual's commitment to a relation, i.e. his degree of identification with the circle in which the interaction occurs, then we must speak circle language. This language is especially well suited to studying the genesis of rules and norms but also role differentiation in social circles. The two viewpoints are complementary, not mutually exclusive, but any confusion will inflict major damage right down to the level of data gathering.

In establishing his renowned distinction between mechanical and organic solidarity, Durkheim's sights were set on role differentiation and the genesis of rules. As an example, we shall reassess his reasoning from a social circle perspective.

Mechanical and Organic Solidarity

In *The Division of Social Labour*, Durkheim (1893) sets out to found 'the science of morality'. Noting that society increased both individual autonomy and solidarity as it evolved from tribal to industrial, he attempted to explain the apparent paradox in terms of changes in the division of labour. He built his model around fundamental rules important enough to warrant punishment if broken. By tracking down a history of law in this way, he came to distinguish two types of solidarity.

His concept of mechanical solidarity is straightforward. A society builds its identity on what it condemns. It stakes out the limits of acceptable behaviour with criminal law. Because the individual is 'part and parcel of the collective personality', society steps in to prosecute and punish lawbreakers even where the victim is a private individual or group, as in larceny or homicide. The collective response to crime designates a guilty party, makes an example of him and isolates him for a shorter or longer time. This is the identity principle in action. Thus, mechanical solidarity ties in with structural equivalence as defined by Harrison White (1963) and Francois Lorrain (1975) when speaking of kinship (see Chapter 4). In that case, marriage and filiation rules are fundamental prohibitions in the social structure (taboos on incest) which lead to obligations of exchange.

Organic solidarity is more subtle. It does not concern membership in a homogeneous group, but participation in a structured system with clearly labelled positions for each actor. Here the rule is grounded in the system of division of labour as an organic whole where civil, not penal, law safeguards the system of interaction and ensures every member obtains his rightful share.

Mechanical solidarity sets up structural opposition between two groups. Organic solidarity plays on the diversity of interactions to assign differentiated roles. Father, boss, teacher and every other role are assigned specific types of interaction. There is also a formal difference at work: every child has a father but does not interact with all fathers, just as every boss has several subordinate employees while most employees have only one boss. Here the operating principle is complementary roles, which amounts to regular equivalence.

So Durkheim's solidarity principles overlap nicely with the principles of social circle building that matrices help bring out: mechanical solidarity fits the identity principle, and organic solidarity fits complementary roles.

Durkheim hypothesizes that interdependence and complementary roles tend to replace identity as a given society becomes increasingly complex. This suggests that the identity principle loses momentum in complex societies and gives way to role differentiation. Figure 8.2 should help put across the concept.

Societies based on mechanical solidarity consist of similar autonomous segments. Segments can be detached without jeopardy to survival. Role differentiation is minimal, so substitutability is high. In segment I, a_1 and b_1 both perform tasks x_1 and y_1. If x and y represent people instead of tasks, then a_1 and b_1 enjoy the same relations to the same people. The same is true for segment II. So we have structural equivalence. But role specialization is greater in the case of organic solidarity and division of labour. Segmentation disappears but individuals become more interdependent: a can only perform x-type tasks while b's know-how is limited to y-type jobs. Actually, we need no distinctions between x_1 and x_2 or y_1 and y_2. We can also do away with nodes of the ax or by types. We have regular equivalence.

Therefore, shifting from one solidarity to the other implies a shift of equivalence too. The first is rigid and the second more flexible. Weak role specialization and high substitutability demand structural equivalence, while more specialized and complementary roles merely require regular equivalence. Industrial society needs less reliance on structural equivalence

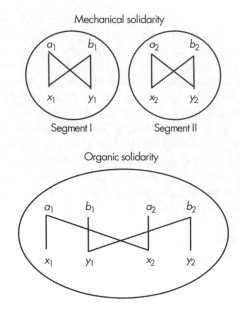

Figure 8.2   Mechanical and organic solidarity

and identity because interdependence underpins social linkage. We still obtain social integration but of a different nature, which we shall review later.

Social Circles, Normative Systems and their Imaging

If the reasoning outlined so far in this chapter is sound, norms are born of interaction. Functionalists dispute this last statement, and the explanations that follow deserve critical reading. We shall start by examining the results of an experiment. The data are from a survey of French sexual behaviour patterns (Spira et al., 1993)[1] which asked respondents the following:

> Now we're going to talk about friends, family and coworkers with whom you have talks. In your opinion, what do your friends think of someone who is having an affair with one person but has a stable relationship with someone else at the same time? What about your coworkers' opinions? What about family members?

1   All would approve.
2   Some would approve, some would not.
3   All would not approve.
4   No comment.

The main results are shown in Table 8.2.

The main lesson from the figures is that the respondents respond. They are well aware of the existence of norms on extramarital relations among

Table 8.2

	All approve (%)	Some approve (%)	All disapprove (%)	No comment (%)	Total no. respondents
Friends					
Men	15.5	52.2	18.3	14.0	1,170
Women	5.6	47.9	28.9	17.6	1,148
Total	10.7	50.1	23.5	15.7	2,318
Coworkers					
Men	13.6	47.2	13.6	25.6	1,170
Women	3.7	38.7	20.3	37.3	1,148
Total	8.7	43.0	16.9	31.4	2,318
Family					
Men	8.2	23.0	50.7	18.0	1,170
Women	4.1	20.4	60.6	14.9	1,148
Total	6.2	21.7	55.6	16.5	2,318

both family and friends. However, the response rate drops when it comes to coworkers. Thus, social circles actually exist in the minds of the respondents as places where norms are at work.

Friends are perceived as more sexually tolerant. Only 23.5% of respondents report unanimous disapproval of unfaithfulness. But family is seen as stricter and 56% of respondents expect unanimous disapproval on this point. Men perceive all circles as more tolerant than women do, and perhaps men do indeed enjoy more leeway.

But in a way, no one in particular actually comes to a respondent's mind when thinking of friends, family and coworkers. The actual people involved are friend to one respondent, coworker to a second and family to a third. When a respondent *lends* a particular opinion to someone, it is actually lending it to the circle the people are cast in. Therefore, the results confirm that social circles are the basic units that generate and operate rules and habits. When a person refers to a family member, she knows what attitudes and behaviour the family circle expects of her. She also knows her circle of friends expect another set of attitudes and behaviour.

Rule Conflict and Circle Combinations

If we accept that social circles are the wombs in which rules develop, operate and evolve, we can also accept that a rule which is operative in one circle also applies to any smaller circle it contains. Thus, the official language of a country also applies to its schools and businesses. But no rule fully governs all actors. A French company could elect to impose English as the company language, which would simply create a conflict with the prevailing national rule. Numerous studies report that speaking one language at home and another at school generates parent/child and parent/school conflicts. The same happens in other contexts. A teacher may apply unorthodox disciplinary measures, but this will trigger conflict with the school. Inversely, top management may decide on a rule that falls foul of existing rules down in the departments and out in the branch offices. It then risks an uphill fight or simply watching the rule become dead letter.

All of the above is consistent with the main point: the rules of a circle cascade onto any smaller circle it contains. Nonetheless, the actual impact of a given rule will vary with how vital that rule is to the survival of the circle. Rules have less impact on affinity circles than on complex societies that comprise a multitude of circles with a wide assortment of roles. As Durkheim (1893) notes on this point: 'Just as personal conflicts can only be contained by the regulatory action of society which envelops individuals, intersocietal conflicts can only be contained by the regulatory action of a society which comprises all others. The only power that can temper the egotism of two groups is another larger group that embraces them.'

At least in some cases, combining circles in this way will crisscross rule systems and affect individual interaction. The more circles two individuals belong to, the greater the number of rules that become applicable to any interaction. The greater the similarity between the individuals as actors, the more we would expect them to behave identically in identical circumstances.

Homogeneity and Integration

Social circles show overlap when some members of one circle belong to a second, or embedding when all members of one circle are members of a bigger circle, some of whose members do not belong to the first.

Industrial societies are awash with such multiple, but not necessarily congruent, affiliations. This can lead to tension and open conflict. Simmel (1908a) was the first to map out social circles in terms of overlap and embedding. At the personal level, we study these configurations by investigating the form and intensity of multiple affiliations as well as the effects.

Overlap   Embedding

Blau (1977) attacked this issue with a theory of social structure based on the properties of relations between circles and their intensity. He wanted to learn the effects of relations on circles and the factors that enhance them.

We shall address the question by applying a criterion such as cohesion to two circles we have identified. The first has n_1 members and the second n_2, where $n_1 > n_2$. We shall also consider that there are r relations, all symmetrical. The $r{:}n_1$ ratio expresses intergroup relations for the larger group, while $r{:}n_2$ does the same for the smaller. We now see

$$n_1 > n_2 \Rightarrow \frac{r}{n_1} < \frac{r}{n_2}$$

The smaller group is necessarily more committed to external relations than the bigger group because of its higher intergroup relations ratio. Applied to mixed marriages, this means the smaller group necessarily has a higher proportion of mixed marriages than the larger. The upshot is that external relations always exert stronger impact on a minority than the majority. Indeed, minorities seem pretty aware of this fact since many institute rules and behaviour codes to curtail external relations. When vested interests come into play as well, segregation becomes a weapon against the power of superior numbers. Here, we have a generally valid truth but, as seen, it is founded solely on arithmetic totals. We now need a few more definitions in order to pursue the issue further by discovering which structural features promote intercircle relations.

There are two standard parameters to break down populations by social positions. First we use nominal parameters that represent discrete variables such as religion, occupation and ethnic origin. Next we have graduated parameters that set up a scale of social positions and appear in studies as numerical, ordinal or qualitative variables such as education and income. In short, nominal or discrete variables express what a person *is* while graduated variables cover what he *has*. You are or are not a member of a given group but you have or do not have the income that helps qualify for a particular social status.

The heterogeneity of a given structure depends on the degree of differentiation between nominal positions. We measure this value as the probability that two individuals selected at random will belong to different groups. This definition implies that heterogeneity increases with the total number of circles and differences in circle sizes. The greater the number of circles in a network, the greater the heterogeneity, if circle sizes are the same. The greater the number of circles of the same sizes, the greater the homogeneity of the network. Inversely, the probability that two individuals will belong to the same group increases if circle sizes differ. Blau's formula for heterogeneity H_e is

$$H_e \approx 1 - \sum_{i=1}^{k} p_i^2$$

where p_i is the probability of affiliation to group i, and k is the total number of groups. Under this formula, a population that is 50% Catholic and 50% Protestant is more heterogeneous than if the split were 80%/20%.

For graduated parameters, differentiation between social positions reflects social inequality, which is defined in relative terms as the difference in social status (e.g. income gap) between any two individuals divided by the average value of the variable for the entire population.

Depending on the nature of the parameter, the problem is to establish whether the level of relations between two circles correlates with heterogeneity or social inequality. Here we need two hypotheses. First, the probability of effective interaction depends on the number of contact opportunities the circles offer. Second, social proximity in the multidimensional scale of social positions increases as the probability of interaction rises. Blau (1977; 1993) goes on to state the following theorems:

I   The probability of intergroup relations increases with the heterogeneity of a structure. In a heterogeneous structure, there is a high chance that two people belonging to different groups will meet and thus heterogeneous societies have a higher probability of intergroup relations than homogeneous societies.

II   The greater the social inequality, the higher the chances of big status gaps between any two people in a relation. The result is that greater inequality increases the chances of relations between partners of differing statuses.

III   The less ordinal or nominal social differences correlate, the greater the chances of intergroup relations. Inversely, strong correlation suggests barriers between homogeneous groups. Therefore, the chances of intergroup relations are lower.

There is an entire series of other theorems that apply to embedded structures and establish that the chances of intergroup relations rise as heterogeneity or inequality at higher levels trickles down to the lower levels or substructures. Inversely, the chances of intergroup relations fall as the correlation between social differences rises. Extensive testing in over 150 metropolises has confirmed the validity of the theorems (Blau and Schwartz, 1984). We shall overlook the details and focus on the implications of Blau's first and third theorems which bear greatest relevance to our subject because, in any event, the argument about inequality runs parallel to that for heterogeneity (Rytina et al., 1988).

We shall stay with an example that matches up only two dimensions but the results readily expand to include many more. We shall assume a study to compare the residential distribution of Catholics C and Protestants P in cities A and B. We graph the relation in standard fashion using a contingency table as follows:

	A	B
C	CA	CB
P	PA	PB

where CA is the number of Catholics living in A, and so on.

Table 8.3

		Individual j			
		CA	PA	CB	PB
	CA	h	C	C	s
Individual i	PA	C	h	s	C
	CB	C	s	h	C
	PB	s	C	C	h

Table 8.4

Type 1 city: $H = 0.75$ (heterogeneity)

	A	B
C	25	25
P	25	25

Type 2 city: $H = 0.50$ (homogeneity)

	A	B
C	50	0
P	0	50

As indicated, heterogeneity is based on the total number of possible dyads. The above four variables can combine into 16 different pairs, as shown in Table 8.3. The h dyads along the diagonal are homogeneous dyads and all others are heterogeneous. Disregard the C and s values for the time being. We shall select the two numerical extremes shown in Table 8.4. The first shows strong heterogeneity according to Blau's index (which is given by $H_{I \times J} = 1 - \sum_{i,j} p_{ij}^2$). In contrast, the second shows minimal heterogeneity (for this marginal structure).

The types in Table 8.4 deserve closer study. Type 2 cities are clearly more homogeneous than type 1 cities but the latter show more homogeneously distributed populations from a *systemic* standpoint. From this standpoint, which is not Blau's but is more commonly held, homogeneity increases as a person's probability of belonging to a given group tends to be identical to that of the other members (as measured by calculating the conditional entropy associated with the table, i.e. the entropy of I given J for the two dimensions of I and J). The paradox arises from the fact that you can form more heterogeneous dyads in an environment of systemic homogeneity, whereas heterogeneity favours greater numbers of homogeneous dyads. If the above two tables reflected marital homogamy, type 1 cities would have more heterogamous couples and thus greater mixing and systemic homogeneity than in type 2 cities, where perfect homogamy would reflect systemic heterogeneity. Both Blau's and the systemic views are soundly argued in their own ways and equally conceivable. One stresses homogeneity in dyads (or in each modality of a classification criterion) while the other bases judgement on global distribution. For simplicity's sake, we will apply Blau but reason inversely for systemic descriptions of cross-distributions.

In type 1 cities, heterogeneity translates into the sort of population distribution you would expect if religion and domicile were independent variables. They correlate weakly. They show strong correlation in type 2 cities, however. More formally, this gives the following identities:

strong status correlation ⇔ homogeneity
low status correlation ⇔ heterogeneity

These identities and their impact on intergroup relations are readily explained by homophilic bias which is definitely far stronger in a homogeneous environment (this bias surfaces when people manifest a preference for establishing relations with persons 'of their own kind' and not in random fashion). Therefore, relations are definitely established between persons of the same religious faith in each type 2 city. Inversely, relations between persons of different faiths are prone to arise in type 1 cities; although levels are not predictable, the probability of interaction between groups is clearly higher. In other words, homophilic bias is lower in heterogeneous environments. The same logic applies to interpersonal relations within each of the two types of cities and even overlaps with interfaith relations under certain conditions. If Catholics only socialize with coreligionists, there are no relations between cities A and B if the cities are homogeneous, but they do exist where A and B are heterogeneous. In summary, homogeneity is conducive to homophily which operates against intergroup relations, while heterogeneity has the opposite effect.

Homophilic tendencies explain why homogeneous social networks are less integrated than heterogeneous ones. Heterogeneous networks show more global integration because weak homophily favours greater numbers of social circles. Connectivity promotes integration here. A network of groups (as defined by a cohesion study) with few or zero intergroup links is considered less globally integrated than a network with such links. We can also distinguish between global integration and local integration within each social circle and disregard the global/local links. This suggests that homogeneity is conducive to local, not global, integration while heterogeneity promotes the latter at the expense of the former.

This leads us to a theory of integration. However, Fararo and Skvoretz (1987) have shown integration theory does not differ fundamentally from Granovetter's theory which bases integration on the strength of weak ties. Before pointing up their common ground, a brief review of Granovetter's position is in order.

Granovetter speaks of a 'forbidden triad' where individual A has strong links to B and C but the latter two share none. Now obviously, B and C have a far higher chance of establishing a relationship than if they had only been vague acquaintances. The triad is only 'forbidden' in the sense that it is unnatural and improbable: a triad with two strong links is very conducive to developing a third strong link. Consequently, if there is no third link, the other ties are very probably weak. The upshot is that strong ties unite members of cliques while links between more isolated individuals tend to be weak. In other words, the chances for a strong tie between two articulators are slim. We can connect to the term 'homophilic bias' used earlier and speak of triadic homophily when we say that B and C have a higher probability of establishing a relationship if they already share a strong tie to A. If weak interpersonal ties stand a poor chance of building a triad, large numbers of weak ties lower triadic bias and simultaneously brighten the outlook for interconnections in the network. Strong ties build strong cohesion groups, even without links among each other, while weak ties connect these groups more securely.

In summary, local integration is made of strong ties, and weak ties ensure global integration of the network. We have also just established that heterogeneity is a key ingredient of integration. This now positions us to accept that the two standpoints boil down to the same thing (see Fararo and Skvoretz, 1987 for a more formal argumentation). Thus we formulate a unified integration theory whose underlying principle is that the greater the heterogeneity, the greater the number of intercircle relationships and the greater the chances they are based on weak ties. In summary, this gives the following:

1   The greater the heterogeneity, the lower the homophily and the greater the probability of weak linkages. Heterogeneity correlates with strong global integration but weak local integration.
2   Inversely, the greater the homogeneity (preference for intragroup relations over intergroup relations) the greater the homophily and the lower the chances of strong linkages. Homogeneity correlates with weak global integration and strong local integration.

Table 8.5 reviews and summarizes the theory of integration following Blau and Granovetter.[2]

This integration theory is compatible with Durkheim's (1893) distinction between integration based on mechanical solidarity and that based on organic solidarity. As seen, mechanical solidarity is proper to a society consisting of similar segments. Each segment shows strong homogeneity

Table 8.5   Theory of integration

Homogeneity	Heterogeneity
Strong social status correlation (systemic heterogeneity)	Weak social status correlation (systemic homogeneity)
Strong homophily	Weak homophily
Few intergroup relations	Many intergroup relations
Strong local integration	Weak local integration
Weak global integration	Strong global integration

and strong social status correlation (i.e. weak social differentiation). Relations between segments are few and homophily is strong. Local integration is strong and global integration is weak (segments can split off without jeopardizing the existence of the entire system). According to Durkheim, increasing differentiation drives the shift into organic solidarity. According to network theory, heterogeneity increases as social status correlation falls. This causes homophily to fall as weak ties proliferate to interconnect groups. The result is weak local integration but far stronger global integration than in the preceding case. The shift from mechanical to organic solidarity is not, as Durkheim claims, the product of higher global density. The shift results from an increase in weak ties and the weakening of homophily that necessarily occur when a social circle becomes more heterogeneous, i.e. what Durkheim calls greater social differentiation.

That said, the definition of dyadic heterogeneity lumps together two somewhat different situations. We shall now return to the Cs and hs in the table of dyadic combinations between Catholics and Protestants. C stands for crisscrossing links, i.e. two individuals who are similar in one dimension but differ in another; and s stands for segmentation, i.e. the dyad has no crisscrossing links, as happens in homogeneous dyads labelled with an h. In the first case the two individuals share no common trait, but they share all in the second. So why not hypothesize that C dyads are better placed to promote intercircle relations than s or h dyads? Many researchers say they are, and the hypothesis deserves detailed treatment.

Crisscrossing and its Effects

The first researchers to pay real attention to crisscrossing links may well have been British anthropologists in the 1940s and 1950s. Evans-Pritchard (1939) describes this sort of link in the preface to a book on the Kipsigi tribe in Kenya. Colson (1955) reports links that cross over between circles of kin and neighbours among the Tanga in Zambia. Gluckman (1965) points out that, in societies with no nation-state, systems of alliance often crisscross such that one man's enemy in one dimension becomes a friend in another.

Social cleavages become relevant as soon as they tangibly modify individual action, such as when membership in the same circle entitles one member to preferential treatment from comembers. In such a case, cleavages dictate allegiances that trigger hostility in the absence of cross-links. The fewer the cross-links, the greater the risk of tension and actual conflict. But we need to measure the degree of crisscrossing if the hypothesis is to be tested.

Links cannot crisscross without a social cleavage of at least two dimensions, and we shall use such an example. Any cleavage differentiates groups according to a predetermined number of modalities. We shall use dichotomous modalities for the sake of simplicity, but without subverting the

Table 8.6

	A	B	Total
X	n_{11}	n_{12}	$n_{1.}$
Y	n_{21}	n_{22}	$n_{2.}$
Total	$n_{.1}$	$n_{.2}$	n

general validity of the example. As for heterogeneity, we start with a cross-tabulation as in Table 8.6.

Now we want to know what degree of crisscrossing exists between two individuals separated by a cleavage. According to Galtung (1966), crisscrossing for a 2 × 2 table is given by:

$$n_{11}n_{12} + n_{11}n_{21} + n_{12}n_{22} + n_{21}n_{22} = (n_{11} + n_{22})(n_{12} + n_{21})$$

The maximum value for this formula is $n^2/4$, while the crisscrossing index ([0,1]) is given by

$$C_G = \frac{4(n_{11} + n_{22})(n_{12} + n_{21})}{n^2}$$

For greater numbers of modalities, we apply Rae and Taylor's (1970) formula:

$$C_{RT} = \frac{1}{n(n - 1)}\left(\sum_i n_i^2 + \sum_j n_j^2 + \sum_{i,j} n_{ij}^2\right)$$

In these relations, C_{RT} is the proportion of crisscrossing dyads to the total number of dyads, and C_G is the proportion of crisscrossing dyads to the maximum possible number of crisscrossing dyads: so

$$C_G = 2C_{RT}(n - 1)/n$$

If we evaluate heterogeneity by feeding the same figures into Blau's formula, we obtain $C_G = 1$ in the first case and $C_G = 0$ in the second. In other words, we have maximum and minimum crisscrossing in the first and second cases respectively. In the second case, we speak of segmentation, i.e. all dyads in the network are perfectly homogeneous or heterogeneous. Obviously, both cases represent extremes and field data will only turn up tendencies one way or another. Nonetheless, the extremes are useful to clarify the distinction between weak and strong crisscrossing.

The structure of network crisscrossing affects individual behaviour in several ways. Hendrik Flap (1988) studied conflicts of allegiance and their impact on violence in social relations. He affirms that conflicting allegiances are less violent in social structures that are rigged to crisscross cleavages than in those where structure and cleavage coincide.

The demonstration of this assertion requires a hypothesis about behaviour. Flap assumes rational actors who choose the option that promises maximum utility. Obviously this utility is both objective and subjective.

However, rational choice theory does not in itself explain actor behaviour adequately. We also need to take into account how the structural context in which the action is committed affects the utility, personal expectations and available options. Individual behaviour is indeed subject to the contours of the institutions and other structural constraints in which it occurs. Therefore, we need to understand how crisscrossing affects the utility and sociometric choices available to actors in the event of conflict.

We shall use a model of a stateless society whose economic capital consists of some scarce resource, symbolic capital consists of honour, and all power falls to the strongest. In such a society, social capital is the assistance an individual can expect from other members of the network. Rational behaviour theory says each individual will act to augment all four kinds of capital. We can fairly assume conflict will arise now and then over the distribution of the scarce resource, and we shall focus exclusively on this. We shall divide all actors into two groups: those apt to fight over the resource and those neutral to the conflict itself but comembers of a network with at least one person likely to pick a fight.

The fighters have four options. They can use violence to appropriate the resource, negotiate a share of a divisible resource, negotiate compensation in the case of an indivisible resource or simply do nothing. What are the respective benefits?

1 Combat will augment their economic wealth but only if they win. It may also increase symbolic capital through the honour that befalls the victor. But there is a cost to social capital if battle requires an ally. There is also a risk of casualties and defeat.
2 Compromise affects the economic capital of fighters according to the deal that is struck, but requires an investment of time and energy (as does battle).
3 Inaction is presumably dishonourable.

Now we shall assume a cleavage in the society that creates two circles based on lineage and locality, as often happens in traditional societies. So we have lineages A and B living in villages X and Y. How easily can fighters enlist support in their network to wage war or negotiate?

We shall accept that neutrals will feel obliged to support the fighters in their network because non-intervention would cost them honour and, more importantly, undermine their capacity to enlist help in other situations. What kind of support will the neutrals provide? Flap shows that their options depend on the degree of crisscrossing, if rational behaviour is assumed.

A conflict between a member of A living in X and a B in Y generates a conflict of allegiance for every B in X and A in Y. This situation would not arise in a segmented society, i.e. where all As live in X and all Bs in Y and fighters could reasonably expect to enlist unanimous support within their respective circles. Any member denying support could be accused of treason, with a resulting loss of social capital. Furthermore, segmentation sharply ups the costs of the transaction because no one enjoys the confidence of both sides to mediate, and anyone appointed to arbitrate would be considered biased. Thus, the chances of a negotiated settlement are slim. Negotiation is not a viable option because of the high risk of failure and the accompanying loss of social capital (bearing in mind that combat is always honourable but botched negotiations are not). Second, inaction is not a viable option because it entails a loss of social and symbolic capital. So maximum utility lies in combat, despite uncertainty about outcome. Flap summarizes the options clearly in the following formulas:

$$U_{\text{combat}} = U_{\text{honour}} + U_{\text{soc. cap}} - (U_{\text{wounded}} \times Prob_{\text{injury}})$$

$$U_{\text{mediation}} = (U_{\text{soc. cap}} \times Prob_{\text{success}}) - U_{\text{transaction}}$$

$$U_{\text{inaction}} = U_{\text{soc. cap}} - U_{\text{honour}}$$

In a segmented society, fighters and neutrals prefer combat to mediation to inaction.

The options take a different order in a crisscrossing environment where neutrals see far better chances for a negotiated settlement. Because of their links to village A and circle Y, neutrals are unlikely to be accused of bias. Transaction costs drop. And fighters will reason the same way. Unlike their segmented counterparts, cross-linked neutrals have no interest in combat that would trigger a conflict of allegiance, forcing them to choose sides. For their part, fighters cannot count on full network support because combat is in nobody's best interests and this should induce them to negotiate. As a rule, crisscrossing makes negotiation preferable to combat.

Given the potential benefits for each option, it seems obvious that network structure will affect actors' order of preferences. Segmentation logically tips the scales toward combat, and crisscrossing toward negotiation.

We can sophisticate this simple example in any number of ways, but the exercise is pointless because we would obtain the same result: the probability of conflict rises with social segmentation, and that of negotiation rises with crisscrossing. If the conflict risks becoming violent, the probability of warfare rises as crisscrossing falls, and greater crisscrossing improves the chances of peace.

This conclusion is not explicitly substantiated in ethnological studies about stateless societies. Those studies were not looking for the effects of crisscrossing and the data require confirmation, however plausible the conclusion may be. For example, we interpret polygamy as a practice that favours crisscrossing among spouses (unless both spouses belong to the same group). Each male belongs to the group he lives with, but establishes multiple alliances to other groups. And indeed, Otterbein (1968) reports that polygamy appears to significantly reduce the frequency of internal conflicts in the 42 societies he investigated. Likewise, patrilinear and patrilocalized societies often correlate with higher levels of infighting than non-patrilinear

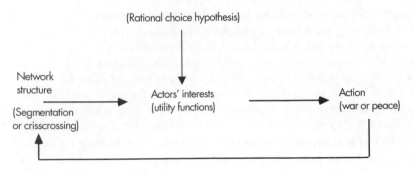

Figure 8.3   Structural interactionism

and non-patrilocalized societies. Thus, we have good reason to believe the model's predictions are most often accurate.

As stated, we are using a bare-bones version of the model. In particular, we have disregarded demographic pressure, 'foreign wars' and other environmental factors or their impact on utility and network structure, the two main elements of the interaction system. Likewise, we have overlooked the boomerang effect of the interaction (war or peace) on the system and its environment. War, for example, may radically alter the proportion of crisscrossing links in the aftermath. But this model also has methodological value. It clearly shows how network analysis and rational choice theory can combine to construct a theory of social conflict. Structure and rational choice are equally important to the theory because structure does not build an adequate model without rational actors, while any model based on utility alone is equally inadequate because structure affects the order of preferences. Figure 8.3 sums up what we mean by structural interactionism.

Ralf Dahrendorf (1957) arrives at broadly the same diagnosis. In his book on conflict in industrial societies, he shows that the interest groups that build up at various levels of society do not necessarily coincide. A plurality of interest groups engenders a plurality of conflicts that have no predetermined reason for aggregating into a single conflict between two social classes. Thus the situation described by Marx only constitutes a special case of aggregated interests, interest groups and the conflicts that oppose them. Dahrendorf says that such was indeed the case in the industrialized societies of the late nineteenth century which, if we accept Flap's theory, means that social circles were strongly segmented. If segmentation becomes strong enough to coalesce into two diametrically opposed macrogroups (i.e. two social classes), you have a powder keg. This leads to structural overhaul through revolution. But Dahrendorf sees post-capitalist society as a series of conflicts among a plurality of interest groups because the interests of any group do not necessarily coincide with the interests of any other group and anyone with a dominant position in one conflict may find herself dominated in another. The result is that conflicts are less violent (but not necessarily less intense) and that structural change comes about gradually without revolution. This amounts to accepting that crisscrossing is much more extensive in post-industrial society and there is more room for negotiation. Flap and Dahrendorf come to the same diagnosis, albeit via very different methodological approaches.

Emerging Norms and Social Order

Hobbes's (1651) problem of social order boils down to how human beings manage to live in peace most of the time if we accept *homo homini lupu*. He says individuals are motivated by self-serving interests and violent conflict must result whenever some precious resource is up for distribution. He says the only way to avoid a state of *natural* ongoing conflict that pits everyone against everyone else is for people to give up some personal freedom and submit to a state, which is the only entity that can impose peace with coercive measures applicable to one and all. However, we now know of traditional societies that survive quite peaceably most of the time without central government, so the state is no prerequisite to peace.

Jean Jacques Rousseau (1762) takes an opposite stance and holds that 'primitive man' is *naturally* good and capable of pity towards fellow beings, but this position is also disappointing because it is an *ad hoc* position and unverifiable in any case. If we return to Hobbes's statement that people act in self-interest, the effect of crisscrossing now becomes far more acceptable. As seen, links that crisscross social circles make it in the best interests of fighters and their supporters to negotiate rather than to open hostilities. Consequently, it does not necessarily follow that stateless societies are doomed to ongoing warfare even if 'people prey upon people' and everyone pursues self-seeking goals.

Our model allows for segmented societies with high conflict levels. We can therefore go on to imagine that the rise of the state is the consequence of network segmentation. It is however clear that segmentation alone will not explain its rise. Evans-Pritchard (1940) amply demonstrates this in his study on the Nuers. This strongly segmented society has a long history of strife between segments but at no time did a state ever manage to assert any long-term global control. In reality, segmentation has little chance of rapid adjustment and conflicts tend to recur regularly among the same belligerents. Over time, they become routine events that may even evolve into ritual. As Evans-Pritchard shows, conflicts build structure, and a very stable structure at that. So conflict is compatible with social order. As soon as conflict ritualizes, there is no need for a state to safeguard social order.

Logically, a given society needs a state only if it is segmented but lacks ritualized conflict. Endogenous factors such as demographic pressure from a given clan, exogenous factors such as 'foreign wars' or ecological imbalances, can destabilize ritualized conflict. Such an imbalance may well be a prerequisite for a state to emerge, but it is by no means a straight-forward case of cause and effect.

We have now reviewed the conditions needed for the emergence of an institutional state, but the emergence itself poses a serious problem. We must explain the very general problem of where norms come from, because any institution is no more than a sum total of norms explicitly recognized by a given group and set up as routines that give the institution its contours.

We tackle this problem and preserve the coherence of our model by continuing to assume that actors behave as a function of objective and subjective self-interest. Here we should remember that socialization describes how to apply a norm but not where it came from. So, what circumstances cause self-interest to establish a norm for everyone? It makes no difference to analysis if the norms become habit patterns that turn into an institution, state, norms or laws. We shall now turn to Coleman (1990) for insight.

We shall assume two groups, X and Y, whose interests are sufficiently homogeneous for two actors, X and Y, to represent them and make decisions on their behalf. We shall further suppose each can elect to invest $900 to a joint profit-making venture. It obviously costs nothing not to invest. However, the $900 will yield a return of $300, and thus they each cash in a net total of $1,200 when the venture winds up. But the net total is divided up equally among both actors, even if one declines to invest (this simulates the problem of the production of collective goods). Under these conditions, each actor is confronted with the options charted in the following table. The first figure in each cell indicates X's net earnings and the second Y's.

	Y invests	Y does not invest
X invests	300; 300	−300; 600
X does not invest	600; −300	0; 0

If X invests $900 and the yield is $300, she nets $1,200 which she then divides in half. But Y is entitled to half of the net total even if her investment is nil. In this case her profit is $600 and X faces a $300 net loss. Neither X nor Y have an interest in investing alone.

If we assume that each actor must decide to commit without knowing the intentions of the other, then she has no special reason to trust the other or to commit. The upshot is that neither invests (lower right-hand cell). The optimization of individual earnings obtains a suboptimal collective result. The optimal collective result (upper left-hand cell) is unachievable under prevailing conditions, so any project that requires an individual investment whose profits benefit one and all, non-investors included, has no chance of succeeding.

The paradox of collective action has generated a great deal of literature because of its broad impact on social psychology, sociology and economics. It is a true paradox because it rules out any collective action at all under certain circumstances, yet simple observation shows collective action occurring all the time. Olson's (1966) position is well known: a collective project only happens if it procures individual profit, material or symbolic, to each investor *over and above* the collective asset it aims to produce. There are other positions. Edna Ullmann-Margalit (1977) notes the prisoner's dilemma leads to the creation of norms that force each actor to invest in collective projects. Everyone will admit that no social optimum can be attained without some coercion and it is therefore reasonable to accept norms that coerce individuals to invest in collective action.

The above line of reasoning does not contradict the theory of rational behaviour because each actor would net more ($300) if both decided to invest than if neither invested ($0). But we could revamp our argument to tie it in with Hobbes: coercion is the only way to obtain collective action. Given our paradox, society needs explicit/implicit norms, rules, laws and institutions (or a state, dear to Hobbes) to coerce people to act in a manner consistent with the collective interest. This reasoning is sound because it incites everyone to accept and help enforce norms. The prisoner's dilemma contains its own solution: society operates to foster norms that make both individual and social optimums attainable.

But Coleman goes on to say that coercion is not the only weapon. So far, we have assumed no contact between the two actors and no special reason to trust one another even if they did communicate. But of course, they can open talks, establish mutual trust and hammer out a deal. In that case, they will reach the social optimum of $300/$300 very quickly, especially since such consensus would be consistent with individual benefit. In short, coercion becomes pointless when trust and communication are viable options. Collective action and joint undertakings can indeed arise out of consensus. This returns us to Rousseau, who says that collective action results from consensus not coercion.

The theories of Hobbes and Rousseau diverge radically and still stand for two antithetical paradigms of the social sciences. It would be futile to take an absolute stand in favour of either, but we can identify the conditions that are relevant to each. Here, the degree of crisscrossing will prove a determining factor.

In a segmented structure, intergroup communication is minimal. Any communication that might exist gives nobody any special reason to trust anyone from another group. We are in a situation where some sort of coercion is a prerequisite to collective action. Inversely, communication and exchange are likely to be intense in a society with numerous crisscrossing circles. Individuals can communicate and reach agreement. There is more scope for trust. Someone is always handy to mediate diverging interests. All the prerequisites of negotiated settlement are at hand. This situation needs no preset norms or coercive institutions.

Norms and their institutional variants are not an inevitable and automatic consequence of the prisoner's dilemma or the paradox of collective action. They only become necessary in segmented networks, while consensus is always an option in a network with multiple legitimate allegiances. Thus, structure determines recourse to coercion or consensus. The critical factor is the degree of multiple allegiances among social groups or circles. Assuming rational behaviour, coercion (i.e. norms and institutions) is the more probable option where multiple allegiances are few and global segmentation prevails in the network. Consensus is the more probable option where multiple allegiances are numerous and social circles intersect, such that there is no *absolute* need for norms to regulate collective action. It is therefore impossible to say either Hobbes or Rousseau is right; the answer to the general issues they each raise depends entirely upon the prevailing structure of the network at hand.

There is no shortage of applications for the broad-brush model we have developed. For example, the model is compatible with Alexis de Tocqueville's model of democracy. If we accept that absolutism is more coercive than democracy, then it follows that this is due to greater segmentation. Under monarchy, French society showed strong segmentation. But it had begun to loosen up in the seventeenth and eighteenth centuries as witnessed, for example, in the rising numbers of titles of nobility that were handed out. As networks intersected more and more, they heralded deep political change because of institutional gridlock. This is what made the French Revolution 'thinkable'. Using different terms from a different standpoint, Tocqueville is saying the same thing when he asserts 'equalizing conditions' go hand in hand with democracy.

We shall close by saying that a discussion of this issue in general terms will not resolve opposition between researchers who feel structures create norms and those who consider norms to be pre-existent. The terms do not fit the issue. No structure necessarily generates norms and no norms necessarily pre-exist structure. Some structures predispose to open warfare, others to negotiation. Obviously, some negotiations collapse or unanimous agreement may be out of reach. In this case, hostilities break out in the absence of institutional intervention to nudge parties toward the social optimum.

The next problem is sanctions, the carrots and sticks of norm enforcement. Coleman speaks of incremental sanctions and heroic sanctions. Group pressure is one example of incremental sanction. Each actor helps enforce the norm by exerting a little individual pressure on the maverick until the sum total of pressures obtains compliance. Heroic sanctions work differently. A person or institution unilaterally steps in to sanction the deviant while other interested parties look on. As Coleman remarks, this theory runs up against the problem of the free rider. However, the free rider problem boils down to the problem of norm emergence, i.e. if no one is prepared to pay the cost of enforcement, the norm probably becomes a dead letter. The possible outcomes are the same as stated earlier and we will not pursue this issue. We still insist that structure will explain the type of sanction imposed. Segmented networks require heroic sanctions and their institutions stand every chance of being highly coercive. On the other

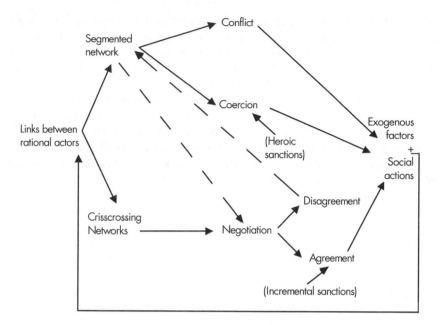

Figure 8.4   Network structure and social action

hand, negotiated settlements are more convenient in strongly cross-linked societies and incremental sanctions therefore become easier to apply (this does not preclude the existence of norms and institutions, it only means they are probably less coercive). Our position maps out as in Figure 8.4.

The figure should not be misunderstood. It is merely a theoretical model or ideal type. All it says is that the greater the segmentation in a given network, the greater the chances it will opt for conflict or coercion (e.g. norms, institutions or a state). Inversely, it also says the greater the prevalence of crisscrossing links, the greater the chances of opting for negotiations and consensus. However, network structure is only a conditioning factor that dictates no particular course of action. All options are theoretically available to both networks, as shown by the dashed lines. Segmentation does not preclude negotiation, it only makes it less feasible and reduces the chances of any peaceful settlement attempted. Crisscrossing does not impose negotiations and negotiations can always collapse, leading back to the options of coercion or conflict. It should therefore be empirically clear by now that cross-linked networks do have norms and conflicts and that segmented networks also have consensus. 'Empirically' is a key word here. We are discussing an empirical question that needs empirical data to substantiate it. Our model theorizes that structure exerts strong impact in the ways shown on the figure.

At 'Exogenous factors + Social actions', we have a line looping back to the starting point. Although we have ignored it so far, the line expresses an essential element of social dynamics. It illustrates that social action can act upon the initial structure. For example, conflict can result in serious structural damage to one of the opposing groups. Exogenous factors and the network's surrounding environment (e.g. demographic pressure and 'foreign wars') affect relations between actors too. But the way the feedback arrow is drawn suggests the dynamics will only be modified to the extent that social action and exogenous factors affect the structure of links between actors. In other words, the feedback arrow is perfectly consistent with the general model that attributes a key role to relational structure.

In practice, this model reads several ways. For example, it can be interpreted in terms of integration theory if we consider the two types of structure as two types of integration. Each structure goes about integration in its own way. It is a mistake to believe that segmented networks are less 'integrated' than multiple affiliation networks. Segmentation leads to the institutionalization of norms and conflicts which, as seen, help structure a society. Social conflict is a powerful force to stimulate identification in modern society, as Gerard Adam and Jean Daniel Reynaud (1978) have shown in studies of labour conflicts. Therefore, norms and conflicts contribute to integration in the vast majority of cases.

This recalls an earlier distinction we made when opposing heterogeneity and global integration to homogeneity and local integration. The concepts coincide imperfectly because multiple affiliations and heterogeneity are not quite the same thing, and nor are homogeneity and segmentation. Still, the overlap is considerable and rounds out the unified theory we have elaborated. Crisscrossing favours heterophily and weak ties. It corresponds by definition to a situation with heterogeneous dyads. The result is that global integration improves as crisscrossing proliferates. Against this, segmentation favours homophily and strong ties (even if all dyads are not necessarily totally homogeneous). Thus, the greater the segmentation, the better the local integration.

Notes

1 The survey was headed by Professor Albert Spira at the INSERM medical research institute and funded by the national AIDS prevention agency. It ran from 1991 to 1992. Alexis Ferrand and Lise Mounier (1993) designed the questionnaire on trust in sexual and affinitive relationships, which is the source of the results presented here.

2 Given the similarities between the weak tie and structural hole theories outlined in Chapter 5, we could even say that Granovetter's weak ties = Blau's heterogeneity = Burt's structural holes.

APPENDIX

Matrix Operations

A matrix is a table of numbers arranged into n rows and p columns. As a rule, matrices are rectangular, but where $n = p$ we have a square matrix. We shall assume that m_{ij} is an element of matrix M which expresses the value where row i intersects column j.

We add two matrices by adding up corresponding elements from each matrix. The same principle applies to subtracting one matrix from another. Obviously, these operations are only valid if both matrices have the same number of rows and columns. We then write that the sum of matrices A and B is matrix C, where all have n rows and p columns, where a_{ij} and b_{ij} are respective elements of A and B, and where we obtain c_{ij}, an element of C, with $c_{ij} = a_{ij} + b_{ij}$.

A row vector is a matrix with p columns and a single row, and a column vector is a matrix with one column and n rows. Convention dictates that unqualified use of 'vector' refers to a column vector. Because vectors consist of either a single row or a single column, double subscripts are not needed to designate a given component (we speak of 'elements' in a matrix and 'components' of a vector). Thus v_i indicates the value in row i of a column vector, and v_j is the value in column j of a row vector. As a rule, vectors are labelled with lower-case letters and upper case is reserved for matrices. A scalar number is a matrix of one row and one column. For example, 5 is a scalar number. Scalar numbers and vectors are simply different kinds of matrices. A matrix can also be seen as a stack of row vectors or an array of column vectors.

Multiplying two vectors element by element is as straightforward as addition or subtraction. The only requirement is that both contain the same number of elements. But matrix multiplication defines a specific and somewhat more complex operation called scalar product.

A prerequisite to scalar multiplication of two vectors taken in a predetermined order is that one vector must have as many rows as there are columns in the other (e.g. you cannot 'multiply' a row vector with three components by a column vector with only two). The scalar product of vector a times vector b is matrix C which will contain as many rows as the first vector and as many columns as the second. Element c_{ij} in C is equal to the product of the components of each vector.

In fact two configurations are possible in the light of this rule:

1 either the first vector is expressed in a row and the second is necessarily a column vector with as many components as elements in the first
2 or the first is expressed in a column and the second is necessarily a row vector.

In the row × column configuration, the scalar product is c (whence the name of the operation) because the resulting matrix has as many rows a as the first vector and as many columns b as the second, i.e. 1 in each case. If p is the number of columns in a given row vector, or of rows in a given column vector, we calculate c as already stated by obtaining the sum of the product of components:

$$c = a_1b_1 + a_2b_2 + \ldots + a_pb_p, \quad \text{or} \quad c = \sum_{i=1}^{p} a_ib_i$$

For example:

$$(1 \ 3 \ 2) \times \begin{pmatrix} 3 \\ 2 \\ 4 \end{pmatrix} = (1 \times 3) + (3 \times 2) + (2 \times 4) + 17$$

In the column × row configuration, the resulting matrix C has n lines and p columns (where n is the number of rows in vector a and p is the number of columns in b). The value c_{ij} at the intersection of line i and column j in matrix C is given by

$$a_i \times b_j = c_{ij}$$

In the next example, $c_{21} = a_2 \times b_1 = (2 \times 4)$:

$$\begin{pmatrix} 3 \\ 2 \end{pmatrix} \times (4 \ 5) = \begin{pmatrix} 12 & 15 \\ 8 & 10 \end{pmatrix}$$

Obviously, the same rule applies to both configurations and they are only presented separately because we are dealing with the special case of a matrix with one row or column. The rule is again the same for matrices of any number of dimensions except that scalar multiplication must be reiterated until the resulting matrix is completed. In short, the above is a special case of what is to follow.

If we are to multiply matrices A and B in that order, the number of columns in the first matrix must equal the number of rows in the second. In other words, if A has n rows and p columns, then B must have p rows and q columns. The resulting matrix C has n rows and q columns (i.e. the same number of rows as A and columns as B). The next diagram summarizes the rule on matrix dimensions:

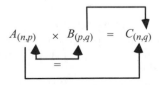

$$A_{(n,p)} \quad \times \quad B_{(p,q)} \quad = \quad C_{(n,q)}$$

c_{ij} is an element of resulting matrix C and, as before, it designates the value for the cell where row i intersects column j. It is calculated by scalar multiplication of row vector i (or row i) in matrix A with column vector j (or column j) in B. One way of remembering this is by thinking of ROCO to recall that you obtain c_{ij} by the scalar product of ROw i in the first matrix and COlumn j in the second. ROCO is also useful to remember that the resulting matrix has the same number of ROws as the first matrix and of COlumns as the second. Note that matrix products are not commutative, i.e. $AB \neq BA$.

Here is a complete example of such a calculation. Let

$$A = \begin{pmatrix} 0 & 1 & 4 \\ 2 & 3 & 5 \end{pmatrix} \quad \text{and} \quad B = \begin{pmatrix} 2 & 3 \\ 4 & 0 \\ 1 & 6 \end{pmatrix}$$

The product is defined since A has three columns and B has three lines. The product of $A \times B$ is C which has two rows and two columns:

$$C = \begin{pmatrix} c_{11} & c_{12} \\ c_{21} & c_{22} \end{pmatrix}$$

where

$c_{11} = (0 \times 2) + (1 \times 4) + (4 \times 1) = 8$ (scalar product of first row in A and first column in B)

$c_{12} = (0 \times 3) + (1 \times 0) + (4 \times 6) = 24$ (scalar product of first row in A and second column in B)

$c_{21} = (2 \times 2) + (3 \times 4) + (5 \times 1) = 21$ (scalar product of second row in A and first column in B)

$c_{22} = (2 \times 3) + (3 \times 0) + (5 \times 6) = 36$ (scalar product of second row in A and second column in B)

Thus we obtain

$$C = \begin{pmatrix} 8 & 24 \\ 21 & 36 \end{pmatrix}$$

Hierarchical Clustering Procedures

Hierarchical clustering is a routine way of processing sociological data (see Jardine and Sibson, 1971; Jambu and Lebeaux, 1982). It obtains a typology of individuals, i.e. a breakdown into a certain number of clusters according to a given criterion. Clusters should be as homogeneous as possible internally and as heterogeneous as possible between each other. Network analysis has the same objective.

The first step of this approach is to take a series of observations about dyadic links, possibly from a sociometric choice matrix, and derive a similarity or distance matrix between individuals. The distance matrix can be based on cohesion, equivalence between two individuals or other criteria covered in this book. The only requirement is that the criterion must lend itself to conversion into a similarity index s between two individuals that varies between 0 and 1 or a distance index d that also varies between 0 and 1. Thus we can toggle back and forth with $s = 1 - d$. The matrix containing these indices lists each network member in both rows and columns and is symmetrical (the distance from a to b equals that from b to a; an individual's distance from herself is nil by convention). One example is Burt's matrix of Euclidean distance given in Chapter 3.

We shall not review similarity criteria here, and we will assume that distance matrix D (or $S = 1 - D$) has been constructed. D is square symmetrical and has a zero trace function. As a rule, the indices are established to verify two other principles:

1 Separation principle: $d_{ih} = 0 \Leftrightarrow i = h$ (individuals i and h are interchangeable).
2 Triangular inequality principle: $\forall\ i, k, h : d_{ih} \leq d_{ik} + d_{kh}$.

An index effectively measures distance if it satisfies the conditions of separation, symmetry and triangular inequality. In a very strict mathematical way, D is a *distance* matrix.

We might pair off and cluster all elements with a dyadic distance below a preset threshold. But the drawback of this simple method is that binary relations are rarely equivalent and the resulting clusters would be heterogeneous. Thus, classification in ascending hierarchical order is often a wiser approach, but we need a few definitions before going further.

1   Partition E is a set of parts of E such that:
    (a) any two parts are disjointed or identical
    (b) the union of all parts of E is the complete set E.
2   A hierarchy of parts of E is a set $H(E)$ of classes such that:
    (a) any part with one element belongs to $H(E)$ where the maximum number of classes is equal to the number of elements in set E
    (b) the set of classes belongs to the hierarchy
    (c) if two elements of $H(E)$ are not disjointed, then one is included in the other.
3   Ultrametric distance must also satisfy Krassner's condition: $\forall\, i, h, k \in E^3 : d_{ih} \leq \max(d_{ik}, d_{hk})$.
4   Any ultrametric distance matrix has a corresponding hierarchical index of parts of E. It is represented as a dendrogram with ultrametric distances between individuals plotted along the abscissa and individuals along the ordinal (see Figure A.3). This approach yields an order of appearance for clusters.
5   The cutoff point for the number of clusters is left to the researcher's discretion. Maximal partitioning yields few real data and clustering should cease as soon as elements in a cluster become too dissimilar.

There are several ways to shift from distance to linkage clustering distance. We start by taking three individuals, i, h and k separated by the following distances (Figure A.1): $d_{ih} = 0.4$, $d_{ik} = 0.6$, $d_{hk} = 0.7$. We cluster the two closest, i and h. They form q, a new object (Figure A.2). The next problem is to determine the distance between k and q. We move point k to the perpendicular centred on ih, which modifies the initial values for distance. The triangle between the three elements is now isoceles with a narrow base (the clustering distance) but k can be positioned at three principal altitudes as follows:

1   $d_{kq} = \min(d_{ik}, d_{hk})$ is *single linkage clustering* that assigns an individual to a cluster if she is closer to any member of that group rather than someone of another cluster.

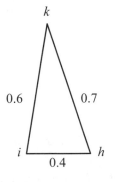

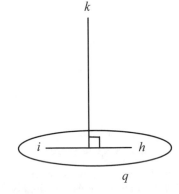

Figure A.1   Figure A.2

2 $d_{kq} = \max (d_{ik}, d_{hk})$ is *complete linkage clustering* that assigns an individual to a cluster if she is closer to all of its members rather than to all members of another cluster.

3 $d_{kq} = \text{mean} (d_{ik}, d_{hk})$ or $d_{kq} = (d_{ik} + d_{hk})/2$ is *average linkage clustering* that assigns an individual to a cluster if she is closer to its average member rather than to his counterpart in another cluster.

We apply this to a p-matrix as follows:

1 Find the shortest distance in D. If i and h are the two closest individuals, they form group N_{p+1}.
2 Calculate the distances between all other remaining individuals ($p - 2$) and N_{p+1} (using any of the three methods given above).
3 Form D_2, a new matrix of order ($p - 1$) that comprises all distances among ($p - 2$) individuals and distances to N_{p+1}.
4 Find the shortest distance and aggregate the two elements into cluster N_{p+2}.
5 Repeat steps 1 to 4 until only one cluster remains.

The next example illustrates the operation. We shall adopt single linkage distance and we give matrix D for distances among five individuals.

		1	2	3	4	5
$D =$	1	0	0.6	0.01	0.09	0.10
	2		0	0.17	0.25	0.02
	3			0	0.04	0.09
	4				0	0.13
	5					0

1 The shortest distance is $d_{13} = 0.01$; we thus add 1 and 3 to form cluster 6.
2 $d_{46} = \min (d_{41}, d_{43}) = 0.04$
   $d_{26} = \min (d_{21}, d_{23}) = 0.16$
   $d_{56} = \min (d_{51}, d_{53}) = 0.10$

3

		6	2	4	5
$D_2 =$	6	0	0.16	0.04	0.10
	2		0	0.25	0.02
	4			0	0.13
	5				0

4 The shortest distance is d_{25}, so 2 and 5 form cluster 7.
5 We repeat the initial operation:
   $d_{47} = \min (d_{42}, d_{45}) = 0.13$
   $d_{67} = \min (d_{62}, d_{65}) = 0.10$

		6	7	4
$D_3 =$	6	0	0.10	0.04
	7		0	0.13
	4			0

The shortest distance is d_{64}, so 4 and 6 form cluster 8.
The distance between 8 and 7 is $d_{87} = \min (d_{74}, d_{76}) = 0.10$.

$$D_4 = \begin{array}{c|cc} & 7 & 8 \\ \hline 7 & 0 & 0.10 \\ 8 & & 0 \end{array}$$

We finally group 7 and 8 into cluster 9. All individuals are now included and the operation stops here. It yields the following positions:

$P(5) = 1,2,3,4,5$
$P(4) = [1,3]\ 2,4,5$
$P(3) = [1,3],[2,5],4$
$P(2) = [1,3,4],[2,5]$
$P(1) = [1,2,3,4,5]$

The result graphs in several ways but we prefer the dendrogram in Figure A.3.

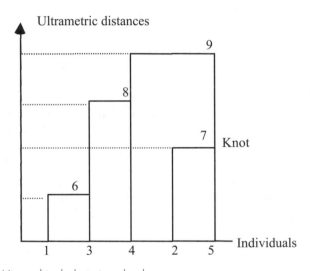

Figure A.3   Hierarchical clustering dendrogram

The resulting clusters are hierarchical because each is associated with an index of distance of increasing value (or a falling value in similarity index). It is an ascending order of hierarchy because we start with as many clusters as individuals and end up with a single cluster after a series of aggregations. The higher we go in the hierarchy, the less the clusters are homogeneous.

It now remains to decide where to set the partition. We want to end up with a small manageable number of clusters but we also want to avoid excessively heterogeneous clusters. There is no easy answer to partitioning. We just go back to the data, see how it processes and make a judgement about when to cut off clustering. If we are clustering at level $n + 1$ and notice that the harvest is too diverse, then we drop back to level n and stop there.

We describe clustering with phrases like 'no easy answer' or 'various algorithms' to insist that there is nothing final about any clustering. Any clustering deserves comparison with the products of other algorithms, if not multidimensional scaling or principal component analysis to see which looks best.

Basic Relational Algebra

This book has presented relations in graph language as mathematical objects which are the building blocks of structure. The following formulas cover the different types of equivalence and other relational algebra (see Pattison, 1993).

Relations

A relation in set X maps out on a graph or matrix. Matrix cells represent all the different possible pairings between elements of X, i.e. the elements of the Cartesian product $X \times X$. The existence of a relation is defined by a 1 in certain cells and thereby selecting a subset of $X \times X$. If X has N elements, $X \times X$ will have N_2 with 2^{N^2} total possible relations. Each relation has a graph. We shall not discuss valued graphs with matrices that use only the figures 0 and 1. All that follows concerns relations on the same set X.

We shall also describe certain properties without the proofs, which interested readers will find in Clifford and Preston (1961), Howie (1976), Boyd (1992) or Pattison (1993).

Relational operations

Set theory applies because relations can be assimilated to subsets of $X \times X$. We shall therefore speak of the union and the intersection of two relations. Any relation may also be embedded in another.

We shall also consider the relational operation of composition. F is a relation expressed as a matrix whose elements are f_{ij}, where i is the row number and j is the column number. Likewise, relation G is represented by a matrix containing element g_{ij}. In the next operations, we shall be using Boolean multiplication and addition subject to the following rules:

addition:		0	1
	0	0	1
	1	1	1

multiplication:		0	1
	0	0	0
	1	0	1

The composition of the two relations $H = FG$ is defined by

$$h_{ij} = \sum_{k=1}^{N} f_{ik} g_{kj}$$

Given the rules of Boolean addition, the composite of two relations is a relation which is itself expressed in another matrix filled with the numbers 0 and 1.

Semigroup of relations for set X

A semigroup is the set of relations defined for set X that are the product of Boolean multiplication. For example, we shall assume X consists of four elements, a, b, c

and *d*. The relations for *X* are mapped out in matrices of four columns and four rows each. Any matrix containing only 0s will be called $\emptyset$ and *I* designates the matrix defined by:

$$ I = \begin{pmatrix} 1 & 0 & 0 & 0 \\ 0 & 1 & 0 & 0 \\ 0 & 0 & 1 & 0 \\ 0 & 0 & 0 & 1 \end{pmatrix} $$

For any matrix *F*, $F\emptyset = \emptyset F = \emptyset$ and $FI = IF = F$. Matrix $\emptyset$ thus operates as a 0 and matrix *I* as a 1 per unit element. The composition operation is associative, which means it can be performed in any order and $F(GH) = (FG)H$. However, it is not commutative in general.

Now we shall build the set of all possible relations in the set. The product of two relations gives a relation for the set. We therefore construct a composition table for this set of relations. The total number of possible relations is obviously going to complicate the problem. Nonetheless, we can reasonably proceed to multiply the relations constructed for set X which contains two elements. This obtains 16 relations, or 512 relations if we use three elements. Table A.1 gives relations for *N* = 2.

Table A.1   Relations for *N* = 2

00	10	01	00	00	11	01	00	10	10	01	01	10	11	11	11
00	00	00	01	10	00	01	11	10	01	10	11	11	10	01	11
$\emptyset$	A	B	C	D	E	F	G	H	I	J	K	L	M	N	O

Composition table

	$\emptyset$	A	B	C	D	E	F	G	H	I	J	K	L	M	N	O
$\emptyset$	$\emptyset$	$\emptyset$	$\emptyset$	$\emptyset$	$\emptyset$	$\emptyset$	$\emptyset$	$\emptyset$	$\emptyset$	$\emptyset$	$\emptyset$	$\emptyset$	$\emptyset$	$\emptyset$	$\emptyset$	$\emptyset$
A	$\emptyset$	A	B	$\emptyset$	$\emptyset$	E	B	$\emptyset$	A	A	B	B	A	E	E	E
B	$\emptyset$	$\emptyset$	$\emptyset$	B	A	$\emptyset$	B	E	A	B	A	E	E	A	B	E
C	$\emptyset$	$\emptyset$	$\emptyset$	C	D	$\emptyset$	C	G	D	C	D	G	G	D	C	G
D	$\emptyset$	D	C	$\emptyset$	$\emptyset$	G	C	$\emptyset$	D	D	C	C	D	G	G	G
E	$\emptyset$	A	B	B	A	E	B	E	A	E	E	E	E	E	E	E
F	$\emptyset$	$\emptyset$	$\emptyset$	F	H	$\emptyset$	F	O	H	F	H	O	O	H	F	O
G	$\emptyset$	D	C	C	D	G	C	G	D	G	G	G	G	G	G	G
H	$\emptyset$	H	F	$\emptyset$	$\emptyset$	O	F	$\emptyset$	H	H	F	F	H	O	O	O
I	$\emptyset$	A	B	C	D	E	F	G	H	I	J	K	L	M	N	O
J	$\emptyset$	D	C	B	A	G	F	E	H	J	I	N	M	L	K	O
K	$\emptyset$	D	C	F	H	G	F	O	H	K	L	O	O	L	K	O
L	$\emptyset$	H	F	C	D	O	F	G	H	L	K	K	L	O	O	O
M	$\emptyset$	H	F	B	A	O	F	E	H	M	N	N	M	O	O	O
N	$\emptyset$	A	B	F	H	E	F	O	H	N	M	O	O	M	N	O
O	$\emptyset$	H	F	F	H	O	F	O	H	O	O	O	O	O	O	O

Raising the matrix through successive powers yields a subset of possible matrices. Table A.2 gives an example. All powers beyond 6 are equal to A^6.

Table A.2

0101	1010	1101	1111	1111	1111
0010	1000	0101	1010	1101	1111
1000	0101	1010	1101	1111	1111
1000	0101	1010	1101	1111	1111
A	A^2	A^3	A^4	A^5	A^6

Permutations

When every row and column contains only a single 1, we have a permutation matrix. Table A.3 illustrates permutation. Relation B changes from the natural order (*abcde*) to (*bcaed*). B^2 changes natural order to (*cabde*). Thus, there are $N!$ permutation matrices for any set of N elements. Here, $N = 5$, $N! = 120$. The table illustrates a cyclical permutation matrix where $B^6 = I$, $B^7 = B$ and so on.

Table A.3

01000	00100	10000	01000	00100	10000
00100	10000	01000	00100	10000	01000
10000	01000	00100	10000	01000	00100
00001	00010	00001	00010	00001	00010
00010	00001	00010	00001	00010	00001
B	B^2	B^3	B^4	B^5	B^6

Relational properties

We shall assume F is a relation, or defines the relation F^{-1} such that if $(x, y) \in F$, $(y, x) \in F^{-1}$. If I is included in F, F is reflexive and all elements are linked to themselves. If F^2 is included in F, F is a transitive relation. A reflexive, transitive relation is a quasi-order. It is equipotent if $F^2 = F$.

A quasi-order relation is equipotent. If indeed F^2 is included in F, then $F \cup I = F$ because a quasi-ordered relation is reflexive. It thus follows that $F(F \cup I) = F2 \cup F = F^2$ and F is included in F^2. The result of this double inclusion is that $F^2 = F$. A relation such that $F^{-1} = F$ is symmetrical.

Equivalences

If F is reflexive, symmetrical and transitive, we have an equivalence relation. We can readily see that equivalence graphs as a set of diagonal blocks filled with 1s that represent equivalence classes:

$$F = \begin{pmatrix} 1 & 1 & 1 & 0 & 0 & 0 & 0 & 0 \\ 1 & 1 & 1 & 0 & 0 & 0 & 0 & 0 \\ 1 & 1 & 1 & 0 & 0 & 0 & 0 & 0 \\ 0 & 0 & 0 & 1 & 0 & 0 & 0 & 0 \\ 0 & 0 & 0 & 0 & 1 & 1 & 1 & 1 \\ 0 & 0 & 0 & 0 & 1 & 1 & 1 & 1 \\ 0 & 0 & 0 & 0 & 1 & 1 & 1 & 1 \\ 0 & 0 & 0 & 0 & 1 & 1 & 1 & 1 \end{pmatrix}$$

This graph shows equivalence in terms of three clusters, *abc*, *d* and *efgh*.

For any F relation, $(F \cup F^2 \cup F^3 \cup \ldots \cup F^{n-1}) = F^*$ is a transitive relation. It is a transitive closure of the F relation. $(I \cup F \cup F^2 \cup F^3 \cup \ldots \cup F^{n-1})$ is the quasi-order of the relation.

Equivalence relation F is said to be greater (or rougher) than equivalence relation G if every cluster in G is included in a cluster of F.

Given that F and G are two equivalence relations, then $F \cap G$ is an equivalence relation. It is the greatest equivalence included in both F and G. FG is not necessarily an equivalence relation, but $(FG)^* = (F \cup G)^*$ is an equivalence relation and is also the smallest to contain both F and G. The set of equivalence relations having the two operations $F \vee G = (FG)^*$ and $F \wedge G = F \cap G$ is a lattice. If F and G are equivalence relations and if $FG = GF$, then FG is an equivalence and it is $F \vee G$.

Given that F is a relation and Φ is an equivalence relation, Φ is a regular equivalence to F if and only if $\Phi F = F \Phi$. An equivalence relation is a relation of strict equivalence for F if and only if $\Phi F = F \Phi = F$.

The product of the relation by regular equivalence operates a kind of saturation that fills out with 1s any blocks containing at least one 1 in any row and column. The corresponding graph and matrix are now given.

$$F = \begin{pmatrix} 0 & 0 & 0 & 1 & 0 \\ 0 & 0 & 0 & 0 & 1 \\ 0 & 0 & 0 & 0 & 1 \\ 1 & 1 & 0 & 0 & 0 \\ 0 & 0 & 1 & 0 & 0 \end{pmatrix}$$

We shall now consider equivalence that generates clusters 1, 2, 3 and 4, 5 for which the matrix is as follows:

$$\Phi = \begin{pmatrix} 1 & 1 & 1 & 0 & 0 \\ 1 & 1 & 1 & 0 & 0 \\ 1 & 1 & 1 & 0 & 0 \\ 0 & 0 & 0 & 1 & 1 \\ 0 & 0 & 0 & 1 & 1 \end{pmatrix} \quad \text{and} \quad F\Phi = \Phi F = \begin{pmatrix} 0 & 0 & 0 & 1 & 1 \\ 0 & 0 & 0 & 1 & 1 \\ 0 & 0 & 0 & 1 & 1 \\ 1 & 1 & 1 & 0 & 0 \\ 1 & 1 & 1 & 0 & 0 \end{pmatrix}$$

Given that F and G are two relations and that Φ has regular equivalence to F and G, then Φ has regular equivalence to FG. In effect, $F\Phi = \Phi F$ and $G\Phi = \Phi G$; thus $(FG)\,\Phi = F(G\Phi) = F(\Phi G) = (\Phi F)\,G = \Phi\,(FG)$. Given that F is a relation, and Φ and Θ show regular equivalence to F, then $\Phi \vee \Theta$ is a regular equivalence to F.

General Properties of Semigroups

We have already said that the relations of set X form a semigroup. Semigroups have numerous properties of specific interest to relations.

We shall assume that R is a set (or 'alphabet') whose elements are letters. We create words by rearranging letter order. Any word set is a semigroup if and only if:

1   The juxtaposition of two words in the set is a word in the set.
2   The juxtaposition operation is associative, i.e. $(st)\,u = s\,(tu)$.

We shall consider the set of all words written with a given alphabet. This is the free semigroup constructed from R. The law of composition allows us to construct a Cayley table for this. Such semigroups are infinite.

We shall assume S is a semigroup. Semigroups can have a 1 element or a neutral element I such that $ss_0 = s_0s = s_0$ for any $s \in S$. Note that such is the case for any element s_0 where $ss_0 = s_0$ (s_0 is a right zero). Thus all words ending in s_0 are equivalents of s_0.

Ideals

We shall assume A is a subset in semigroup S. A is an ideal to the right of S if SA is included in A, i.e. if any two elements s in S and a in A are such that sa is an element of A. A is an ideal to the left of S if AS is included in A. A is only an ideal if it is an ideal both left and right of S.

As an example, we shall take semigroup T that expresses the relations of a set of two elements which we have already used. Relations [K, L, M, N, O] constitute a sub-semigroup of the complete semigroup. Likewise, [I, J] is a sub-semigroup of T. We can easily identify others such as [$\emptyset$, A, B, C, D, E, G].

We shall consider the following equivalence relations S and R to elements of T. Two relations x and y are equivalent to R, xRy, if and only if $xT = yT$, i.e. if the set of elements in the row for x of the Cayley table is the same as the set in the row for y. Likewise, we construct equivalence classes S from columns containing the same elements. For example, rows A, B and E all contain elements $\emptyset$, A, B and E; rows C, D and G all contain $\emptyset$, C, D and G; and rows F, H and O all contain $\emptyset$, F, H and O. Thus all three sets are equivalent to R and the same is true of I, J. The elements of a single class engender the same ideals to the right. The equivalence classes for columns are B, C, F; A, D, H; E, G, O; K, N; L, M; and I, J.

1   The following clusters are equivalent relations for R:
       A, B, E/C, D, G/F, H, O/I, J/K/L/M/N/$\emptyset$
2   The S relation contains the following:
       A, D, H/B, C, F/E, G, O/I, J/K, N/L, M/$\emptyset$
3   The following are $R \vee S = U$ equivalences:
       A, B, C, D, E, F, G, H, O/I, J/K, N, L, M/$\emptyset$
4   The following are $R \wedge S = U$ equivalences:
       A/B/C/D/E/F/G/H/I, J/K/L/M/N/O/$\emptyset$

These four equivalences are called Green semigroup relations. We now rearrange Table A.1 as a function of these relations to obtain the exceptionally structured representation in Table A.4.

I and J engender a true ideal (both left and right) that is T. [K, L, M, N] engender the ideal [A, B, C, D, E, F, G, H, K, L, M, N, O, $\emptyset$]. The smallest ideal for this semigroup is [$\emptyset$].

Structural Investigation Sampling

We are all familiar with random sampling for opinion polls. Individuals in the source population are presumed to be independent of one another. Each person has her own attributes. We select a sampling method, constitute a survey population and set about exploring individual traits. Sociability studies use the same approach

Table A.4

	∅	ADH	BCF	EGO	IJ	KN	LM
∅	∅	∅∅∅	∅∅∅	∅∅∅	∅∅	∅∅	∅∅
A	∅	A∅A	B∅B	E∅E	AB	BE	AE
B	∅	∅AA	∅BB	∅EE	BA	EB	EA
E	∅	AAA	BBB	EEE	EE	EE	EE
C	∅	∅DD	∅CC	∅GG	CD	GC	GD
D	∅	D∅D	C∅C	G∅G	DC	CG	DG
G	∅	DDD	CCC	GGG	GG	GG	GG
F	∅	∅HH	∅FF	∅OO	FH	OF	OH
H	∅	H∅H	F∅F	O∅O	HF	FO	HO
O	∅	HHH	FFF	OOO	OO	OO	OO
I	∅	ADH	BCF	EGO	IJ	KN	LM
J	∅	DAH	CBF	GEO	JI	NK	ML
K	∅	DHH	CFF	GOO	KL	OK	OL
L	∅	HDH	FCF	OGO	LK	KO	LO
M	∅	HAH	FBF	OEO	MN	NO	MO
N	∅	AHH	BFF	EOO	NM	ON	OM

to measure the size of a given network of people who know each other or go on holiday together.

Formally, a network consists of a population and the relation(s) that link them up. From this observation, Ove Frank (1988) designates the composition of a network as a set of individual traits and a structure as the features of the edges. He then classifies various situations which require that relational structure be taken into account according to whether the population and structure of relations are predetermined or random as follows:

	Predetermined structure	Random structure
Predetermined composition	1	2
Random composition	3	4

Case 1 corresponds to studying a complete network. This is a determinist model in the sense that it rules out any probability calculations. Case 2 has a predetermined population in a structure assumed to be random. This would apply to an investigation of who knows whom in a city setting. Here we take a sample and observe relations among sample subjects. From there we draw conclusions about global structure. Case 3 has a preset structure but individuals are assumed to be in a random state. Diffusion models are of this type. We start with a friendship network and observe if it explains the diffusion of a new gadget, piece of information or lifestyle pattern. Markov chain models are also of this type. Case 4 has random structure and composition. This model is useful in longitudinal surveys where we select a sample at the outset but some subjects drop out and new subjects hop on along the way. Thus, our conclusions will depend on the composition of the graph. For example, if we construct a model to describe the spread of HIV infection, we need to take account of the fact that respondents who establish links at one point in time will eventually develop AIDS and disappear from the survey population.

The sampling techniques for exploring any given structure are therefore relevant to case 2. We constitute a sample to observe certain structural features at work in the sample and provide insight about the structure. But what is the significance of this operation and, more importantly, what are the risks? Let's take another example.

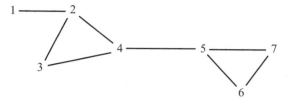

We shall assume this graph represents the relational structure for a group of seven persons. We shall use simple features. This graph only shows one connected component but as a rule the number of connected components is an obvious indicator to estimate. The number of individuals in relation to a single individual is also valuable data. This leads us to consider the distribution of values for node degrees.

Degree values	0	1	2	3	4	5	6
No. nodes	0	1	3	3	0	0	0

The seven nodes combine into a total of 21 potential dyads. Some nodes will be edges and we shall call them 'type 1', while those which are not edges will be 'type 0'. This gives us the following distribution by type of dyad:

Dyad type	0	1
Total no. dyads	13	8

We can go on to examine triads in terms of four categories that vary as a function of node type. Here, we have a total of 35.

Triad type	1	2	3	4
Total no. of triads	5	22	6	2

Obviously, we cannot reconstruct a graph from the statistics but they offer insight nonetheless. If we put ourselves in the position of a researcher trying to understand the structure from her sample, she will choose some of the nodes and then turn to the corresponding subgraph to see the edges. Our example is based on a sample of four nodes with a potential of 35 distinct samples. For each sample, we look at the distribution of degrees, dyad and triads and fit them into different types. We shall take three subgraphs in Table A.5 as examples.

We immediately see that some samples misrepresent the working universe. But if we review all possible samples, we soon realize the most frequent distributions best approach the features of the working universe. Bernouilli's theorem is at work here and helps pick out the estimators that will satisfactorily evaluate the number of edges on a graph as a function of the type of sample at hand, or the mean, or the variances of degree distribution, or the number of components. Frank (1981), who churned out enormous amounts of results on this subject, has introduced a broad overview of estimators and the polling techniques that go with them. Thus a sample

Table A.5

	Subgraphs											
	1234				2356				1346			
Degree	0	1	2	3	0	1	2	3	0	1	2	3
Total	0	1	2	1	0	4	0	0	2	2	0	0
Dyad type		0	1			0	1			0	1	
Total		2	4			4	2			5	1	
Triad type	1	2	3	4	1	2	3	4	1	2	3	4
Total	0	1	2	1	0	4	0	0	2	2	0	0

of a structure should theoretically yield valuable data, but reality is often more complex unfortunately.

Granovetter (1976) uses Frank's results to examine the feasibility of estimating the social density of a graph. In practice, the technique involves producing a list of names of reachable people from a given population. We then extract a sample and invite each respondent to identify who he knows. Performing several successive samplings will improve the accuracy of estimates. Granovetter says this technique is the best way to learn 'who knows who in a given population'.

If respondents study the handout lists seriously, we should harvest reliable data in addition to avoiding forgetfulness, rationalization and other scourges of direct interviewing. However, one unknown replaces another and we have little control over the effects of long interrogations that have respondents reeling off 'No, don't know him' name after name. Granovetter has worked out optimum sample sizes as a function of total population size and average number of relations per member respondent (Table A.6).

Table A.6   Optimum sample sizes according to population and network size

Total population	Average individual network size	Optimum sample size
1,000,000	100	1,465
1,000,000	500	705
1,000,000	1,000	477
100,000	100	522
100,000	500	292
100,000	1,000	181
10,000	100	233
10,000	500	178
10,000	1,000	93

The values for sample sizes will obtain an estimate that is within 20% of the value to be estimated in 95% of cases. Sample sizes are only indicative and any actual survey requires precise calculations based on Frank (1981). But the table does show that the operation is feasible because we can reasonably expect any respondent who reads the list studiously to reel off at least 100 ties if not 500+ in a good number of cases.

The drawback of this approach is that the researcher is left with a nagging doubt about information loss. If we assume the average respondent knows 500 persons in a given population of 100,000, she stands a 1:200 chance of recognizing someone on a list of 300 names, and will recognize 1.5. This means we would be startled by anyone recognizing, say, five names. Had we asked her to list who she knew in town, she would have spontaneously named far more contacts and given us a better idea of her actual personal network. However, we would still have no reliable estimate for the average number of persons anyone knows.

Morgan and Rytina (1977) have also raised the case of a segmented population. Northern Ireland has a population of 1.5 million with a 60/40 split between Protestants and Catholics. We could decide to compare the densities of links among Protestants with those for Catholics. Assuming each person knows an averages of 500 others, we would need a list of 575 Catholics and 700 Protestants. However, Morgan and Rytina point out that it would be more sociologically relevant to learn the density of links *between* Catholics and Protestants. To evaluate this, we would need a random list of 800 names. If responses are matched between respondents, we would need a total of 800 × 799 name queries, i.e. 639,200 questions. This figure daunts. Morgan and Rytina throw up their arms and find this approach only workable with small populations. Granovetter protests. But the bottom line is that nobody has ever applied this technique on a large scale.

Surveys

So far we have assumed the sample consists of a *selected* set of nodes and that we have observed the edges existing between them.

Studies based on name generators operate very differently. They start by defining a subset X and studying all edges adjacent to at least one node. If we call a given node a 'star', E is the set of edges adjacent to her and their connecting nodes. The resulting graph includes all stars originating in each node.

The snowball survey is a variant of the name generator. Starting with a set of X nodes, we use the nodes around the stars to obtain a new set of nodes that become stars and repeat this operation as often as needed (see Goodman, 1961; Snijders, 1992).

For his part, Klovdahl (1989) has developed yet another technique. His random walk strategy starts with a set of nodes X and determines the star of each node, but gleans at random only one node to establish a new star. And so on. We thus obtain a sample of nodes and edges that correspond to a set of chains. This approach is very useful but runs up against the fact that we have no way of calculating appropriate standard estimators because we still have a poor statistical under-standing of this type of sample. Here again, we still have a long way to go before we bridge the gap between observations of complete networks and samplings of personal networks.

Galois Lattices and Hypergraphs

Social network analysis sometimes needs qualitative studies of similarity between people and objects. We shall assume we know which members of a given popu-lation have attended a certain series of parties or other social events or belong to a youth club or other social circle. The network thus consists of a family of fragments in set X, i.e. a hypergraph. The nodes of this hypergraph are the elements of set X and the edges are the subsets. Likewise, we construct maximal cliques on a graph by identifying which sets show outstanding cohesion and it becomes interesting to seek out the structure that clique memberships infer. In all of the above cases (and others too) this type of structure is a Galois lattice or concept lattice.

We shall borrow the Meylan graphs of maximal cliques from Chapter 4 for an example. There we found five maximal cliques of at least two nodes apiece (Figure 4.2). Here again we label them a, b, c, d and e. Table A.7 below maps out clique memberships.

Table A.7   Maximal cliques for Meylan example

		Clique				
		a	b	c	d	e
APACH	(1)	1	1	1	1	0
APEDI	(2)	1	1	0	0	0
Grand Pré	(3)	1	0	0	0	0
MJC	(4)	1	1	1	1	0
Haut-Meylan	(5)	0	1	0	0	0
Revirée	(6)	0	0	1	0	0
Centre Musical	(7)	1	0	0	1	0
Harmonie	(8)	0	0	0	1	1
Saint-Valentin	(9)	0	0	0	0	1

Columns indicate cliques. For example, the 'word' ad designates 'comprehensibly' the intersection of cliques a and d. We can also list cliques 'extensionally' as sets of elements, e.g. a: $\{1, 2, 3, 4, 7\}$, or d: $\{1, 4, 7, 8\}$. When we examine what cliques a and d have in common, we obtain $\{1, 2, 3, 4, 7\} \cap \{1, 4, 7, 8\} = \{1, 4, 7\}$.

If we rearrange Table A.7 so that a and d are side by side and rows 1, 4 and 7 follow one another, we obtain a block with a 1 in every cell. Furthermore we have a maximal block because it would cease to contain only 1s as soon as an extra row or column is added. Figure A.4 shows all maximal blocks with a 1 in every cell which are possible for this table. Every node is a block. It is designated as a comprehensive block (by the right-hand element of its label) and as extensive (by the left-hand element). Two blocks toward the bottom combine to unite the right-hand fraction with the intersection of the left-hand fraction. The opposite is true toward the top.

This graph is a Galois lattice for the table (Duquenne, 1992; 1996). It displays up the data in a different manner and can be used to reconstruct the original table. It also highlights the implications. For example, every clique that contains 2 also contains 1 and 4. Likewise $6 \Rightarrow (1, 4)$, $7 \Rightarrow (1, 4)$ and $9 \Rightarrow 8$.

Although Galois lattices are symmetrical by definition, we usually work on either the rows or the columns. For example, we can use them to work on diseases in terms of sets of symptoms or even the questions on a questionnaire in terms of respondents' responses. However, Galois lattices become unwieldy once the number of elements in the columns or rows exceeds 20.

Galois lattices do not just show up individuals sharing strong links because of common traits; they also identify these traits. They are therefore a tool of

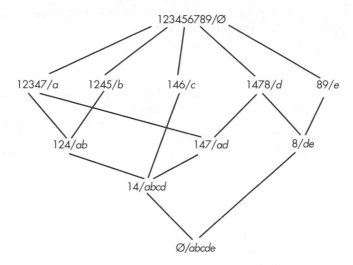

Figure A.4   Galois lattice for Meylan example

qualitative analysis. Freeman (1992) finds it a worthwhile way of studying the content of social groups.

Software

Several software packages are commercially available to process network data, and we shall review Ucinet® and Structure®, the two most popular.[1]

Ucinet®

Ucinet® is by Linton Freeman, Steve Borgatti and Martin Everett. It contains a good number of standard multivariate analysis tools and routines such as multi-dimensional scaling (MDS), correspondence analysis and hierarchical clustering.

Data import/export is via ASCII. The software performs matrix symmetrization, row/column selection and other transformations. An integrated spreadsheet function makes for convenient data input to matrices and matrix modification.

Features specific to network analysis are as follows:

1   Connectivity functions include geodesic distances, node accessibility and path studies. Built-in algorithms give path lengths on valued graphs, link strengths and the costs as well as the probabilities of links.
2   Centrality functions include degree, closeness and betweenness for valued and unvalued graphs. Also included are centrality and power scoring based on matrix-specific vectors.
3   Subgroup search functions include maximal and n-cliques, n-clans, lambda sets, factions, k-plex and k-cores. It will also identify graph components and calculate densities for each.

4   Role and position analysis functions include searches for regular, structural, automorphic and other equivalence searches

Structure®

This software package is by Ronald Burt. The latest version offers two new utilities: Jedit®, which simplifies the processes of affiliation data (e.g. actor/event matrices); and Assistant®, a user-friendly wizard to write batch programs that set up data for input to Structure®. Here too, data import/export is via ASCII.

  This package also offers a wide range of powerful features and the following six are specific to the network analyst's needs:

1   Cohesion functions include clique searches for weak/strong cohesion by weak/strong connectivity, social circle overlap, hierarchical clustering and spatial charting with distance maps.
2   Structural equivalence functions include distance maps, automatic clustering, and density tables that obtain optimum distribution of individuals into equivalences after the wizard sets up the data. The output in density tables is handy to construct the block models of a network. Obviously, all these functions are built around Burt's approach.
3   Diffusion functions include several ways of testing the effects of relations on diffusion which can be based on either cohesion or equivalence.
4   Individual autonomy analysis functions cover a set of personal indicators including non-redundant contacts, contact efficacy, density, constraints and hierarchy.
5   Power and equilibrium functions cover a set of personal indicators including prominence, centrality and eigenvectors. Actual equilibrium analysis operates using models with or without actor substitution.
6   Monte Carlo functions include all manner of analyses just mentioned that lend themselves to Monte Carlo analysis. They serve to compare randomized results against empirical data.

Notes

1   UCINET® is available from Pro GAMMA bv, P.O. Box 841, 9700 AV Groningen, The Netherlands
Phone: +31 50 363 69 00, Fax: +31 50 363 66 87
WWW: http://www.gamma.rug.nl, e-mail: gamma.post@gamma.rug.nl

  Structure® is distributed by Columbia University, Center of Social Sciences, 420 West 118th Street, 8th Floor, New York, NY 10027, USA.

BIBLIOGRAPHY

Adam, G. and Reynaud J.-D. (1978) *Conflits du travail et changement social*. Paris: PUF.

Agulhon, M., Gemelli, G. and Malatesta, M. (1982) *Forme di sociabilità nella storiografia francese contemporanea*. Milan: Feltrinelli.

Alba, R. and Kadushin, C. (1976) 'The intersection of social circles', *Sociological Methods and Research*, 5: 77–102.

Allan, G. (1979) *A Sociology of Friendship and Kinship*. London: Allen and Unwin.

Allan, G. (1989) *Friendship: Developing a Sociological Perspective*. Hemel Hempstead: Harvester Wheatsheaf.

Baechler, J. (1992) 'Groupes et sociabilité', in R. Boudon (ed.), *Traité de sociologie*. Paris: PUF.

Barnes, J.E. (1954) 'Class and committees in a Norwegian island parish', *Human Relations*, VII (1): 39–58.

Barnes, J.E. (1972) *Social Networks*. Reading, MA: Addison-Wesley.

Bavelas, A. (1948) 'A mathematical model for group structures', *Human Organization*, 7: 16–30.

Bavelas, A. (1950) 'Communication patterns in task oriented groups', *Journal of the Acoustical Society of America*, 22: 271–82.

Beauchamp, M.A. (1965) 'An improved index of centrality', *Behavioural Science*, 10: 161–3.

Becker, G.S. (1971) *Economic Theory*. New York: Knopf.

Becker, G.S. (1976) *The Economic Approach to Human Behaviour*. Chicago: University of Chicago Press.

Berge, C. (1967) *Théorie des graphes et ses applications*. Paris: Dunod. Translated as *The Theory of Graphs and its Applications*. Westport, CT: Greenwood, 1982.

Berge, C. (1970) *Graphes*. Paris: Gauthier-Villars. Translated as *Graphs*. Amsterdam: Elsevier North-Holland, 1985.

Berge, C. (1987) *Hypergraphes*. Paris: Dunod. Translated as *Hypergraphs: Combinatorics of Finite Sets*. Amsterdam: Elsevier North-Holland, 1989.

Berkowitz, S.D. (1988) 'Markets and market-areas: some preliminary', in B. Wellman and S.D. Berkowitz (eds), *Social Structures: a Network Approach*, Cambridge: Cambridge University Press.

Bertin, J. (1967) *Sémiologie graphique, les diagrammes – les réseaux – les cartes*. Paris: Gauthier-Villars.

Bidart, C. (1997) *L'Amitié: un lien social*. Paris: La Découverte.

Blau, P. (1977) *Inequality and Heterogeneity*. New York: Free Press.

Blau, P. (1993) 'Multilevel structural analysis', *Social Networks*, 15 (2): 201–15.

Blau, P. and Schwartz, J. (1984) *Crosscutting Social Circles*. Orlando, FL: Academic Press.

Bonacich, P. (1972) 'Factoring and weighting approaches to status scores and clique identification', *Journal of Mathematical Sociology*, 2: 113–20.

Bonacich, P. (1987) 'Power and centrality: a family of measures', *American Journal of Sociology*, 92 (5): 1170–82.

Bonvalet, C., Maison, D., Le Bras, H. and Charles, L. (1993) 'Proches et parents', *Population*, 1: 83–110.

Bott, E. (1957) *Family and Social Networks*, 2nd edn 1971. New York: Free Press.

Boudon, R. (1988) 'Individualisme ou holisme: un débat méthodologique fondamental', in H. Mendras and M. Verret (eds), *Les Champs de la sociologie française*. Paris: Armand Colin.

Bouglé, C. (1897) 'Qu'est-ce que la sociologie', *Revue de Paris*.

Bourdieu, P. (1980) 'Le capital social', *Actes de la Recherche en Sciences Sociales*, 31: 2–3.

Boyd, J.P. (1992) *Social Semigroups*. Fairfax, VA: George Mason University Press.

Bozon, M. (1984) *Vie quotidienne et rapports sociaux dans une petite ville de province*. Lyon: PUL.

Bozon, M. and Héran, F. (1987) 'La découverte du conjoint', *Population*, 6: 943–87.

Bozon, M. and Lemel, Y. (1990) 'Les petits profits du travail salarié', *Revue Française de Sociologie*, XXXI (1): 101–27.

Brain, R. (1976) *Friends and Lovers*. London: Hart-Davis, MacGibbon. Translated as *Amis et amants*. Paris: Stock, 1980.

Breiger, R., Boorman, S. and Arabie, P. (1975) 'An algorithm for clustering relational data with applications to social network analysis and comparison with multidimensional scaling', *Journal of Mathematical Psychology*, 12: 328–83.

Burt, R. (1982) *Toward a Structural Theory of Action*. New York: Academic Press.

Burt, R. (1992a) *Structural Holes: the Social Structure of Competition*. Cambridge, MA: Harvard University Press.

Burt, R. (1992b) *Structure, Version 4.2, Reference Manual*. New York: Columbia University Center for the Social Sciences.

Caplow, T. (1968) *Two against One: Coalitions in Triads*. Englewood Cliffs, NJ: Prentice-Hall.

Caplow, T. and Forman, R. (1950) 'Neighborhood interaction in a homogeneous community', *American Sociological Review*, 15.

Choquet, O. (1988) 'Les sorties, une occasion de contacts', *Economie et Statistique*, 214: 19–25.

Clifford, A.H. and Preston, G.B. (1961) *The Algebraic Theory of Semigroups*. Providence, RI: American Mathematical Society.

Cohn, B.S. and Mariott, M. (1958) 'Networks and centres of integration in Indian civilization', *Journal of Social Research*, 1: 1–9.

Coleman, J.S. (1966) 'Foundations for a theory of collective action', *American Journal of Sociology*, 71: 615–27.

Coleman, J.S. (1973) *The Mathematics of Collective Action*. Chicago: Aldine.

Coleman, J.S. (1990) *The Foundations of Social Theory*. Cambridge, MA: Harvard University Press.

Coleman, J.S., Katz, E. and Menzel, H. (1966) *Medical Innovation: a Diffusion Study*. New York: Bobbs-Merrill.

Colson, E. (1955) 'Social control and vengeance in Plateau-Tonga society', *Africa*, 23: 119–212.

Cook, K. and Emerson, R. (1978) 'Power, equity and commitment in exchange networks', *American Sociological Review*, 43: 721–39.

Cook, K., Emerson, R., Gillmore, R. and Yamagishi, T. (1983) 'The distribution of power in exchange networks: theory and experimental results', *American Journal of Sociology*, 89: 275–305.

Cook, K. and Yamagishi, T. (1992) 'Power in exchange networks: a power-dependence formulation', *Social Networks*, 14 (3–4): 245–65.

Courgeau, D. (1972) 'Les réseaux de relations entre personnes, étude d'un milieu rural', *Population*, 4–5: 641–84.

Crozier, M. and Friedberg, E. (1977) *L'Acteur et le système*. Paris: Seuil. Translated as *Actors and Systems: the Politics of the Collective*. Chicago: University of Chicago Press, 1980.

Czepiel, J.A. (1974) 'Word of mouth processes in the diffusion of a major technological innovation', *Journal of Marketing Research*, 11: 172–80.

Dahl, R.A. (1957) 'The concept of power', *Behavioural Science*, 2: 201–15.

Dahl, R.A. (1958) 'Critique of the ruling elite model', *American Political Review*, 52: 463–9.

Dahl, R.A. (1961) *Who Governs? Democracy and Power in the American City*. New Haven, CT: Yale University Press.

Dahrendorf, R. (1957) *Class and Class Conflict in Industrial Society*. Stanford, CT: Stanford University Press.

Dalud-Vincent, M., Forsé, M. and Auray, J.-P. (1994) 'An algorithm for finding the structure of social groups', *Social Networks*, 16 (1).

Davis, A., Gardner, B.B. and Gardner, M.R. (1941) *Deep South*. Chicago: University of Chicago Press.

Degenne, A. (1986) 'Un langage pour l'étude des réseaux sociaux', in OCS, *L'Esprit des lieux*. Paris: Editions du CNRS. pp. 291–312.

Degenne, A., Fournier, I., Marry, C. and Mounier, L. (1991) 'Les relations au coeur du marché du travail', *Sociétés Contemporaines*, 5: 75–98.

Degenne, A. and Lebeaux, M.-O. (1991) 'L'Entraide entre les ménages, un facteur d'inégalité sociale?', *Sociétés Contemporaines*, 8: 21–42.

Degenne, A. and Lebeaux, M.-O. (1993) 'Les rôles conjugaux dans leur environnement social', *L'Année Sociologique*, 43: 253–68.

De Graaf, N. and Flap, H. (1988) 'With a little help from my friends', *Social Forces*, 67: 453–72.

Doreian, P. (1988) 'Equivalence in a social network', *Journal of Mathematical Sociology*, 13 (3): 243–82.

Doreian, P. and Stokman, F. (eds) (1997) *Evolution of Social Networks*. Amsterdam: Gordon and Breach.

Doreian, P. and Woodward, K.L. (1994) 'Defining and locating cores and boundaries of social networks', *Social Networks*, 16 (4): 267–93.

Dubar, C., Gayot, G. and Hidoux, J. (1982) 'Sociabilité minière et changement social à Sallaumines et à Noyelles-sous-Lens (1900–1980)', *Revue du Nord*, LXIV (253): 363–463.

Dujardin, P. (1988) *Du groupe au réseau*. Paris: Editions du CNRS.

Duquenne, V. (1992) *GLAD (General Lattice Analysis and Design): a Fortran Program for a Glad User*. Paris: MSH-Maison Suger.

Duquenne, V. (1996) 'On lattice approximations: syntactic aspects', *Social Networks*, 18: 189–99.

Durkheim, E. (1893) *De la division du travail social*. Paris. Republished by PUF, 1930, 1973. Translated as *The Division of Labor in Society*. New York: Free Press, 1984.

Emerson, R.M. (1962) 'Power–dependence relations', *American Sociological Review*, 27: 31–40.

Emerson, R.M. (1972) 'Exchange theory part 1: a psychological basis for social exchange. Exchange theory part 2: exchange relations and network structures', in J. Berger, M. Zelditch and B. Anderson (eds), *Sociological Theories in Progress*, Vol. 2. Boston: Houghton Mifflin.

Epstein, A.L. (1969) 'The network of urban organization', in J.C. Mitchell (ed.), *Social Networks in Urban Situation*. Manchester: Manchester University Press. pp. 77–116.

Evans-Pritchard, E. (1939) 'Introduction', in J.G. Peristiany, *The Social Institution of the Kipsigis*. London: Routledge.

Evans-Pritchard, E. (1940) *The Nuer*. London: Oxford University Press. Translated by L. Emard as *Les Nuers*. Paris: Gallimard, 1968.

Fararo, T.J. and Skvoretz, J. (1987) 'Unification research programs: integrating two structural theories', *American Journal of Sociology*, 92 (5): 1183–209.

Ferrand, A. (1982) *Parents, habitants, citoyens. Meylan banlieue grenobloise*. Lyon: Editions du CNRS.

Ferrand, A. (1991) 'La confidence: des relations au réseau', *Sociétés Contemporaines*, 5: 7–20.

Ferrand, A. and Mounier, L. (1993) 'L'échange de paroles sur la sexualité: une analyse des relations de confidence', *Population*, 5: 1451–76.

Firth, R. (1954) 'Social organization and social change', *Journal of the Royal Anthropological Institute*, LXXXIV: 1–18.

Fisher, C.S. (1948) *To Dwell among Friends*. Chicago: Chicago University Press, 2nd edn, 1982.

Flament, C. (1991) 'Associations-réseaux et réseaux d'associations, *Sociétés Contemporaines*, 5: 67–74.

Flament, Cl. (1963) *Application of Graph Theory to Group Structures*. Englewood Cliffs, NJ: Prentice-Hall.

Flament, Cl. (1979) 'Independent generalization of balance', in P.V. Hollandt and S. Leinhardt (eds), *Perspectives in Social Network Research*. New York: Academic Press.

Flap, H. (1988) *Conflict, Loyalty and Violence*. Frankfurt: Peter Lang.

Ford, L.R. and Fulkerson, D.R. (1957) 'A simple algorithm for finding maximal network flows and an application to the Hitchcock problem', *Canada Journal of Mathematics*, 9: 210–18.

Forsé, M. (1981a) 'La sociabilité', *Economie et Statistique*, 132: 39–48.

Forsé, M. (1981b) 'Les réseaux de sociabilité dans un village', *Population*, 6: 1141–62.

Forsé, M. (1984) 'Les créations d'associations: un indicateur de changement social', *Observations et diagnostics économiques, Revue de l'OFCE*, 6: 125–45.

Forsé, M. (1991) 'Contribution à une morphologie des rôles réticulaires', *Sociétés Contemporaines*, 5: 43–53.

Forsé, M. (1993a) 'Les créations d'associations progressent selon un rythme ralenti', in Louis Dirn (ed.), *Chronique des tendances de la société française*, special issue of *Observations et Diagnostics Économiques, Revue de l'OFCE*, 46: 272–4.

Forsé, M. (1993b) 'La fréquence des relations de sociabilité: typologie et évolution', *L'Année Sociologique*, 43: 189–212.

Forsé, M. (1997) 'Capital social et emploi', *L'Année Sociologique*, 47 (1): 143–81.

Forsé, M. and Chauvel, L. (1995) 'L'évolution de l'homogamie en France', *Revue Française de Sociologie*, XXXVI (1): 123–42.

Foster, B.L. and Seidman, S.B. (1982) 'Urban structures derived from collections of overlapping subsets', *Urban Anthropology*, 11 (2).

Frank, O. (1981) 'A survey of statistical methods for graph analysis', in S. Leinhardt (ed.), *Sociological Methodology*. San Francisco: Jossey-Bass. pp. 110–55.

Frank, O. (1988) 'Random sampling and social networks, a survey of various approaches', *Mathématiques et Sciences Humaines*, 26 (104): 19–33.

Freeman, L. (1979) 'Centrality in social networks. Conceptual clarification', *Social Networks*, 1: 215–39.

Freeman, L. (1992) 'La résurrection des cliques: applications du treillis de Galois', *Bulletin de Méthodologie Sociologique*, 37: 3–24.

Freeman, L., Borgatti, S. and White, D. (1991) 'Centrality in valued graphs. A measure of betweenness based on network flow', *Social Networks*, 13: 141–54.

Freeman, L. and Thompson, C.R. (1989) 'Estimating acquaintanceship volume', in M. Kochen (ed.), *The Small World*. Norwood, NJ: Ablex. pp. 147–58.

Friedkin, N.E. (1991) 'Theoretical foundations of centrality measures', *American Journal of Sociology*, 96 (6): 1478–504.

Galaskiewicz, J. (1979a) 'The structure of community interorganizational networks', *Social Forces*, 57: 1346–64.

Galaskiewicz, J. (1979b) *Exchange Networks and Community Politics*. Beverly Hills, CA: Sage.

Galtung, J. (1966) 'Rank and social integration: a multidimensional approach', in B. Berger, M. Zelditch and B. Anderson (eds), *Sociological Theories in Progress*, Vol. 1. Boston: Houghton Mifflin. pp. 145–98.

Gamson, W.A. (1961) 'A theory of coalition formation', *American Sociological Review*, 26 (3): 373–83.

Gans, H. (1962) *The Urban Villagers*. Glencoe, IL: Free Press.

Gans, H. (1967) *The Levittowners*. London: Allen Lane.

Girard, A. (1964) *Le Choix du conjoint*. Paris: PUF.

Gluckman, M. (1965) 'Stateless society and maintenance of order', in M. Gluckman (ed.), *Politics, Law and Ritual in Tribal Society*. Oxford: Blackwell.

Goffman, E. (1959) *The Presentation of Self in Everyday Life*. New York: Doubleday Anchor. Also *Relations in Public*, Basic Books. Translated as *La Mise en scène de la vie quotidienne*. Paris: Vols 1 and 2, 1973.

Goffman, E. (1967) *Interaction Ritual*. Translated as *Les Rites de l'interaction*. Paris: Minuit, 1974.

Goodman, L.A. (1961) 'Snowball sampling', *Annals of Mathematical Statistics*, 32: 148–70.

Gould, R.V. and Fernandez, R.M. (1989) 'Structure of mediation: a formal approach to brokerage in transactions networks', *Sociological Methodology*, 89–126.

Granovetter, M.S. (1973) 'The strength of weak ties', *American Journal of Sociology*, 78: 1360–80.

Granovetter, M.S. (1974) *Getting a Job: a Study of Contacts and Careers*. Cambridge, MA: Harvard University Press.

Granovetter, M.S. (1976) 'Network sampling, some first steps', *American Journal of Sociology*, 81: 1287–303.

Granovetter, M.S. (1982) 'The strength of weak ties: a network theory revisited', in

P.V. Marsden and N. Lin (eds), *Social Structure and Network Analysis*. Beverly Hills, CA: Sage.

Granovetter, M.S. (1985) 'Economic action and social structure: the problem of embeddedness', *American Journal of Sociology*, 91: 481–510.

Guilbaud, G.T. (1970) 'Système parental et matrimonial au Nord Ambrym', *Journal de la Société des Océanistes*, 26: 9–32.

Guilbot, O. (1979) 'Vers une analyse stratégique de la sociabilité', *Archives de l'OCS*, 1: 7–32.

Gurvitch, G. (1950) *La Vocation actuelle de la sociologie*, Vol. 1. Paris: PUF.

Hage, P. and Harary, F. (1995) 'Eccentricity and centrality in networks', *Social Networks*, 17: 57–63.

Hall, A. and Wellman, B. (1985) 'Social networks and social support', in S. Cohen and J. Syme (eds), *Social Support and Health*. New York: Academic Press. pp. 23–41.

Harary, F. (1959) 'On the measurement of structural balance', *Behavioural Science*, 4: 316–23.

Harary, F., Norman, R. and Cartwright, D. (1965) *Structural Models: an Introduction to the Theory of Directed Graphs*. New York: Wiley. Translated as *Introduction à la théorie des graphes orientés*. Paris: Dunod, 1968.

Heider, F. (1946) 'Attitude and cognitive organisation', *Journal of Psychology*, 21: 107–12.

Heider, F. (1979) 'On balance and attribution', in P.V. Hollandt and S. Leinhardt (eds), *Perspectives in Social Network Research*. New York: Academic Press.

Héran, F. (1987) 'Comment les Français voisinent', *Economie et Statistique*, 195: 43–60.

Héran, F. (1988a) 'Un monde sélectif: les associations', *Economie et Statistique*, 208: 17–31.

Héran, F. (1988b) 'La sociabilité, une pratique culturelle', *Economie et Statistique*, 216: 3–21.

Hobbes, T. (1651) *Léviathan*. New York: Collier, 1962.

Hoggart, R. (1957) *The Uses of Literacy*. London: Chatto and Windus. Translated as *La Culture du pauvre*. Paris: Minuit, 1970.

Homans, G. (1951) *The Human Group*. London: Routledge and Kegan Paul.

Howie, J.M. (1976) *An Introduction to Semigroup Theory*. London: Academic Press.

Hunter, F. (1953) *Community Power Structure*. Chapel Hill, NC: University of North Carolina Press.

Jambu, M. and Lebeaux, M.-O. (1982) *Cluster Analysis for Data Analysis*. Amsterdam: North-Holland.

Jamous, H. (1968) *Contribution à une sociologie de la décision: la réforme des études médicales et des structures hospitalières*. Paris: Copédith.

Jardine, N. and Sibson, R. (1971) *Mathematical Taxonomy*. New York: Wiley.

Jobson, J.D. (1992) *Applied Multivariate Data Analysis. Volume II: Categorical and Multivariate Methods*. New York: Springer.

Johnsen, E. (1986) 'Structure and process: agreement models for friendship formation', *Social Networks*, 8: 257–306.

Kadushin, C. (1966) 'The friends and supporters of psychotherapy: on social circles in urban life', *American Sociological Review*, 31: 786–802.

Kadushin, C. (1968) 'Power influence and social circles. A new methodology for studying opinion makers', *American Sociological Review*, 33 (5): 685–99.

Kadushin, C. (1982) 'Social density and mental health', in P.V. Marsden and N. Lin (eds), *Social Structure and Network Analysis*. Beverly Hills, CA: Sage. pp. 147–58.

Katz, E. (1953) 'A new status index derived from sociometric analysis', *Psychometrika*, 18: 39–43.

Katz, E. and Lazarsfeld, P.F. (1955) *Personal Influence: the Part Played by People in the Flow of Mass Communication*. Glencoe, IL: Free Press.

Killworth, P.D. and Bernard, H.R. (1978) 'The reverse small world experiment', *Social Networks*, 1: 159–92.

Killworth, P.D., Bernard, H.R. and McCarthy, C. (1984) 'Measuring patterns of acquaintanceship', *Current Anthropology*, 25: 381–97.

Klovdahl, A.S. (1989) 'Urban social networks. Some methodological problems and possibilities', in M. Kochen (ed.), *The Small World*. Norwood, NJ: Ablex. pp. 176–210.

Klovdahl, A.S., Potterat, J., Woodhouse, D., Muth, J., Muth, S. and Dazzow, W.W. (1992) 'HIV infection in a urban social network', *Bulletin de Méthodologie Sociologique*, 36: 24–33.

Knoke, D. (1983) 'Organization sponsorship and influence reputation of social influence associations', *Social Perspectives*. Cambridge: Cambridge University Press.

Knoke, D. (1990) *Political Networks: the Structural Perspective*. Cambridge: Cambridge University Press.

Knoke, D. and Burt, R.S. (1983) 'Prominence', in R.S. Burt and M.J. Minor (eds), *Applied Network Analysis*. Beverly Hills, CA: Sage. pp. 195–222.

Knoke, D. and Kuklinski, J. (1982) *Network Analysis*. London: Sage.

Kochen M. (ed.) (1989) *The Small World*. Norwood, NJ: Ablex.

Lagrange, H. (1992) 'Appréhension et préoccupation sécuritaire', *Déviance et société*, 16 (1): 1–29.

Langlois, S. (1977) 'Les réseaux personnels et la diffusion des informations sur les emplois', *Recherches sociographiques*, XVIII (2): 213–46.

Laumann, E.O. and Pappi, F.U. (1976) *Networks of Collective Action: a Perspective in Community Influence Systems*. New York: Academic Press.

Lazarsfeld, P.F. and Merton, R.K. (1982) 'Friendship as social process: a substantive and methodological analysis', in P. Kendall (ed.), *The Varied Sociology of Paul F. Lazarsfeld*. New York: Columbia University Press.

Lazega, E. (1992) 'Une analyse de réseaux: les avocats d'affaire', *Revue Française de Sociologie*, XXXIII (4): 559–89.

Lazega, E. (1994) 'Analyse de réseaux et sociologie des organisations', *Revue Française de Sociologie*, XXXV (2): 293–320.

Leavitt, H.J. (1951) 'Some effects of communication patterns on group performance', *Journal of Abnormal and Social Psychology*, 46: 38–50.

Leinhardt, S. (1977) *Social Networks: a Developing Paradigm*. New York: Academic Press.

Lemel, Y. and Paradeise, C. (1974) 'Appartenance et participation à des associations', *Economie et statistique*, 55: 41–6.

Lemel, Y. and Paradeise, C. (1976) *La sociabilité*. Paris: INSEE.

Lemieux, V. (1982) *Réseaux et appareils*. Québec: Edisem. Paris: Maloine.

Lévi-Strauss, C. (1949) *Les Structures élémentaires de la parenté*. Paris: PUF. Translated as *The Elementary Structures of Kinship*. Boston: Beacon, 1969.

Levine, J. (1972) 'The sphere of influence', *American Sociological Review*, 37: 14–27.

Levine, J. (1985) *Atlas of Corporate Interlocks*. Worldnet.

Levine, J. (1987) 'The methodology of the *Atlas of Corporate Interlocks*', *Bulletin de Méthodologie Sociologique*, 17: 20–58.

Leydesdorff, L. (1991) 'The static and dynamic analysis of network data using information theory', *Social Networks*, 13 (4): 301–45.

Lin, N. (1982) 'Social resources and instrumental action', in P.V. Marsden and N. Lin (eds), *Social Structure and Network Analysis*. Beverly Hills, CA: Sage.

Lorrain, F. (1975) *Réseaux sociaux et classifications sociales*. Paris: Hermann.

Lorrain, F. and White, H.C. (1971) 'Structural equivalence of individuals in social networks', *Journal of Mathematical Sociology*, 1: 49–80.

Lynd, R.S. and Lynd, H.M. (1937) *Middletown in Transition*. New York: Harcourt Brace.

Maisonneuve, J. (1966) *Psycho-sociologie des affinités*. Paris: PUF.

Maisonneuve, J. and Lamy, L. (1993) *Psychosociologie de l'amitié*. Paris: PUF.

Marry, C. (1983) 'Origine sociale et réseaux d'insertion des jeunes ouvriers', *Formation-Emploi*, 4: 3–15.

Marsden, P.V. (1982) 'Brokerage behaviours in restricted exchange networks', in P.V. Marsden and N. Lin (eds), *Social Structure and Network Analysis*. Beverly Hills, CA: Sage.

Marsden, P.V. and Laumann, E.O. (1977) 'Collective action in a community elite: exchange, influence processes, and issue resolution', in R.J. Liebert and A. Imershein (eds), *Power, Paradigms and Community Research*. London: Sage. pp. 199–250.

Mayo, E. (1933) *The Human Problems of an Industrial Civilization*. Cambridge: Macmillan.

McKenzie, R.D. (1921) 'Le voisinage, une étude de la vie locale à Columbus, Ohio', in Y. Grafmeyer and I. Joseph (eds), *L'Ecole de Chicago*. Paris: Aubier, 1984.

Mendras, H. (1967) *La Fin des paysans*. Paris: Sedeis. New edition *Le Paradou*. Paris: Actes Sud, Babel, 1991. Translated as *The Vanishing Peasant: Innovation and Change in French Agriculture*. Cambridge: MIT Press, 1970.

Mendras, H. (1976) *Sociétés paysannes*. Paris: Armand Colin.

Merton, R.K. (1949) *Social Theory and Social Structure*. Glencoe, IL: Free Press. Translated as *Eléments de théorie et de méthode sociologiques*. Paris: Plon, 1965.

Merton, R.K. (1954) 'Friendship as a social process', in M. Berger, T. Abel and C.H. Page (eds), *Freedom and Control in Modern Society*. Princeton: Van Nostrand.

Milgram, S. (1967) 'The small world problem', *Psychology Today*, 1: 61–7.

Mintz, B. and Schwartz, M. (1981a) 'The structure of intercorporate unity in American business', *Social Problems*, 29: 87–103.

Mintz, B. and Schwartz, M. (1981b) 'Interlocking directorates and interest group formation', *American Sociological Review*, 46: 851–69.

Mitchell, J.C. (1969) *Social Networks in Urban Situation*. Manchester: Manchester University Press.

Mizruchi, M., Mariolis, P., Schwartz, M. and Mintz, B. (1986) 'Techniques for disaggregating centrality scores in social networks', in N. Tuma (ed.), *Sociological Methodology*. San Francisco: Jossey-Bass.

Mokken, R. (1979) 'Cliques, clubs and clans', *Quality and Quantity*, 13: 161–73.

Moreno, J.L. (1934) *Who Shall Survive*. Translated as *Fondements de la sociométrie*. Paris: PUF, 1954.

Morgan, D. and Rytina, S. (1977) 'Comment on "Network sampling, some first steps" by Mark Granovetter', *American Journal of Sociology*, 83 (3): 722–7.

Nadel, S.F. (1957) *The Theory of Social Structure*. London: Cohen and West.

Naville, P. (1982) *Sociologie et logique*. Paris: PUF.

OCS (1986) *L'Esprit des lieux*. Paris: CNRS.

Olson, M. (1966) *The Logic of Collective Action*. Cambridge, MA: Harvard University Press. Translated as *Logique de l'action collective*. Paris: PUF, 1978.

Ossowski, S. (1963) *Class Structure in the Social Consciousness*. London: Routledge and Kegan Paul. Translated as *La Structure de classe dans la conscience sociale*. Paris: Anthropos, 1971.

Otterbein, K. (1968) 'Internal war: a cross-cultural study', *American Anthropologist*, 70.

Palmer, D., Friedland, R. and Singh, J.V. (1986) 'The ties that bind: organizational and class bases of stability in a corporate interlock network', *American Sociological Review*, 51: 781–96.

Paradeise, C. (1980) 'Sociabilité et culture de classe', *Revue Française de Sociologie*, XXI (54): 571–97.

Park, H.J., Chung, K.K., Han, D.S. and Lee, S.B. (1974) 'Mothers' clubs and family planning in Korea'. Seoul National University, School of Public Health, mimeo report.

Park, R. and Burgess, E.W. (1925) *The City*. Chicago: University of Chicago Press.

Parlebas, P. (1986) *Eléments de sociologie du sport*. Paris: PUF.

Parlebas, P. (1992) *Sociométrie, réseaux et communication*. Paris: PUF.

Parrochia, D. (1993) *Philosophie des réseaux*. Paris: PUF.

Passaris, S. and Raffi, G. (1984) *Les Associations*. Paris: La Découverte.

Pattison, P. (1993) *Algebraic Models for Social Networks*. Cambridge: Cambridge University Press.

Pinçon, M. (1986) 'Autoproduction, sociabilité et identité dans une petite ville ouvrière', *Revue Française de Sociologie*, XXVII (4): 629–53.

Piore, M. (1975) 'Notes for a theory of labor market stratification', in R. Edwards, M. Reide and D. Gordon (eds), *Labor Market Segmentation*. Lexington, MA: Heath.

Radcliffe-Brown, A.R. (1940) 'On social structure', *Journal of the Royal Anthropological Society of Great Britain and Ireland*, LXX: 1–12.

Rae, D. and Taylor, M. (1970) *The Analysis of Political Cleavages*. New Haven, CT: Yale University Press.

Rapoport, A. and Yuan, Y. (1989) 'Some experimental aspects of epidemics and social nets', in M. Kochen (ed.), *The Small World*. Norwood, NJ: Ablex. pp. 327–48.

Reitz, K.P. (1988) 'Social groups in a monastery', *Social Networks*, 10 (4): 343–57.

Reitz, K.P. and White, D.R. (1989) 'Rethinking the role concept: homomorphisms on social networks', in L.C. Freeman, D.R. White and A. Kimball Romney (eds), *Research Methods in Social Networks Analysis*. Fairfax, VA: Georges Mason University Press.

Roché, S. (1993) *Le Sentiment d'insécurité*. Paris: PUF.

Roethlisberger, F.J. and Dickson, W.J. (1939) *Management and the Worker*. Cambridge, MA: Harvard University Press.

Rogers, E.M. (1979) 'Network analysis of the diffusion of innovations', in P.W. Holland and S. Leinhardt (eds), *Perspectives on Social Network Research*. New York: Academic Press. pp. 137–64.

Rogers, E.M. and Shoemaker, F. (1971) *Communication of Innovations: a Cross-Cultural Approach*. New York: Free Press.

Rogers, E.M. and Thomas, P.C. (1975) 'Bibliography on the diffusion of innovations'. Ann Arbor: University of Michigan, mimeo report.

Rosenbaum, J.E., Karitya, T., Settersten, R. and Maier, T. (1990) 'Market and network, theories of transition from high school to work', *Annual Review of Sociology*, 16: 263–99.

Rousseau, J.-J. (1762) *Du contrat social*. Ed. M. Halbwachs. Paris: Aubier Montaigne, 1943. Translated as *The Social Contract*. Baltimore: Penguin, 1968.

Roy, W. and Bonacich, P. (1985) 'Centrality and power in a balkanized network: interlocking directorates among American railroads, 1886–1905', paper presented at the Annual Meeting of the American Sociological Association, Washington, DC.

Ryan, B. and Gross, N.C. (1943) 'The diffusion of hybrid seed corn in two Iowa communities', *Rural Sociology*, 8: 15–24.

Rytina, S., Blau, P., Blum, T. and Schwartz, J. (1988) 'Inequality and intermarriage: a paradox of motive and constraint', *Social Forces*, 66 (3): 645–75.

Sabidussi, G. (1966) 'The centrality index of a graph', *Psychometrika*, 31: 581–603.

Sainsaulieu, R. (1977) *L'Identité au travail*. Paris: Presses de la Fondation nationale des sciences politiques.

Salais, R. (1990) 'Emploi et chômage', in X. Greffe, J. Mairesse and J.-L. Reiffers (eds), *Encyclopédie économique*. Paris: Economica. pp. 847–83.

Salais, R., Baverez, N. and Reynaud, B. (1986) *L'Invention du chômage*. Paris: PUF.

Sampson, S. (1969) 'Crisis in a cloister'. PhD dissertation, Cornell University.

Sansot, P. (1991) *Les Gens de peu*. Paris: PUF.

Scott, J. (1987) 'Intercorporate structure in Western Europe', in M.S. Mizruchi and M. Schwartz (eds), *Intercorporate Relations: the Structural Analysis of Business*. Cambridge: Cambridge University Press. pp. 208–32.

Scott, J. (1991) *Social Network Analysis*. London: Sage.

Seidman, S.B. (1981) 'Structures induced by collections of subsets: a hypergraph approach', *Mathematical Social Sciences*, 1: 381–96.

Seidman, S.B. (1983) 'Network structure and minimum degree', *Social Networks*, 5: 269–87.

Seidman, S.B. and Foster, B.L. (1978) 'A note on the potential for genuine cross-fertilisation between anthropology and mathematics', *Social Networks*, 1: 65–72.

Silvestre, J.-J. (1990) 'Formation et qualification', in X. Greffe, J. Mairesse and J.-L. Reiffers (eds), *Encyclopédie économique*. Paris: Economica. pp. 885–911.

Simmel, G. (1900) *Philosophie des Geldes*. Leipzig: Duncker and Humblot. Translated as *Philosophie de l'argent*. Paris: PUF, 1987. Translated as *The Philosophy of Money*. London: Routledge, 1990.

Simmel, G. (1903) 'Métropoles et mentalité', translation in Y. Grafmeyer and I. Joseph (eds), *L'École de Chicago*. Paris: Editions du Champ Urbain, 1979. pp. 61–78.

Simmel, G. (1908a) *Die Kreuzung Sozialer Kreise*. Translated by R. Bendix as *The Web of Group Affiliations*. New York: Free Press, 1955.

Simmel, G. (1908b) *Soziologie*. Leipzig: Dunkeel and Humblot. Part translated as 'Digressions sur l'étranger', in Y. Grafmeyer and I. Joseph (eds), *L'École de Chicago*. Paris: Editions du Champ Urbain, 1979. pp. 53–9.

Simmel, G. (1911) 'Soziologie der Geselligkeit', in *Verhandlungen des I. Deutschen Soziologentages*. Translated by H. Everett as 'The sociology of sociability', *American Journal of Sociology*, 55 (3), 1949.

Simmel, G. (1918) *Grundfragen der Soziologie*. Translated by J. Freund in *Simmel G: Sociologie et épéstimologie*. Paris: PUF, 1981.

Simmel, G. (1950) Translated by K.H. Wolff as *The Sociology of Georg Simmel*. New York: Free Press.

Snijders, T.A. (1992) 'Estimation on the basis of snowball samples: how to weight?', *Bulletin de Méthodologie Sociologique*, 36: 59–60.

Sola Pool, I. de (1978) 'Contacts and influence', *Social Networks*, 1: 5–51. Republished in M. Kochen (ed.), *The Small World*. Norwood, NJ: Ablex, 1989.

Spinoza (1677) *L'Ethique*, Oeuvres III. Paris: Garnier–Flammarion, 1965. Translated as *Ethics*. New York: Philosophical Library, 1957.

Spira, A., Bajos, N. and the ASCF group (1993) *Les Comportements sexuels en France*. Paris: La Documentation Française. Translated as *Sexual Behaviour and AIDS*. Aldershot: Avebury, 1994.

Spreen, M. (1992) 'Rare populations, hidden populations and link tracing designs: what and why?', *Bulletin de Méthodologie Sociologique*, 36: 34–58.

Stokman, F.N. and Wasseur, F.W. (1985) 'National networks in 1976: a structural comparison', in F.N. Stokman, R. Ziegler and J. Scott (eds), *Networks of Corporate Power: a Comparative Analysis of Ten Countries*. Cambridge: Polity.

Stokman, F.N. and Van den Bos, J.M.M. (1992) 'A two stage model of policy making with an empirical test in the U.S. energy policy domain', in G. Moore and J.A. Whitt (eds), *The Political Consequences of Social Networks*. Greenwich, CT: JAI. pp. 219–54.

Tarde, G. (1895) *Les Lois de l'imitation*. Réimpression Geneva: Slatkine Reprints, 1979.

Travers, J. and Milgram, S. (1969) 'An experimental study of the small problem', *Sociometry*, 32: 425–43.

Ullmann-Margalit, E. (1977) *The Emergence of Norms*. Oxford: Clarendon.

Valade, B. (1990) 'De la civilité à la sociabilité', in *Symposium Encyclopaedia Universalis*. Paris. pp. 1180–3.

Valente, T.W. (1995) *Network Models of the Diffusion of Innovations*. Cresskill: Hampton.

Warner, W.L. and Lunt, P.S. (1941) *The Social Life of a Modern Community*. New Haven, CT: Yale University Press.

Warner, W.L. and Lunt, P.S. (1942) *The Status System of a Modern Community*. New Haven, CT: Yale University Press.

Wasserman, S. and Faust, K. (1994) *Social Network Analysis: Methods and Applications*. Cambridge: Cambridge University Press.

Waters, M. (1989) 'Collegiality, bureaucratization and profesionalization: a Weberian analysis', *American Journal of Sociology*, 94: 945–72.

Weber, M. (1922) *Wirtschaft und Gesellschaft*. Translated as *Economie et société*. Paris: Plon, 1971.

Wellman, B., Carrington, P.J. and Hall, A. (1988) 'Networks as personal communities', in B. Wellman and S.D. Berkowitz (eds), *Social Structure: a Network Approach*. Cambridge: Cambridge University Press.

Wellman, B. and Leighton, B. (1981) 'Réseau, quartier et communauté', *Espaces et Sociétés*, 38–39.

White, D. and Borgatti, S. (1994) 'Betweenness centrality measures for directed graphs', *Social Networks*, 16: 335–46.

White, D. and Jorion, P. (1992) 'Representing and computing kinship, a network approach', *Current Anthropology*, 33: 454–62.

White, H.C. (1963) *An Anatomy of Kinship*. Englewood Cliffs, NJ: Prentice-Hall.

White, H.C., Boorman, S.A. and Breiger, R.R. (1976) 'Social structure from multiple networks. I: Block models of roles and positions', *American Journal of Sociology*, 81 (4): 730–80.

Willer, D. (1992) 'Predicting power in exchange networks: a brief history and introduction to the issues', *Social Networks*, 14 (3–4): 187–211.

Wippler, R. (1978) 'The structural-individualistic approach in Dutch sociology', *The Netherlands Journal of Sociology*, 14: 135–55.

Young M. and Willmott, P. (1957) *Family and Kinship in East London*. London: Routledge and Kegan Paul.

Author Index

Subject Index